William L. Buchanan, Ph.D.
200 S. Enota Dr.
Suite 400
Gainesville, GA 30501

William L. Buchanan, Ph.D.
200 S. Enota Dr
Suite 400
Gainesville, GA 30501

Psychology and Health
Second Edition

Donald A. Bakal, Ph.D., is a Professor in the University of Calgary Department of Psychology. He received his doctorate in psychology in 1971 from the University of Manitoba.

PSYCHOLOGY AND HEALTH
Second Edition

Donald A. Bakal, PhD

Springer Publishing Company
New York

Springer Publishing Company, Inc.
536 Broadway
New York, NY 10012

92 93 94 95 96 / 5 4 3 2 1

Library of Congress Cataloging-in-Publication Data

Bakal, Donald A.
    Psychology and health / Donald A. Bakal: — 2nd ed.
      p.   cm.
    Rev. ed. of: Psychology and medicine. c1979.
    Includes bibliographical references and index.
    ISBN 0-8261-7900-2
    1. Clinical health psychology.   2. Medicine and psychology.
3. Medicine, psychosomatic. I. Bakal, Donald A. Psychology and medicine. II. Title.
    [DNLM: 1. Disease—psychology. 2. Mental Disorders.
3. Psychology, Clinical. WM 100 B166p]
R726.7.B35   1992
616'.001'9—dc20
DNLM/DLC
for Library of Congress   91-5241
                                              CIP

Printed in the United States of America

For Janice, Jeff, and Chris
To my parents and
In memory of Cathy

Contents

Preface

The initial version of this book, titled *Psychology and Medicine: Psychobiological Dimensions of Health and Illness* (1979) was published at a time when psychology's relation to medicine was in transition. Traditional psychoanalytic and personality formulations of disease were experiencing difficulty, while the new fields of behavioral medicine and health psychology were exploding in popularity. The "paradigm shift" from the biochemical model of disease to the biopsychosocial model of disease was well under way. The strength of the movement is evident from the widespread acceptance of psychology in medicine today.

The present book has undergone more than a title change. The psychobiological emphasis has been strengthened through a decade of research and clinical experience. The content is far more clinical and the topics cover a wide number of clinical conditions, which include somatization disorders, chronic pain, migraine, anxiety, mood disorders, and cancer. In this volume, there is a much greater effort toward developing both a theoretical and clinical appreciation of the role played by a patient's thoughts, feelings, and ways of coping in the context of disorder development and treatment.

The book is directed primarily to health care students and professionals with a desire to improve their understanding of the psychology-medicine interface. Nursing, psychology, and medical students will find the material directly relevant to their professional training and goals. They will discover the content and approach to be of value in their individual efforts to develop, within their respective professions, a holistic approach to health, illness, and patient care.

Acknowledgment

The author expresses appreciation to the Killam Resident Fellowship Program for the support provided to assist with the completion of the manuscript.

1
Integrating Body and Mind

INTRODUCTION

This book provides an overview of current thinking on the role of psychobiology in health. A union has taken place between psychology and medicine that embraces every aspect of health care, including disease onset, prevention, treatment, and rehabilitation. Health and wellness are terms which now compete directly with disease and illness for public attention. This reflects a dramatic change in the direction of society's approach to health issues. The World Health Organization (WHO, 1964) has defined health as "a state of complete physical, mental, and social well-being and not merely the absence of disease or infirmity." This definition emphasizes the biopsychosocial nature of health as well as the position that health is more than the absence of disease. Wellness and prevention are now part of our value system and we are repeatedly encouraged to avoid health-impairing habits such as poor diet, lack of exercise, and alcohol consumption. A person's thoughts, feelings, and general coping styles are also under continued study and in many cases are seen as requisite to achieving and maintaining physical health.

The content of this book is focused on the individual and deals exclusively with the health and illness issues which reflect the interface between mind and body. It is this interface which constitutes "psychobiology" and it is the understanding and appreciation of the interface which constitutes the soul of this book. Emotionality, nonemotionality, body awareness, stress, and distress are psychological concepts that are applied to virtually all disorders and diseases ranging from pervasive migraine headache to life-threatening cancer. Without a thorough understanding of the potential psychobiological determinants of these conditions, it is very doubtful that we can know what to do when faced with such a condition within ourselves or within someone we are attempting to assist.

Psychobiology represents one facet of a field known as behavioral medicine. Behavioral medicine is defined as follows:

> The *interdisciplinary* field concerned with the development and integration of
> behavioral and biomedical science, knowledge and techniques relevant to the

understanding of physical health and illness and the application of this knowledge and these techniques to prevention, diagnosis, treatment, and rehabilitation. (Schwartz & Weiss, 1978, p. 250)

The psychobiological or behavioral medicine approach represents a particular emphasis within the larger field of health psychology—a field which
often approaches health issues from a broad social perspective.

The need to develop better understandings of human functioning based
on the integration of both psychological and physiological principles in
health processes and disease processes is not a new phenomenon. Even
Louis Pasteur, the founder of the germ theory of disease, wrestled with the
relative significance of the disease microbe in the context of the person's
overall health or resistance to disease. Eventually, he was to emphasize
personal variables in making the statement, "Bernard avait raison. Le germe
n'est pas rien, c'est le terrain qui est tout." ("Bernard was right. The germ is
nothing, the soil is everything"; Ornstein & Sobel, 1987.) In 1859 Claude
Bernard had proposed the concept of "milieu interieur" or internal environment, and suggested that the stability of that environment was essential for
health. From our perspective, this stability can best be understood through
models which integrate both the psychological and biological domains of
human behavior.

Modern health care centers have widely embraced holistic patient
approaches. In most centers, it is possible to find programs that encourage
patients to utilize a variety of mental strategies which include stress management, relaxation, biofeedback, guided imagery, and hypnosis to control
disorders and diseases that include migraine, hypertension, irritable bowel,
heart disease, and cancer. The initial enthusiasm for these approaches is
often very high, even though the patients themselves seldom fully understand the connection between their particular medical condition and the
self-control technique that they are using. In all instances, claims for success
are being made, in spite of the fact that we do not understand exactly what
is taking place between the various mental and physical processes involved.
Moreover, there are still far too many patients who, after showing some
initial improvements following some form of self-regulation therapy, relapse
to their pretreatment symptom level. In addition, it is still very common to
hear patients being told to "learn to live" with their particular symptom. The
situation can be drastically improved if we can learn to better appreciate the
psychobiologic processes which build wellness within the individual.

PSYCHOBIOLOGY AND HOLISTIC EXPERIENCE

Until very recently, the term "psychobiology" was used in a narrow sense to
refer to physiological psychology. The guiding objective within this

framework was to explain human and animal behavior at a physiological level. This approach is known as reductionism and had its beginnings in the 17th century. In 1637 the influential philosopher René Descartes presented a philosophical position which clearly separated mind from body. Known as Cartesian dualism, the thinking mind became separate from the body and the concept of holism was relegated to the back burner. According to Cassel (1982), Cartesian dualism "made it possible for science to escape the control of the church by assigning the noncorporeal, spiritual realm to the church, leaving the physical world as the domain of science."

Descartes believed that mind and body were two distinct entities and that each was subject to different laws of causality. The body was viewed as a machine and was governed by mechanical principles known at the time. The example involves the perception of pain, which Descartes suggested operated like a bell-ringing mechanism in a church: a rope is pulled at the bottom of the tower and a bell rings in the belfry (Figure 1.1).

> Just so, when I sense pain in the foot, physics teaches me that this feeling took place because of nerves scattered throughout the foot. These nerves, like cords, are extended from that point all the way to the brain; when they are pulled in the foot, they also pull on inner parts of the brain to which they are stretched, and produce a certain motion in these parts of the brain. This motion has been constituted by nature so as to affect the mind with a feeling of pain, as if it existed in the foot. (Descartes, 1637, p. 98)

Descartes also attempted to explain "psychogenic" pain which, for him, meant that the bell was rung in the brain rather than in the foot:

> For if some cause, not in the foot but in some other part through which the nerves are stretched from the foot to the brain—or perhaps even in the brain itself—were to produce the same motion that would normally be produced by a badly affected foot, then the pain will be felt as if it were in the foot, and the senses will naturally be deceived, because it is reasonable that the motion should always show the pain to the mind as something belonging to the foot rather than to some other part . . . (p. 99)

Although mind and body were separate, Descartes recognized the necessity of allowing some communication, especially for the senses. Otherwise, how would we know "pain"? He was forced to acknowledge that there might be a small portion of the brain, a kind of sensory communication channel, that permitted conscious awareness of bodily sensations. There was, however, no causal relationship between the two entities.

The concept of holism took a battering following Descartes' writings, but managed to survive—largely as a philosophical rather than a scientific issue. With developments of technological medicine in the 19th century and continuing to the present, there was little scientific inquiry directed by a

Figure 1.1. Descartes' concept of the pain pathway. (MEDICINE North America 1989; 3(36):6525)

holistic view of human health and disease. Science, in fact, became extremely reductionistic, with all energies shifted toward understanding the biological and biochemical aspects of human functioning.

In spite of the current popularity of holistic ideas at the clinical level, scientific medical knowledge remains largely reductionistic, preferring to study and treat illness at the biochemical level. This is understandable given the difficulty of dealing with human functioning at a holistic level. The quintessential belief in reductionism is often found in genetics, where many scientists believe that the origins for most diseases and disorders reside. Significant discoveries of genetic abnormalities are taking place, and yet it is doubtful that genetics alone will account for many forms of disease. For example, family (and presumably genetic) history is a strong predictor of heart disease and cancer but we do not inherit heart disease or cancer; what we do inherit are enzymes which control individual differences in disease susceptibility. Whether disease develops or not is dependent on the interactions that take place between genetically-determined predispositions and life history variables, usually referred to as environmental and experiential factors.

The clinical management of a patient's presenting problems are still frequently attempted solely at the biological level. Biological measures of a patient's condition through clinical tests are considered essential whereas psychological or behavioral measures are considered secondary to the medical condition. Biological measures based on blood pressure and blood chemistry are seen as being more reliable and valid than subjective and behavioral measures. Kaplan (1990) argued that the biological assessment "bias" is not always valid and needs to be balanced with psychological and behavioral perspectives. With arthritis, for example, it is often assumed that biologic measures such as erythrocyte sedimentation rate (ESR) are "true" measures of the patient's disease. And yet such measures often do not reflect the degree of pain or disability present:

> An elevated ESR means little to a patient who feels fine and can conduct his or her life without pain. The ESR characterizes current inflammation but does not give information about future dysfunction. Conversely, a patient with disabling arthritic pain is not well when the ESR is normal. Clinical tests are useful only when they identify treatment to remedy current dysfunction or predict future problems. (p. 1214)

Hypertension is another medical condition that can be associated with vastly different behavioral outcomes. Elevated blood pressure (systolic blood pressure exceeding 140 mmHG or diastolic pressure exceeding 90 mmHg) characterizes about 30% of the population. Severe elevated blood pressure is a risk factor for heart disease and stroke, whereas mild hypertension is much less of a problem and in most cases does not lead to medical complications. Yet the medical treatment of hypertension can be associated with a number of problems, including dizziness, tiredness, impotence, and health preoccupation. Efforts to reduce blood pressure need be undertaken; the point being made is that medical symptom management in isolation may not be sufficient to improve the health of the patient.

Psychiatry is an example of a medical specialty which at times has difficulty knowing which philosophical position to take. At a clinical level, psychiatrists are faced with individuals who present with a multitude of difficult mental and behavioral problems, making adoption of a holistic perspective mandatory. And yet they have a need to be as scientific as their other medical colleagues and will often as a result embrace reductionistic models in the understanding and management of their patients. Some psychiatrists believe that at some time in the future it will be possible to fully explain and treat psychological disorders through the identification of relevant underlying biochemical and neurophysiological processes. Biological psychiatry, for example, is based on the notion that psychiatric illness is caused by alterations in neurotransmitter function. Based on this view, it should be possible to fully explain and manage a psychiatric disorder at the biochemical level, without accounting for the interaction of mental and physical events (Charlton, 1990). To explain psychiatric illness in terms of biochemistry is not to describe its underlying cause but rather to redescribe it at another level of analysis. Different sciences are not saying the same things in different ways, but are about different things. The mind-body problem is dissolved rather than solved. Aspects of behavior such as free will, for example, involve conscious issues surrounding morality and responsibility; neurotransmitters are concerned with biochemical functioning of the brain.

The difficulty with a reductionist position is that it maintains a dualism between mind and body very similar to the perspective first established by Descartes. It does little to promote a holistic view of human functioning. Consider the following analogy first used by Frankl (1969) to illustrate the distortion that occurs when human functions are dissected into physical and mental events. As shown in Figure 1.2, a cylinder projected out of its own three-dimensional space with lower horizontal and vertical properties results in two new dimensions with different properties. In one case, the result is a circle; in the other case, a rectangle; and in both cases, something is lost. Similarly, if a person with a physical symptom is viewed solely from a biochemical frame of reference or solely from a psychological frame of reference, the same limitations occur. In one case, the outcome is biologic information; in the other, psychologic information; yet, in both cases, the holistic or psychobiologic perspective is lost. The cylinder analogy provides a convincing illustration of the distortions inherent in studying separate functions of persons rather than integrated living humans. The properties

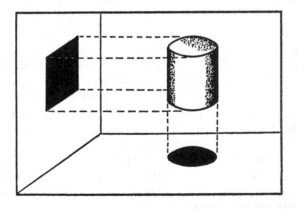

Figure 1.2. Projection of cylinder out of its three-dimensional space to form a circle and a rectangle; in both cases, something is lost (Frankl, 1969). Copyright © by Hutchinson Publishing Group Limited. Reprint permission granted by Peters Fraser & Dunlop Ltd.

inherent in the cylinder represent psychobiologic processes within the individual that cannot be identified from study of the components alone.

Central to the present use of the term psychobiology is the persons' total awareness or experience of themselves, involving thought, feeling, and body sensations. Whether we are dealing with emotional conditions involving anxiety or depression, stress, chronic pain disorders, or life-threatening disease, we are seeking to identify very subtle experiences within persons which can be tapped directly and indirectly to provide a degree of personal symptom management and improve health. In effect, we are speaking of individual awareness of the integration or union of a person's thoughts, feelings, sensations, and bodily reactions. Many factors impede awareness of this state but its importance in maintaining health in a complex world is without question.

Emergent Determinism

The ability to adequately describe human conditions from a psychobiologic perspective presents a problem as we do not have a satisfactory class of concepts for depicting the indivisible union of our physical and psychological realities. Sperry (1987) has long argued for the importance of holistic concepts for understanding mind-body functioning. Sperry's view that the mind consists of more than a collection of cells began with his observations of split-brain experiments. In the 1960s Sperry and his colleagues were conducting psychological studies of patients that had undergone commissurotomy or "split-brain" surgery. The patients had undergone surgical sectioning of the corpus callosum and other forebrain commissures as a last-resort effort to control severe epilepsy. The corpus callosum is a massive fiber tract consisting of some 200 million nerve fibers that relays information between the hemispheres of the brain. Thus the surgery removed all possibility of direct communication between the left and right hemispheres. Through a series of ingenious experiments, Sperry and his colleagues were able to demonstrate that although deficient in speech, the right hemisphere was quite capable of reading and comprehending. In addition, each disconnected hemisphere operated as if it were not conscious of cognitive events in the opposite hemisphere. Further, each hemisphere appeared to have its own separate cognitive domain, with its own private perceptual, learning, and memory experiences. The notion that the right hemisphere also had specialized functions followed with demonstrations of its superiority over the left hemisphere in performing spatial and imagistic tasks (e.g., reading faces, sorting block sizes and shapes, judging whole pictures). Galin (1974) described a film segment in which a postcommissurotomy subject is tested with a tachistoscope and photographed by Sperry and associates. The patient is seen performing a block design task and trying to match a colored geometric design with a set of painted blocks. Galin described how the left hand (right hemisphere) quickly carries out the assigned task. When the right hand (left hemisphere) is given the same task, it performs it with difficulty. Galin described seeing the left hand on the screen quickly intrude itself and correct an error the right hand is in the process of making. This film report demonstrated "not only that the processing capabilities for a given task may differ between the hemispheres, but also, at least in this example, that one hemisphere will monitor, evaluate, and attempt to change or overcome the actions of the other hemisphere."

Sperry early on cautioned about making too much of the left-right specialization (such as "left brain equals consciousness" and "right brain equals unconsciousness") as in the normal state the two hemispheres work closely together as a unit, rather than one being turned on while the other idles. However, he also recognized the significance of these observations for further understanding of nonverbal intellect. In addition his observations suggested that the brain processes information in an almost modular fashion. Moreover the left hemisphere acts as an "interpreter," and at times attempts to explain behaviors more under the control of right hemisphere function. Other modules likely exist as well. An analogy has been made to the orchestra conductor who seems (to himself or herself) to be the undisputed director or leader, but who must interact with players in the orchestra who he or she does not fully know or understand, but for whom he or she must assume leadership. The members of the orchestra may have distinct purposes, agendas, and "lives" of their own. This interpretive function is found in the left hemisphere of right-handed individuals. There may be a number of conductors, each waiting in the wings for an opportunity to be recognized.

The fact that the left hemisphere is generally responsible for speech and language comprehension fostered the notion of a dominant left-hemisphere and a nondominant or subordinate right hemisphere. The left hemisphere was also regarded as dominant for organized movement, calculation, and arithmetic reasoning. The right hemisphere is capable of an equally high degree of intellect, and Sperry has called for methods to study human intellect beyond those reflected in the three Rs of linguistic communication. In maintaining health, it may be necessary to have the two hemispheres function closely together as a single unit or at least not in opposition. In the intact person, it may happen that the qualities of conscious experience associated with each hemisphere become functionally separated or disconnected. In order to understand what is meant by functional dissociation, consider first the following example of a patient whose hemispheres had been anatomically disconnected:

One film segment shows a female patient being tested with a tachistoscope. . . . In the series of neutral geometric figures being presented at random to the right and left fields, a nude pinup was included and flashed to the right (nonverbal) hemisphere. The girl blushes and giggles. Sperry asks "What did you see?" She answers, "Nothing, just a flash of light," and giggles again, covering her mouth with her hand. "Why are you laughing, then?" asks Sperry, and she laughs again and says, "Oh, Dr. Sperry, you have some machine!" The episode is very suggestive; if one did not know her neurosurgical history, one might see this as a clear example of perceptual defense and think that she was "repressing" the perception of the conflictual sexual material—even her final response (a socially acceptable non sequitur) was convincing. (Galin, 1974, p. 573)

The same kind of behavior in the intact person might appear when the experiences of one hemisphere are in conflict with the experiences of the other hemisphere:

Imagine the effect on a child when his mother presents one message verbally, but quite another with her facial expression and body language: "I am doing it because I love you, dear," say the words, but "I hate you and will destroy you," says the face. Each hemisphere is exposed to the same sensory input, but because of their relative specializations, they each emphasize only one of the messages. The left will attend to the verbal cues because it cannot extract information from the facial gestalt efficiently, the right will attend to the nonverbal cues because it cannot easily understand the words. (Galin, 1974, p. 576)

After spending years wrestling with the problem of conscious unity in the presence and absence of cerebral commissures, Sperry (1987) became convinced that consciousness is causal rather than noncausal in brain activity. Rather than attempt to reduce human existence to some final common denominator, such as might be found in subatomic physics, he proposed that we complement the natural science philosophy of examining control from below upward with a humanist-mentalist philosophy of examining control from above downward. In advocating this approach, Sperry is not rejecting the efforts of medical science to explain phenomena at lower or micro levels but rather encouraging the recognition of "new, previously nonexistent, emergent properties, including the mental that interact causally at their own higher level and also exert causal control from above downward."

The advantage of Sperry's conceptual framework is that it allows for an integration of both humanistic values and natural science thinking. It allows reductionism and holism to live side by side. Conscious properties (thoughts, feelings, attitudes, beliefs) remain determined by neuronal events (factors below exerting upward control) but as newly emergent properties they become more than simple "swamp gas" and are now seen as capable of influencing physical events below them. That is, by having conscious mental function not only arise from but also influence physical brain/body action, it becomes possible to integrate some uniquely human attributes with objective brain function and its consequences. Courage, moral values, self-reflection, purpose, human spirit, religion, and feeling are elevated from epiphenomena to mental forces at the top of the brain's control hierarchy. As an explanatory concept for mind-body interaction, Sperry's notion of emergent determinism might appear less than satisfactory. However, the concept does emphasize the importance of the continued study of holistic conscious attributes for understanding health and illness.

Other writers have noted the necessity of studying holistic properties of the human condition. In a commentary on the search for specific determinants of human behavior, Maddi, Bartone, and Puccetti (1987) concluded:

> In the final analysis, variables useful in studies of human behavior are more likely to be analogous to chemical compounds than elements. Compounds such as water exist in our everyday world, whereas elements, such as hydrogen and oxygen, exist outside of the laboratory only in very rare circumstances. We can learn much of value to us by considering the properties of water, such as its boiling and freezing points and its importance for physical survival, without ever breaking it down into its elements. And we can study those elements separately for a long time without discovering much about the emergent properties of water. (p. 840)

The importance of recognizing the potential power of emergent properties is evident in a recent study of brain lesions and cognitive function in elderly individuals (Fein et al., 1990). Normally, greater atrophy of cortical tissue is associated with greater cognitive loss. This is not always the case, however, as the presence of cortical atrophy by itself is not diagnostic of dementia. The study in question examined subcortical or deep white matter lesions in a small group of elderly individuals and correlated the presence of such lesions with level of cognitive function. Deep white matter lesions are detectable through the use of magnetic resonance imaging and are frequently observed in elderly individuals. The clinical significance of deep white matter lesions is unknown. Cognitive function was assessed with a battery of tests which measured attention and concentration, memory, language, and nonverbal reasoning. Of interest were the brain images of individuals that showed evidence of considerable deep white matter lesions. Two of the three subjects with extensive lesions showed high performance on all the cognitive measures and no evidence of cognitive loss. The brain image for one of the subjects is shown in Figure 1.3. The individual behind the brain

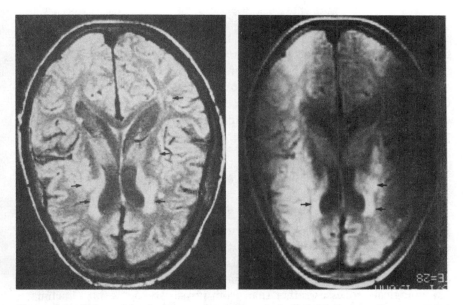

Figure 1.3. Selected brain images for subject 1. Left, initial magnetic resonance imaging scan when subject was 80 years old. Arrows indicate extensive white-matter lesions. Right, repeated magnetic resonance imaging when subject was 83 years old, illustrates persistence of deep white-matter lesions (Fein et al., 1990). Reproduced from Archives of General Psychiatry, 47, 220–223. Copyright 1990, American Medical Association. Reprinted by permission.

image was a retired schoolteacher in her eighties, who still took care of her house alone, enjoyed reading, walking, gardening, and playing bridge. She was clearly maintaining an active and rich intellectual and emotional life, in spite of considerable loss of brain tissue. The case study is not presented as evidence of "mind-without-matter" but as an illustration that many human experiental attributes are under the control of high-order emergent properties that are not necessarily controlled by a specific region within the brain. The property in question may be a general interest in learning which the individual cultured throughout her life.

TRADITIONAL PSYCHOSOMATIC THEORY

Traditional psychosomatic medicine developed in the 1930s as a special branch of medicine because a small group of physicians were dissatisfied with attempts to explain their patients' symptoms solely in biochemical terms. These physicians were struck by how often their patients seemed to be troubled by negative thoughts and feelings, both at conscious and unconscious levels. The term "psychosomatic medicine" was first introduced in 1818 (Lipowski, 1986a). This new branch of medicine developed as a reaction against biologic medicine and represented a scientific effort to study ideas that had their origins in ancient times, in folklore, as well as in clinical observation. There were two essential features to the early psychosomatic approach: psychosomatic diseases were viewed as distinct from other diseases; and psychosomatic explanations were heavily influenced by psychoanalytic or Freudian psychology.

Classification of Disorders

In the early days, there were clearly perceived boundaries between disorders with a psychological component and disorders without such a component. Those with a psychological component were classified as *psychosomatic* or *conversion reaction* disorders while those without a psychological component were classified as *organic* disorders. Historically, psychosomatic disorders were defined as physiological dysfunctions that resulted from psychological processes rather than from physical toxic agents (Lachman, 1972). The psychological processes most often listed involved frustrating circumstances, interpersonal conflict situations, and emotion-provoking situations. Note from the definition that physiologic changes do underlie the symptoms. An unfortunate tendency, never intended by founders of the psychosomatic approach, was to view symptoms with psychosomatic origins as less significant or real than symptoms with a presumed organic origin. Not surprisingly, therefore, people were reluctant to embrace a psychosomatic explanation for their condition, especially if it implied that the symptom was "all in their head." Even today, people are reluctant to accept causal explanations for their condition which go beyond physical factors.

The second category of psychologically-determined illness, *conversion reaction disorder,* often occurs in the absence of underlying physical changes. Traditionally, conversion reactions (otherwise known as hysterical disorders) are characterized by the onset of a physical symptom, which usually involves a loss of a sensory or motor function. The symptom may appear very suddenly and the individual may not remember what was happening at the time the symptom appeared. Thus the individual may suddenly develop a tremor, paralysis of a limb, or the loss of vision. Malmo (1970) described a young girl named Anne who, after having many angry disputes with her mother, finally left home but, upon returning, began to complain of fainting, dizziness, and buzzing in the ears. Then one morning she awoke to find herself totally deaf. Conversion reaction disorders, unlike psychosomatic disorders, are not associated with tissue damage. They are viewed as occurring solely at a cortical level and are seen as solving a problem for the individual at an unconscious level. The patient with a conversion disorder is often capable of functioning, in spite of the disorder. For example, patients with bilateral blindness are still capable of walking about freely without harming themselves or bumping into things. Classic conversion reaction disorders involving sensory loss are seldom seen in clinic and hospital settings, possibly because the populace has become more sophisticated with respect to symptoms and associated anatomy and physiology. The concept of conversion reaction is still present in medicine but has become much more complex in meaning.

Freudian Theory

Initial psychobiologic approaches to medicine were heavily influenced by Freudian ideas. Freud attempted to explain, at a mental level, the problems created when an individual is prevented from expressing thoughts and feelings which often had their origins in biological processes. He represents the first modern theorist to emphasize that physical disorders may occur when an individual cannot *discharge* his emotional impulses in some acceptable manner. According to Freud, a definite relationship existed between an individual's personality and the defensive style with which the individual dealt with emotional and instinctual impulses. In fact the adult personality is largely defined by the kinds of defense mechanisms an individual uses. Defense mechanisms are defined as "intrapsychic coping mechanisms which have the function of keeping anxiety within manageable limits." There are a number of defense mechanisms, some of which contribute to a neurotic personality and some of which are considered healthy in nature. Neurotic defenses are common in normal individuals and appear to the observer as "quirks" or "hang-ups." Repression is a common neurotic defense mechanism and consists of memory lapse or failure to acknowledge ideational input (e.g., weeping for no apparent reason). An example of a mature defense is sublimation which consists of the indirect expression of aggressive and sexual drives without negative consequences (e.g., sports, courting). Humor is also considered a mature defense as it allows the expression of aggressive feelings, often in a direct manner, without fear of consequences.

The best known and most influential extension of Freudian thinking to psychosomatic disorders is the *nuclear conflict theory* of Alexander (1950). Psychosomatic ailments are viewed as the defensive outcome of a central, or nuclear, emotional conflict. In general terms, unconscious feelings of hostility are believed to trigger cardiovascular disorders (migraine headaches, hypertension), whereas unconscious feelings of dependency or desires to be loved are believed to trigger respiratory and gastrointestinal disorders (asthma, ulcers, spastic colon, irritable bowel syndrome).

With hypertension, migraine, and cardiovascular disorders, the central conflict has to do with the inhibition or repression of self-assertive hostile impulses. Because the impulses are repressed or inhibited, the corresponding behavior (aggression) is never consummated. In other words, although the physiological processes have been activated for aggression, they are not brought to action and the individual remains in a state of physiological preparedness. Similarly, on the other side of the model, persons with unconscious conflicts associated with dependency are never quite able to acknowledge and express these feelings in consciousness and the underlying physiologic systems once again remain in a state of perpetual activation. Alexander described the emotional style of hypertensives as follows:

> The damming up of his hostile impulses will continue and will consequently increase in intensity. This will induce the development of stronger defensive measures in order to keep pent-up aggressions in check. . . . Because of the marked degree of inhibitions, these patients are less effective in their occupational activities and for that reason tend to fail in competition with others, so that envy is stimulated and their hostile feelings toward more successful competitors is intensified. (Alexander, 1950, p. 150)

Anger, aggression, and hostility have been linked to heart disease, arthritis, and other disorders involving the vascular system. An example of how anger is handled by these individuals is illustrated by the following patient example:

> A 55-year-old woman with painful arthritis described herself as having "good days" and "bad days." On good days, she was able to perform her duties as an executive secretary for a vice-president within a large corporation. She considered herself to be a top-flight secretary and remarked that she had never experienced anger at work or at home. She said that she learned at a very young age to "keep my mouth shut." Although her boss did very little for her of a personal nature, she was extremely loyal and would never acknowledge resentment or negative feelings toward him during a clinical session. On bad days, she was in severe pain with extreme swelling and yet would struggle to work and not acknowledge the symptoms to herself. Eventually, she had to leave the company and be placed on permanent disability.

We cannot say how much, if any, of this individual's arthritic condition was the result of repressed hostility. Alexander described the mental traits of arthritic women as emotionally controlling, demanding, and domineering. They are also rejecting of feminine attributes, competitive with men, and driven to serve other people. The disease begins when the unconscious hostility toward men has been increased and threatens to erupt (e.g., when a man threatens to leave), or when guilt feelings cannot be relieved by serving others.

The problem is that not all patients with any of these medical conditions exhibit excessive anger and/or hostility. With hypertension, for example, some patients exhibit high levels of anger and hostility while others do not. The current psychophysiologic evidence linking anger/hostility to hypertension is examined in the next chapter; suffice it to say, however, that there continues to be very considerable evidence that such a relationship exists. Behavioral medicine researchers involved in cardiovascular research are coming closer and closer to Alexander's original formulation of a link between hostility and hypertension.

Peptic ulcer is an example of a gastrointestinal disorder associated with emotional withdrawal. The term *peptic ulcer* refers to both gastric and duodenal ulcers. An ulcer is a lesion of the mucous lining of the stomach or of the duodenum. In humans, ulcers are most frequently duodenal. Such ulcers are quite common, but in many instances they are "quiet," causing no pain or distress, and are, therefore, unnoticed and unreported. However, ulcers often cause severe pain, and when they perforate, serious internal bleeding results, which can be fatal. The stereotype of ulcer patients is of "harried executives chewing on antacid tablets, as well as neurosurgeons interrupting an operation to gulp down a glass of milk." According to Oken (1985), Alexander's description of the ulcer patient as a hyperindependent, striving, ambitious, and competitive person developed largely because middle-class male patients over-represented patients who sought out psychoanalysis:

> Based on detailed psychoanalytic observations of middle-class men with duodenal ulcer, he postulated that the ulcer patient experienced a characteristic unconscious conflict over intense, dependent, oral-receptive longings to be cared for and loved, which was defensively overcompensated for by accentuation of the overt personality traits described. He believed that the persisting, ungratified, unconscious dependency, aggravated by the additional frustration of the defensive posture, resulted in a chronic unconscious "hunger." This hunger, he further postulated, was manifested physiologically by persistent vagal hyperreactivity, leading to acid hypersecretion and, then, to ulcer formation. (Oken, 1985, p. 1125)

As noted with the anger/hostility-cardiovascular arm of this theory, these psychodynamic descriptions sometimes characterize gastrointestinal patients and sometimes do not. A study in support of the hypothesis was reviewed by Oken (1985). In the study, the constitutional factor of gastric secretion was added to the predictive equation. Alexander maintained that psychodynamics were not the sole cause of disease as he acknowledged that genetics, injury, and other factors might set the stage for the organ to be involved in psychosomatic illness. In this particular study, subjects were initially screened for pepsinogen levels and given a battery of psychological tests. Predictions as to which subjects were hypersecretors and which were hyposecretors were made from the tests: "These predictions correctly identified 71% of hypersecretors and 51% of hyposecretors." Other studies have found some support for the dependency hypothesis, but only for men.

Irritable bowel syndrome (IBS) is another category of gastrointestinal disorder related to dependency. IBS is also called irritable colon syndrome, mucus colitis, spastic colitis, nervous diarrhea, and colon neurosis. The disorder is involved in more than half the patients who seek medical attention for gastrointestinal complaints. The primary symptoms include abdominal pain or discomfort, usually associated with constipation, diarrhea, or both (Walker, Roy-Byrne, & Katon, 1990). IBS is presumed to be a disorder of intestinal motility and yet it has proved difficult to isolate the precise nature of this disorder. There have been suggestions that IBS patients have a higher proportion of "slow" myoelectric activity in the colon and this may constitute part of the vulnerability toward the disorder. The problem is that many patients without IBS also exhibit this motility marker. In any case, Alexander's model viewed the IBS symptoms of constipation and diarrhea as two aspects of the dependency conflict. Diarrhea was linked to aggressiveness, riddance and giving, and constipation to the reverse. There is no solid evidence for this formulation. Psychological research indicates that IBS patients, although generally more anxious and distressed than nonpatients, do not exhibit a common psychological profile.

Both Freud's and Alexander's notions are likely to continue to survive in some form. The idea that specific conflicts lead to specific disorders will need modification as conscious and unconscious thought is too fluid and varied in content to be characterized in terms of constellations of relatively fixed unconscious conflicts. In addition, it is highly unlikely that specific psychological conflicts can be correlated with specific bodily changes and resultant symptoms. Emotions and personality traits involving resentment, frustration, hostility, depression, and anxiety are frequently reported correlates of illness, regardless of the disorder. The suggestion has been made (Friedman & Booth-Kewley, 1987) that we should be looking for a *disease-prone personality* that is present across a number of diseases—a nonspecific rather than a specific disease influence. "Personality may function like diet, where imbalances can predispose one to all sorts of diseases." Certain personalities may tip the scale toward disease-proneness more than other personalities but it is unlikely one personality will predict specific disorders/disease.

Although current psychosomatic research has moved away from psychoanalytic formulations linking specific conflicts and personalities to disease, the field continues to follow the general premise that a person's responses to his or her interactions with others, as well as his or her personality, are factors influencing illness. The research questions of today are generally more specific than those of the past. A sample of current issues are the following (Lipowski, 1986b):

1. If one assumes that psychological (or psychosocial) factors do impact on an individual's health, then which of them are most likely to do so?
2. Are there specific psychophysiological response patterns which follow exposure to a particular environmental event, situation, or emotion?
3. To what extent is such a response specific to the individual and to the stimulus situation, respectively?
4. Are there life events or situations which are likely to increase the risk of becoming ill?
5. Are there psychological attributes and behaviors of a person which increase his or her susceptibility to a specific disease?
6. Which personality features enhance resistance to disease and adaptive coping with it if it does occur?
7. What are the mediating physiological pathways and mechanisms whereby psychosocial factors may effect changes in the organism and hence increase or reduce vulnerability to illness?

SIGNS, SYMPTOMS AND SOMATIZATION

One of the greatest challenges facing clinicians is teasing out the relative contributions of psychological and physiological determinants of bodily changes associated with medical disorders and disease. This issue is even more important to the afflicted individuals as they must often decide on the basis of limited information whether a symptom is indicative of a particular disease, or the result of some psychobiological process. Physiologists often make a distinction between signs and symptoms in dealing with this issue (Cacioppo et al., 1989). Signs are defined as bodily events which are detectable by another person and sometimes by the patient himself. Signs have an objective physical referent such as a lump or fracture. Symptoms, on the other hand, are subjective events which are most often only apparent to the affected person. Symptoms are more difficult to communicate accurately and to understand. Although some bodily changes can be classified both as symptoms and signs (e.g., fever), many changes constitute only symptoms (e.g., pain) or signs (e.g., elevated blood pressure). Physiological signs cannot be used as the sole standard by which to judge symptoms. For example, two individuals who have undergone similar surgeries and tissue damage may experience vastly different levels of postsurgical pain.

Greater problems arise in dealing with patients who present with symptoms and no signs. Many psychophysiologic conditions are not associated with organic/tissue damage and show no evidence of organicity, as detected by current technology and understanding (e.g., low back pain, migraine, irritable bowel). What happens in these situations is often less than desirable as the affected patients may feel misunderstood and physicians are at a loss to account for the symptoms. Many back pain patients, for example, believe that their physicians do not really believe in their expressed levels of pain. On the other side, physicians and nurses often have difficulty understanding how a patient with little or no objective evidence of injury could hurt so much.

In dealing with patients, it is important to understand that all physical symptoms are complex cognitive-perceptual phenomena and are subject to complex psychosocial processes that go beyond biosensory mechanisms alone (Cioffi, 1991). A patient with Raynaud's disease can be used to illustrate this approach. Raynaud's disease is a vascular disorder of the skin which has as its most characteristic symptom cold hands and feet. It is believed to result from spasmodic contraction of arteries and arterioles of the extremities. The vasosconstriction is often so severe that the fingers become pallid and painful. Cold stimuli are considered a major trigger for symptom onset. Initially the cold hands and feet were attributed solely to the disease itself and the patient would not consider the hypothesis that falling hand temperature was related to her psychological condition. She would attempt to ignore the symptom, as best she could, and get on with caring for her husband and family. She frequently wore gloves and extra-warm socks to bed to lessen the symptoms. She noted several situations which reliably led to a drop in hand temperature. One involved getting out of bed in the morning and the second involved entering the refrigerator in order to begin meal preparation. To examine the possibility that psychological factors might cause the symptoms, she was invited to monitor her thoughts and feelings when entering the refrigerator. She discovered, to her amazement, that the sensation of cold hands had less to do with the air temperature and more to do with feelings of resentment that she had to prepare dinner alone. The example illustrates how the physical symptom of cold hands, resulting from vasoconstriction, is subject to psychobiologic and situational influence.

There is a strong tendency to interpret such symptoms as indicative of underlying psychological rather than psychobiological problems. Similar to Freudian theory, physical symptoms of many kinds are often interpreted as a "defense" against emotional acknowledgment or expression. Patients suffering from undiagnosed pain may, for example, be seen as needing to learn to deal with repressed anger, guilt, grief, or some other emotional condition. These individuals are frequently advised by their physicians as "needing to come to terms with some emotional issues" or, at a simpler level, "needing to learn to deal with stress." In psychiatry, any physical symptom that is not due to organic factors or known pathophysiologic mechanisms, but for which medical attention has been sought, may lead to a diagnosis of *somatization disorder*. The organ systems involved may include the respiratory, gastrointestinal, reproductive, and cardiovascular systems. The afflicted person is not malingering or consciously producing the symptoms. An example of this condition is the somatoform pain disorder, which is defined as "preoccupation with pain in the absence of adequate physical findings to account for the pain or its intensity" (American Psychiatric Association, 1987):

> A young college student; 23 years of age began developing severe back spasms while an undergraduate. The spasms persisted and, after consulting a neurosurgeon, he was advised to have surgery. After several unsuccessful operations, he became convinced that he could no longer move, that he in fact was experiencing all the symptoms of a degenerative disease that could not be cured. His pain was experienced in a very nonspecific fashion and described as a burning sensation which moved up and down his legs, back, and shoulders. His pain was very difficult to manage and not helping the cause was the fact that he was an extremely demanding individual. While in the hospital he made continual requests for pain-relieving medication, played quasi-religious mind-control audiotapes at a level which annoyed other patients, and demanded repeated body rubs from the nurses to ease the burning pain. Several weeks of his demands led a number of student nurses on the unit to consider another profession. Specialist after specialist was called in to convince him that there was absolutely no evidence of degenerative disease. At the same time, he insisted that he was moving toward total paralysis and that he should be moved to a long-term care facility, a move which would make him totally dependent on others for the rest of his life.

This patient illustrates the features of painful symptoms in the absence of identifiable signs. From his perspective, physicians were "missing something" in their search for the signs and from their perspective the patient was inventing the symptoms to solve some emotional problem. Interestingly, the symptom had no known anatomical basis. The young man was also experiencing, prior to the pain becoming severe, major difficulties with both his academic and interpersonal life, which reinforces the notion that the pain and accompanying disability may have served to "solve" these problems. In this case, however, as with other patients presenting with psychosomatic and conversion reaction symptoms, the patient is not faking the symptoms or malingering. There is a condition called the "Munchausen syndrome" in which individuals deliberately feign physical symptoms and medical conditions in order to gain specific benefits from compensation or some other source (Fishbain et al., 1988).

With somatoform pain and other somatization conditions, the operation of psychological variables generally takes place outside the individual's awareness, making it very difficult for him or her to understand why no one believes that the pain or other symptoms are "real." According to Kirmayer (1984), somatization is a universal occurrence and is not unique to a particular culture or personality. He believes that, worldwide, it is more acceptable to report physical complaints than emotional complaints. In China, for example, there is a social and moral stigma associated with emotional complaining and as a result few individuals complain directly of anxiety or depression. Patients seen in general practice, however, complain of symptoms very similar to those reported in America (sleep disturbance, general malaise, dizziness, and menopausal symptoms). The Japanese as well, especially Japanese women, complain frequently of headache, coldness, shoulder stiffness, back pain, and premenstrual pain.

Close to 80% of college students, when surveyed in class, reported then experiencing some degree of at least one of ten common symptoms: headache, upset stomach, sore muscles, nasal congestion, flushed face, dizziness, sweaty hands, shortness of breath, watering of the eyes, ringing in ears. In 1960, Raymond Prince described the *brain fag syndrome* in Nigerian students, consisting of an inability to concentrate and retain learned material, burning or peppery sensations most often associated with "brain work," and an unhappy, tense facial expression. The same symptoms have been found in those engaged in nonintellectual work, which challenges the notion that the symptoms are the result of excessive intellectual brain work. Symptoms of burning eyes, bodily heat, and pain in the back and chest are very common in a number of cultures and the somatization connection is often reflected in the language. A tribe in Nigeria, for example, describes depression as "bad heart." A number of cultures equate psychological distress with heart distress.

The most common presenting symptoms of patients attending medical clinics include abdominal and chest pain, dyspnea, headache, fatigue, cough, back pain, dizziness, and nervousness. These symptoms are also the symptoms most often attributed to "psychiatric disturbance." Pain is by far the most common symptom, especially that involving the back, abdomen, chest, head, and pelvis. Also common are complaints of fatigue, dizziness, shortness of breath, and palpitations. Sufferers from such symptoms are often desperate for a nonpsychological explanation of their condition. There was much recent media interest in the possibility that chronic mononucleosis or chronic Epstein-Barr virus (EBV) was the condition responsible for chronic fatigue symptoms. Research was generally unable to verify any correlation between the symptoms experienced and immune system measures indicative of EBV activity (Greenberg, 1990). In fact, patients with the symptoms, under careful examination, have in many instances been found to exhibit symptoms of depression. The condition is now called chronic fatigue syndrome and is likely to have multiple determinants which include both anxiety and depression. College students, for example, who complained of excessive fatigue also reported considerable symptoms of anxiety and/or depression. Interestingly, psychoanalytic writers have cited helplessness, fruitless effort, and frustration as the psychic conditions most often leading to chronic fatigue.

There are a number of definitions of somatization, with each definition reflecting varying degrees of inference about the psychological significance of the presenting somatic symptoms. The simplest definition resembles very closely the definition of conversion reaction:

> Somatization is defined here as a tendency to experience and communicate somatic distress and symptoms unaccounted for by pathological findings, to attribute them to physical illness, and to seek medical help for them. It is usually assumed that this tendency becomes manifest in response to psychosocial stress brought about by life events and situations that are personally stressful to the individual. This interpretation represents an *inference* on the part of outside observers, since somatizing persons usually do not recognize, and may explicitly deny, a causal link between their distress and its presumed source. They respond primarily in a somatic rather than a psychological mode and tend to regard their symptoms as indicative of physical illness and hence in need of medical attention. (Lipowski, 1988, p. 1359)

Susan Sontag (1979) described somatization as an emotional body language, a metaphor for social and personal experience, a tendency to avoid the use of emotional language in describing feelings in favor of descriptions of bodily sensations. Many of the elderly, for example, experience the loneliness and social isolation accompanying physical decline in terms of their physical aches and pains. In clinic, the symptoms of somatizing patients are also called "hysterical," "hypochondriacal," "functional," and "psychogenic." All these terms imply that however strongly such symptoms suggest physical illness, they belong to a different realm and are but an imitation of the "real" thing. Persistent somatizers have been given various names, such as "crocks," "turkeys," and "problem patients." These labels express the frustration of doctors faced with patients who claim to be physically ill, clamor for medical diagnosis and treatment, tend to be dissatisfied with any therapy they get, and are inclined to "doctor shop." Pilowsky (1990) viewed such patients as presenting with abnormal illness behavior, which he defined as:

> the persistence of a maladaptive mode of experiencing, perceiving, evaluating, and responding to one's own health status, despite the fact that a doctor has provided a lucid and accurate appraisal of the situation and management to be

followed (if any), with opportunities for discussion, negotiation, and clarification, based on adequate assessment of all relevant biological, psychological, social, and cultural factors. (p. 207)

Pilowsky devised an Illness Behavior Questionnaire which measures a number of dimensions of this construct, including hypochondriasis, disease conviction, somatization, and emotional denial. For Pilowsky, the concept of illness behavior is vital for understanding the patient's psychosocial as well as biological difficulties. There are also patients at the other end of the continuum who show abnormal denial of illness:

> Mr. B, a 56-year-old man who had suffered his third massive myocardial infarction two days earlier, was found doing pushups and other strenuous exercises in the hospital. When he requested to leave the hospital later the same day, he explained to the psychiatric consultant that he had had a 'small heart attack' but believed that the best way to manage the continuing chest pain was to 'exercise through it.' (Strauss, Spitzer, & Muskin, 1990, p. 1170)

We need to be careful in working with concepts such as somatization not to downgrade the nature of symptoms reported by the patient. Some theorists believe that patients scoring high on measures of somatization are not really sick and that that their symptoms are less than real. Costa and McCrae (1987), for example, proposed that *neuroticism* may represent a form of somatization. They described neuroticism as a chronic condition of irritability and distress-proneness which operates *independently* from signs of real physical illness. That is, neuroticism or negative affectivity is associated with the verbal report of both psychological and physical problems but is not necessarily associated with the presence of more physical disease. For example, they referred to a number of studies linking anxiety, depression, and other negative affective traits to hypertension while noting a number of other studies reporting no relation or even an inverse relation between neuroticism and degree of arterial blockage or stenosis as determined by arteriography. In their terms, this means that neuroticism is not a causal agent in the development of heart disease but simply that neuroticism is related to somatic concerns and health care-seeking behavior. "The anxious, irritable, dejected individual seeks out and amplifies bodily sensations." Thus, one reason given for the greater incidence of reported hypertension in these individuals is based on their greater tendency to visit clinics. Individuals high in somatic concerns are more likely to visit their physicians.

Some patients do present with a variety of symptoms for which no objective signs can be detected. However, it would be a serious mistake to conclude that there is no relationship of consequence between psychological variables and "real" disease processes. For example, the observation that measures of neuroticism correlate *negatively* with degree of arterial damage might point to an important link between nonemotional expressive style and disease processes, rather than to no relationship between such variables. At this stage of knowledge both positive and negative findings need to be carefully examined for elements of concepts which will help improve our understanding of the complex linkages between mental and physical processes. Also, how people cope with disease profoundly affects the course of the disease. Multiple sclerosis, for example, is a progressive disease which destroys the nervous system. The symptoms are unpredictable in onset and associated with sensory and motor disruptions, visual disturbances, urinary and sexual dysfunction, tremor, and profound fatigue. Severe life stress can lead to the onset of the disease as well as worsen the symptoms; whereas periods of calm can result in temporary remission of the symptoms. Thus, psychological and physical correlates of stress and anxiety can exacerbate the already present symptoms of the disease. Finally, fear, anxiety, and depression about the disease can severely limit one's ability to optimally manage the disease.

The recommended view, with all disorders and diseases, is to consider illness and illness behavior or signs and symptoms as integrated events and to encourage the search for variables which link these dimensions in a causal fashion. Mechanic's (1986) definition of illness and illness behavior comes close to this perspective:

> The concept of illness or disease refers to limited scientific models for characterizing constellations of symptoms and the conditions underlying them. The concept of *illness behavior,* in contrast, describes the ways in which people respond to bodily indications and the conditions under which they come to view them as abnormal. Illness behavior thus involves the manner in which individuals monitor their bodies, define and interpret their symptoms, take remedial action, and utilize sources of help as well as the more formal health care system. It is also concerned with how people monitor and respond to symptoms and symptom change over the course of an illness and how this affects behavior, remedial actions taken, and response to treatment. (p. 1)

The objective in this book is to develop a balanced perspective of the interface or two-way flow that occurs between our psychological experiences of physical symptoms and to use these experiences to facilitate health. Some writers believe that our society has already "gone funny" with its quest for mind-body understanding and "wellness." Barsky (1988), in his book *Worried Sick,* stated that society has developed a "dis-ease about disease," that we have become a nation of hypochondriacs. By constantly focusing on potential threats to our bodies (e.g., fat and sodium content of foods, weight, lack of exercise), we run the risk of being crippled by fear of disease. Because of this fear, bodily sensations and symptoms have a potential "fatal" significance. In addition, there is also a growing expectation that we are each somehow responsible for our own illness and, conversely, wellness. Our society has come to believe in the healing power of the mind, in the control of health not just through behavior but through attitude, thought, and emotion. It is important therefore that, as individuals, we develop a perspective, based, not on fear, but on theory, research, and personal experience. Only then will we be able to develop a feeling of confidence in our internal and external environments.

The approach advocated may facilitate a general condition vital to health which has been described by Antonovsky (1987) as a "sense of coherence." Sense of coherence (SOC) is defined as:

> . . . . a global orientation that expresses the extent to which one has a pervasive, enduring though dynamic feeling of confidence that (1) the stimuli deriving from one's internal and external environments in the course of living are structured, predictable, and explicable; (2) the resources are available to one to meet the demands posed by these stimuli; and (3) these demands are challenges, worthy of investment and engagement. (p. 19)

Antonovsky derived this concept after examining the characteristics of a large number of individuals who managed to cope well following a major trauma. Three cognitive characteristics are contained in the definition of SOC: (1) comprehensibility—the degree to which demands make sense; (2) manageability—a high probability that things will work out as well as can be expected; and (3) meaningfulness—the extent to which one feels that life makes sense emotionally, that some of the problems of life are worthy of commitment and challenge. Inner feelings, interpersonal relations, major activities, and existential issues involving death, conflict, and isolation, are all at the heart of SOC. Interview excerpts from a person with a weak SOC and one with a strong SOC are provided below:

Example of a weak SOC:

> I'm a sick woman, I always suffered from something, even before the tragedy three years ago when my husband died. . . . They tossed him out of the hospital, as if there was nothing wrong. But I knew from his looks that he was sick . . . I believe in fate. . . . My life has been full of losses even from before. . . . Things are rough, I don't have any faith left in anyone. . . . All of life is full of problems, only in dying there are no problems. . . . I don't even think of going out with a man or of getting married again. (p. 72)

Example of a strong SOC:

> I would walk a great deal intentionally, even against doctor's orders. . . . I laugh a great deal, laugh with everyone. . . . When my first serious boyfriend

left me because of his family's pressure, it hurt, but I knew it was for the best, because there would only be problems with his family. . . . I love to dance, to swim. . . . My husband's family loves me. . . . I got pregnant right after we were married but lost the baby. . . . So far I'm doing fine. . . . I always had a strong will, never felt that there was something wrong with me. . . . You have to know how to use your life. (p. 69)

Antonovsky hypothesized that the channel by which SOC is related to health and illness is based in part on underlying psychic tension. Regardless of the source of intra and interpersonal difficulties, the message to the brain is the same, "You have a problem." "Tension, then, reflects the recognition in the brain that some need one has is unfulfilled, that a demand on one has to be met, that one has to do something if one is to realize a goal." Tension also has a physiologic and biochemical substrate. Learning to identify and regulate the psychobiology of tension in ourselves and others is a theme that runs throughout this book.

SYMPTOMS WITHIN SYSTEMS

The theoretical and clinical themes of the material which follows emphasize psychobiological processes within the individual. The "searchlight" is on the processes that mediate between psychological and physiological variables within the person rather than processes which mediate between the person and his or her environment. Although the focus is on the interplay of thoughts, feelings, and physiological processes "inside the skin," it is recognized that individuals cannot always "go it alone" and have a strong need for supportive social relationships. Some attention will be devoted to the individual's interpersonal world, as health and illness issues cannot be fully understood without consideration of the individual's family, work, and social environments. This broad approach is referred to as *system's theory,* which has been used by numerous theorists to describe the multitude of factors contributing to health and illness.

Angyal (1941) described a system as *unitas multiplex,* that is multiple components bound together by a unifying structure in which each subsystem is an integral part of the whole. The most important tenets are that (a) systems are composed of interrelated parts, (b) no part of the system functions independently of the whole system, (c) change in one part is associated with change in all others, and (d) systems maintain a regular state of balance or homeostasis. The key issue is that the health of the components is as much determined by the "health" of the other components as it is by the condition of the component in question.

Systems theory was originally adapted from the biological sciences. Hu-

man-systems models draw heavily on the concepts of hierarchical organization and cybernetic processes of communication and control (Seeman,
1989). The cybernetic concept (Wiener, 1954) is needed to account for the
dynamic and bidirectional interactions that occur among the subsystems.
Moreover, it is assumed that living systems have self-regulating properties
and a healthy system is one characterized by information exchange and
self-correction. From a systems perspective, problems arise when "regula-
tory processes go askew, disregulation prevails, and the harmonious working of the system is disrupted" (Seeman, 1989).

Personal applications of systems models are at times difficult to com-
prehend, both in knowing where the "system" resides (i.e., within the
person or within the environment at large) and also what the individual's
role is in terms of self-regulating the system(s). Angyal, for example, viewed
the critical system in terms of a "biosphere" which developed from the
dynamic interplay between individual and environmental variables. The
biosphere resided neither in the individual or in the environment but rather
represented a new property based on both environmental and individual
properties.

Knowing which level of system analysis to use in understanding ourselves
and others is often a difficult issue. To illustrate with an everyday example,
let us examine a hypothetical college student who is bothered by frequent
migraine headache attacks which are interfering both with her ability to
listen attentively in class and to study effectively for examinations. She lives
at home with two loving parents who have high expectations of their
daughter, and has a caring boyfriend who tries to be supportive but at times
resents the disruption of their relationship created by the headaches. No one
can understand the cause of her increasing headache activity and the student is finding it increasingly difficult to balance the scholastic and interpersonal demands in her life.

A systems model for understanding the student's plight is presented in
Figure 1.4. The model, adapted from Seeman (1989) has three characteristics found in most systems models: a hierarchical structure shown by the
arrangement of the subsystems; the reciprocal communications as indicated
by the bidirectional arrows; and the longitudinal aspects of the entire
system. The horizontal dimension of the model shows that health and illness
need to be mapped in longitudinal developmental terms so as to emphasize
that the continuum of health and illness is an ongoing process.

The various subsystems may be grouped as representing *intraindividual*
(biochemical, physiological, sensory, cognitive) systems and *interpersonal*
(person-to-environment, person-to-person) systems. Systems theorists vary
considerably in the emphasis placed on these larger categories. With children, for example, symptoms such as headache are often seen as indicative
of dysregulation in the interpersonal subsystems and family therapy is

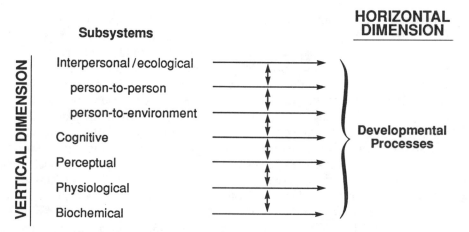

Figure 1.4. A human-system health framework (Seeman, 1989). Reproduced from American Psychologist, 44, 1099–1109. Copyright 1989 American Psychological Association. Reprinted by permission.

prescribed. The emphasis in adults generally shifts to the other end of the continuum, with regulation attempted through medication at the biochemical level.

A developmental sequence for our hypothetical student with migraine may be as follows: Her headaches may have begun or at least become more noticeable in adolescence and finally surfaced as a problem in adulthood. Rest and analgesics may have helped initially but now the problem seems to resist all forms of chemical control. The headaches may have their onset early in the morning, making it difficult for the student and her boyfriend to understand why this is happening. Neurological examinations of such individuals are almost invariably negative and the medical specialist may advise the patient to learn to live with the problem since nothing more can be done. Such advice generally fails and the student may try some form of physical intervention, such as acupuncture or psychological interventions such as relaxation and/or biofeedback training. These techniques may also have limited value, especially in the context of a student with high personal goals, university demands, family issues, and the distress associated with the disorder itself. The student will likely attempt to ignore the pain, not bother others with whining, and attempt to focus on university demands while at the same time fight off the relentless pain and suffering. Over time, this becomes an extremely frustrating and exhausting experience, with a strong likelihood of worsening of symptoms.

To understand the occurrence of these headache symptoms in a systems context, we need to appreciate the (a) physiochemical individuality that makes one person more susceptible to headache than another, (b) the physiological-biochemical interactions that occur in the developing attacks, (c) the sensory-physiological interactions, (d) the cognitive coping styles in use, and (e) the interpersonal demands and constraints that are taking place. Ultimately, we may need to go even further in understanding the condition and examine the larger culture. Prior to the development of women's consciousness groups for example, many women attributed a variety of somatic and psychic symptoms to personal inadequacy. The symptoms were often viewed as solely a "personality" problem or deficit within the woman. Now, there is a greater tendency to view such conditions as resulting from social constraints, exploitive relationships, and blocked opportunities to achieve career goals. From this perspective, the system explanation for a particular condition extends to society at large.

For someone with headache, there are no easy answers as to which component of the system needs to be altered in order to control the condition. By adopting a systems position, we are recognizing that illness is a condition that is influenced by a multitude of factors within and outside the skin. How should treatment decisions be determined? At present, they are generally attempted solely at the biochemical level, without due regard to the impact of the individual's thoughts, feelings, and bodily reactions to situations and events. Systems thinking teaches us to appreciate the complexity of factors which may be contributing to the development and maintenance of particular disorders.

2
Emotions

A large part of living involves emotional experience—some would say that "living" is synonymous with emotional experience. We observed in the opening chapter that emotions have been implicated in health and illness throughout the history of ancient and modern medicine. Negative emotions have been associated with migraine, hypertension, ulcer, irritable bowel, and other diseases, including cancer. We still do not know, for certain, whether emotional processes contribute to the onset of such disorders or, instead, are the consequence of having such disorders. In spite of lacking evidence, the conviction that emotional health and physical health go hand in hand continues to gain strength. Even in the absence of physical illness, the severe occurrences of negative emotions involving anxiety and/or depression constitute major health problems and can have devastating consequences on afflicted individuals and their families.

Freud recognized that emotions have both constructive and destructive potential. Freudian theory laid the foundation for formulas of emotional health which advocate emotional expressiveness and, conversely, not "bottling up" feelings within oneself. Many people believe that it is not emotions that cause human problems but rather our way of handling the emotions. If we feel angry or depressed because of mistreatment, it is not the feelings that cause difficulties but rather our inability to respond appropriately to the emotional signals while the feelings are still at a low or moderate intensity. Historically, our culture has placed a premium on emotional control. An individual's success and survival often depend on maintaining very tight control in demanding situations. Women in particular often describe having to maintain very tight control over their feelings, reflecting an internal code not to display anger or become visibly upset. Many women patients with somatic complaints comment that they feel that they have to "be right or certain" before expressing themselves for fear of being "put down." For both men and women, there is increasing appreciation of the importance to health of emotional expressiveness. Growing numbers of behavioral scientists are pointing to the motivational and adaptive function of emotional expression. Parents, teachers, and therapists are also recognizing the importance of acknowledging negative emotions as a healthy alternative to suppressing or eliminating them.

This chapter explores what is currently known of emotions as they relate to day-to-day experience. In understanding emotions within ourselves and others, we need to know something of their physiologic origins as well as their psychologic function. We also need to know how to recognize subtle psychobiologic processes that occur during emotional activity. Thought is normally directed toward the object of our emotion rather than toward internal changes that accompany the emotion. Seldom do we reflect on the internal processes that underlie emotional experience.

PERIPHERAL DETERMINANTS OF FEELING

Most emotion theorists believe that peripheral physiologic systems contribute to both the intensity and quality of emotional experience. The peripheral nervous system is comprised of two major subsystems that are important to this discussion, the *autonomic nervous system* and the *somatic nervous system*. The autonomic nervous system activates smooth muscles of internal organs, glands, heart, and lungs. It is composed of afferent fibers which carry signals from the organs of the body to the central nervous system, and efferent fibers which carry signals from the central nervous system back out to the body. The system generally operates outside of our awareness in the control of bodily functions (e.g., regulation of heart rate, gastrointestinal peristalsis). The somatic nervous system is tied to sensory and motor functions of the body and regulates activity in striated or skeletal muscles in day-to-day interactions with the external world. It too is composed of afferent nerves which carry sensory information from receptors in the skin, eyes, ears, and joints to the central nervous system, and the efferent nerves, which carry signals from the central nervous system to the skeletal muscles. Both systems are involved in emotional behavior and likely work in a high degree of concert. Their interaction becomes especially important when we are trying to understand relationships between stress, tension, and emotionality as well as symptom onset and self-regulation.

The autonomic nervous system itself has two major subdivisions: the sympathetic nervous system and the parasympathetic nervous system, with each division originating from different sections of the brainstem and spinal cord. In the sympathetic division, the nerve fibers originate in the middle part of the spinal cord, in the segments between the neck and lower spine. These nerves run to a vertical chain of ganglia (collection of nerve cells that lie outside the central nervous system) that exists on each side of the spinal cord. Fibers that enter the chain are called preganglionic and those that leave are called postganglionic. In the sympathetic nervous system, every preganglionic fiber connects to several ganglion cells, which means that there is much "cross-talk" between sympathetic fibers. In fact, the name *sympathetic,* meaning "in sympathy," indicates that the system works as a unit or in an all-or-nothing fashion when stimulated. When a person is threatened or angry, or is engaging in strenuous exercise, the sympathetic nervous system prepares the body for action by increasing heart rate, causing the liver to release sugar for the muscles, stimulating the release of epinephrine, and inhibiting the digestive processes so that blood can be diverted to the periphery.

The fibers in the parasympathetic division originate above and below the sympathetic nerve fibers. Unlike the sympathetic nervous system, the parasympathetic nervous system has preganglionic fibers that are long and that run right up to the target organ before forming a junction. Because there is little opportunity for interconnection among the fibers, the parasympathetic system tends to function much more discretely. Basically, the parasympathetic system carries out bodily functions that conserve and protect bodily resources such as digestion and the elimination of wastes.

James-Lange Theory of Emotion

The James-Lange theory of emotion represents one of the earliest theoretical efforts to relate peripheral bodily changes to emotions. In 1890 William James proposed that physiological changes in the peripheral nervous system, when perceived in consciousness, resulted in the emotional experience. A Danish physiologist named Carl Lange proposed a similar explanation of emotion, and the position is now referred to as the James-Lange theory. The theory is essentially a sensory feedback model of emotion and assumes that (a) the peripheral physiological changes precede the actual emotional experience, and (b) the pattern of peripheral physiological change is different from one emotion to the next. To quote James:

> We have a scheme perfectly capable of representing the process of the emotions. An object falls on a sense organ, affects a cortical part, and is apperceived [perceived below awareness] by the appropriate cortical center; or else the latter, excited inwardly, gives rise to an idea of the same object. Quick as a flash, the reflex currents pass through their preordained channels, alter the condition of muscle, skin and viscus; and these alterations, perceived like the original object, in as many portions of the cortex, combine with it in consciousness and transform it from an object simply apprehended into an object emotionally felt. (James, 1890, p. 474)

This theory was quickly criticized by Walter Cannon (1929–1970) who argued that:

1. Separation of the autonomic nervous system from the central nervous system does not alter emotional behavior.

2. Artificial induction of autonomic responses that are characteristic of strong emotion does not produce the emotions.

3. Autonomic responses are basically the same across different emotional states.

It is instructive to examine these criticisms in detail.

Criticism 1: Separation of the viscera does not alter emotional behavior. James offered the following possibility for a demonstration of support for his position:

> A positive proof of the theory would . . . be given if we could find a subject absolutely anesthetic inside and out, but not paralytic, so that emotion-inspiring objects might evoke the usual bodily expressions from him, but who, on being consulted, should say that no subjective emotional affection was felt. Such a man would be like one who, because he eats, appears to bystanders to be hungry, but who afterwards confesses that he had no appetite at all. (p. 455)

James was saying that support for his theory might come from examining a patient who, as a result of some injury, no longer had afferent feedback from the autonomic nervous system. James thought that someone with a damaged spine in the neck region would meet this requirement because it was believed that the autonomic system, at least in terms of the sympathetic division, is controlled primarily from fibers entering the middle part of the spinal cord. Dana (1921) described a patient who had a broken neck at the third and fourth cervical level. She was a complete quadriplegic and had very few muscles at her command. Her parasympathetic system was functioning, but her sympathetic was not. Dana reported that she was still capable of showing emotions of grief, joy, displeasure, and affection. More recent observations of spinal cord-injured patients are consistent with this observation as it appears that individuals deprived of sensory feedback from the neck down still experience the full range of emotions. Afferent feedback may not have a causal influence in the origin of emotions.

Criticism 2. Drug-induced physiological changes do not produce emotions. A direct test of the James-Lange theory would be to induce autonomic nervous changes artificially and determine if subjects become emotional. Such a study was carried out very early by Maranon (cited in Lader & Tyrer, 1975). In the study, 210 subjects were injected with epinephrine and then asked to report their feelings. Of the subjects, 71% reported physical symptoms with no emotional overtones; 29% responded with what Maranon labeled as "cold" or "as if" emotions ("I feel as if I were awaiting a great happiness," "as if moved," "as if going to weep," and "as if I had a great fright"). This study indicated that drug-induced peripheral changes are not sufficient for emotional experience.

Criticism 3. Autonomic responses are the same across different emotions. Cannon based this criticism on observations of hormonal changes in cats which had been exposed to a barking dog. Reading his description of the changes observed makes it clear that there is nothing that would differentiate one emotion from another:

> The visceral changes wrought by sympathetic stimulation may be listed as follows: acceleration of the heart, contraction of arterioles, dilation of bronchioles, increase of blood sugar, inhibition of activity of the digestive glands, inhibition of gastrointestinal peristalsis, sweating, discharge of adrenin, widening of the pupils, and erection of hairs. These changes are seen in great excitement under any circumstances. (Cannon, 1929–1970, p. 351)

We cannot know, of course, what Cannon's cats were experiencing during these confrontations with barking dogs.

Studying physiological changes associated with emotions in humans is not an easy task. A significant difficulty is inducing emotion within the constraints of an artificial laboratory setting. In the 1950s there were efforts to induce the most primitive emotions, anger and fear, through laboratory manipulations. These studies were derived from what is still known as the *Funkenstein hypothesis* (Funkenstein, 1955). Funkenstein hypothesized that it was possible to differentiate anger and fear on the basis of hormonal responses. Fear was believed to be associated with an adrenaline- or epinephrine-like response while anger was believed to be associated with a noradrenaline- or norepinephrine-like response. These two hormones were further hypothesized to produce different cardiovascular responses, with epinephrine leading to increases in heart rate and norepinephrine leading to increases in diastolic blood pressure.

Efforts to experimentally induce emotions typically involved frightening and/or criticizing subjects during some difficult or unsolvable problem (Ax, 1953; Funkenstein, 1955). In general, these studies showed nonspecific arousal of the physiological measures being recorded. That is, cardiovascular, respiratory and muscular activity all tended to increase under anger or fear conditions. Some differentiation did occur which was generally consistent with the epinephrine-norepinephrine hypothesis in that heart rate increases were generally greater under fear and diastolic blood pressure increases were generally greater under anger. The changes in physiological measures, however, were far from the degree of specificity required to differentiate anger from fear.

One of the few clinical examples of specificity of emotion and peripheral physiology occurs with blood phobia. Most phobics show generalized physiological arousal in the presence of fearful stimuli. Blood phobics, however, show a unique pattern of response, which has been documented by Ost and colleagues (Ost & Sterner, 1987). Blood phobics, when presented with a film depicting surgical procedures, exhibited a diphasic cardiovascular response. Initially, the subjects displayed increases in both heart rate and blood pressure, which were followed by large decreases in both measures and occasional fainting. This response pattern represented a high degree of stimulus-response specificity in that these individuals did not faint in the presence of other frightening stimuli. The fainting may reflect a historic adaptive response to bleeding (Barlow, 1988) in which decreases in blood pressure and heart rate accompanying fainting may serve to minimize blood loss and shock. Ost and Sterner treated blood phobics with a technique called "applied tension." Blood phobics were instructed to tense major muscle groups at the first signs of hypotension. They were then instructed to apply this tension while viewing a series of slides depicting wounds and considerable gore. Finally, they were taken to a blood donor center where they not only observed others giving blood but gave blood themselves. In the last session they witnessed thoracic surgery. The treatment was highly successful.

In general, researchers have had a most difficult time isolating physiological changes that would clearly differentiate one emotion from the next. Statistical differentiation, when observed, has not been strong enough to permit one to examine the physiological profile and state, with confidence, which emotion was likely being experienced. In fact, the repeated finding of small magnitude and statistically nonsignificant correlations between self-report and physiological measures has led to use of terms such as "disconcordance," "desynchrony," and "dissociation" to account for the apparent independence or "imperfect coupling" of the physiological and psychological (as well as behavioral) response systems. Clinicians often see desynchrony in patients that have undergone behavioral treatment for anxiety reduction. Exposure treatment, for example, is commonly used to treat a number of specific fears. A person with a fear of flying may with exposure treatment show behavioral signs of improvement but subjectively and/or physiologically may still exhibit considerable fear while flying. Although terms like desynchrony are not favored within a psychobiologic framework, they are useful for emphasizing the importance of studying emotions at more than one level. In clinic, for example, it is often important to recognize with the patient the somatic, cognitive, and behavioral components of a negative emotion such as anxiety and to design modality-specific therapies which deal with each component, that is, cognitive techniques for cognitive symptoms, somatic techniques for somatic symptoms, and behaviorally-oriented techniques for behavioral symptoms.

Efforts to isolate the physiological correlates of different emotional experiences assume that emotions, whether induced or studied naturally, occur in a discrete fashion. However, most occurrences of human emotion are likely a mixture of several feeling states. Emotion theorist Izard (1977) views anxiety, for example, as a combination of fear with distress/sadness, shame, guilt, interest, and even anger. Furthermore, the blend may vary from one situation to the next; on one occasion, fear, anger, and distress may comprise anxiety while on another occasion, fear may combine with shame and guilt. Some emotions, like joy, anger, and fear are considered "basic" emotions while others like jealousy and guilt are considered a mixture or combination of the basic emotions. White and Mullen (1989) listed six affective components of romantic jealousy:

Anger (hate, disgust vengefulness, contempt, annoyance, rage)
Fear (anxiety, tenseness, worry, distress)
Sadness (blueness, depression, hopelessness, suffering, melancholy)
Envy (resentment, covetousness, begrudging)
Sexual arousal (lust, desire, passion)
Guilt (regret, shame, remorse, embarrassment)

According to White and Mullen, romantic jealousy, although often accompanied by physiological reactions experienced as a "jealous flash," is not accompanied by physiological changes which are unique to the feeling.

Jealousy as well as other human emotions are very complex conditions and not likely to be analyzable in terms of specific physiological changes, either within the peripheral nervous system or, for that matter, within the central nervous system. Jealous persons as well as angry or anxious persons engage in a variety of complex patterns of responding, including engaging in more frequent intimate communication, withholding affection, verbal and /or physical assault, denial that there is a threat, and actions such as getting drunk or taking a long drive, which distract from unpleasant feelings. Jealousy must be analyzed and treated from a biopsychosocial systems perspective.

Facial Feedback

The majority of research dealing with physiological differentiation of emotion has focused on autonomic nervous system parameters. However, more recent efforts have dealt with muscles, particular the voluntary striated muscles of the face. There is some evidence that sensory feedback from facial expression contributes to emotional experience. This hypothesis has its origins with Darwin (1872–1965) who viewed emotional expressiveness as innate. He noted that facial expressions are the same in those born blind as in those who are normally sighted, and that similar emotional expressions are present in different cultures. Darwin also believed that even voluntary emotion expression is capable of causing an emotional feeling:

> The free expression by outward signs of an emotion intensifies it. On the other hand, the repression, as far as this is possible, of all outward signs softens our emotions. He who gives way to violent gestures will increase his rage; he who does not control the signs of fear will experience fear in a greater degree. (Darwin, 1872–1965, p. 365)

Our reactions to faces appears to be innate, especially faces which are angry, critical, or rejecting in nature. Ohman (1986) demonstrated that conditioning to such faces is established very quickly and seems to occur outside of conscious awareness. Such conditioning is also highly specific and occurs only when the stimulus person stares directly at the subject.

Izard (1977, 1990) emphasized the importance of afferent input from facial muscles in determining emotional experience. He noted that the Vth cranial nerve, the trigeminal nerve, is an afferent nerve which provides sensory feedback from facial muscles and the skin. There are three main branches to the trigeminal nerve, one for each major region of the face. Each of these regions also contains muscle groups that contribute differentially to the emotion-specific components of the facial expressions of the emotions.

Research by Ekman and Friesen (1986) on facial expressions of emotion has identified several patterns of facial muscle movements that are reliably associated with specific emotions across a variety of cultures. These universal or pan-cultural facial expressions of emotion include facial expressions of happiness, surprise, anger, fear, disgust, and sadness. Contempt has also been added to the list. Facial expressions are analyzed using the Facial Action Coding System (FACS) which was developed by Ekman and Friesen. FACS is an anatomically based system which codes facial expressions using a set of 44 action units or AUs. Each AU represents the movement of a single muscle or a group of muscles that function as a unit. Ekman, Levenson, and Friesen (1983) performed an interesting study of facial feedback by having subjects contract specific muscle groups known to be associated with the emotions of anger, fear, sadness, happiness, surprise, and disgust. They were told to hold these expressions for 10 seconds while autonomic measures were recorded. No specific instruction was given to mimic or image an emotion, they were simply told to focus on specific muscle groups. Physiologic changes were greater for negative emotion than positive emotion. Within anger and fear, the only real difference occurred in terms of finger temperature, which was significantly greater for anger than fear. Fear and anger produced similar heart rate increases but colder fingers in fear. None of the physiologic changes was of large magnitude.

The implications of the facial feedback research for emotion theory remain to be specified. Some people believe that emotion expression plays no causal role in determining internal states and represents, instead, a social-communicative function. There are others, however, who are pursuing the possibility that facial expression is directly involved in the activation and regulation of emotion. Known as the facial feedback hypothesis, it is maintained that sensory feedback from receptors in the facial muscles and skin contribute to the affective experience. Researchers in this area have either manipulated the expressions in their subjects (as with the Ekman & Friesen study) or had subjects engage in self-managed expressions through the use of emotional and non-emotional imagery.

We all know that there is more to happiness or anger than simply smiling or frowning. We also know, especially in situations where there is social obligation to smile, that it is possible to facially simulate a feeling and experience either no feeling or a contrary feeling. In addition, it may be that innervation of voluntary and involuntary facial expressions involves different neural pathways (Izard, 1990). Even so, this research has drawn attention to the importance of expressiveness and adds some credence to the advice to "smile when you feel blue" and "whistle a happy tune when you're afraid."

BRAIN PROCESSES

Full understanding of the role of peripheral physiological responses in emotion depends on the link such responses have with processes within the brain. Although notions of emotion centers within the brain have lost favor, there is ongoing research into physiochemical processes that contribute to emotion. Much of the research points to emotional pathways or "circuits" within the brain that are part of our evolutionary past. Some years ago, MacLean (1967) proposed that the human brain is actually comprised of three brains, each different in structure and chemistry and yet interacting and functioning as a single organ. The "brains" are stacked on top of one another and represent different points in the phylogenic development of the human nervous system. The reptilian brain is the oldest brain structure and consists of systems in the upper spinal cord, brainstem, and parts of the midbrain. MacLean considered the reptilian brain to be responsible for stereotyped behaviors based on ancestral learning and ancestral memories. The second structure, the paleomammalian brain, refers to the limbic system, while the third structure, the neomammalian brain, refers to the cortex. The cortex refers to the "gray matter" of the brain or the thin layer of cells 2–5 mm deep in which sensations, muscle control, and problem-solving thought occur. MacLean hypothesized that each of the three divisions has "its own special kind of intelligence, its own memory, its own sense of time and space, and its own motor and other functions."

Emotions are influenced by a number of limbic forebrain structures. The word *limbic* is derived from the Latin word meaning border and the system itself refers to structures that outline the inner surfaces of the cerebral hemispheres. Anatomical regions within the limbic system that are known to play a major role in emotional behavior include the hippocampus, hypothalamus, thalamus, and amygdala. Cannon was one of the first researchers to demonstrate the importance of the hypothalamus in emotion. He found that surgical removal of the cerebral cortex seemed to intensify reactions driven by the hypothalamus whereas surgical destruction of the hypothalamus seemed to eliminate most emotional behavior. For Cannon, the hypothalamus became the seat of emotional behavior.

Decades of animal research attempted to locate areas or structures within the limbic system that are unique to different emotional states. For example, the amygdala has been implicated in anger and aggression. Surgical destruction of this region in monkeys, however, often produced unpredictable rather than predictable emotional changes. Some monkeys became less aggressive as predicted but others became more aggressive, suggesting that the surgery had not removed some fundamental mechanism for aggression but instead seemed to have disrupted some brain process sensitive to helping the animal maintain appropriate social interactions with others in the environment (Pribram, 1976).

Neurobiologists are presently focusing less on specific anatomical sites within the brain and more on the various neurotransmitter systems involving multiple areas of the brain which contribute to emotions (LeDoux, 1987). These transmitter systems are at the basis of efforts to identify systems unique to anxiety and depression and are discussed in Chapter 5. Understanding how these systems contribute to emotions represents a formidable challenge. One research strategy in favor is to identify organized neurobehavioral systems rather than specific locations within the brain. Gray (1982), for example, postulated the existence of a behavioral inhibition system to be at the basis of anxiety. The system has a complex neurochemical basis and involves a number of brain structures, which are collectively referred to as the septo-hippocampal system. The system is activated by stimuli that signal punishment, novel stimuli, and fear stimuli. When activated, the system leads to inhibition of behavior, increased attention to the environment, and increased level of arousal. Norepinephrine and serotonin are major transmitters within the behavioral inhibition system. Antianxiety drugs are believed to exert their effects within this system. Depue (Depue et al., 1989) described a second major system, termed the behavioral facilitation system, which is designed to "mobilize behavior so that active engagement with the environment occurs under appropriate stimulus conditions." The behavioral facilitation system has two major components, initiation of motor activity and incentive-reward motivation. Activation of the system, in humans, is generally associated with positive mood. Dopamine is considered the major transmitter within this system. The involvement of this system in addictive behaviors is examined in Chapter 5.

It is still unknown why some individuals are more or less "emotional" than other individuals. With respect to anxious persons, for example, there is the possibility that these individuals have a more sensitive noradrenergic system. The term noradrenergic refers to neurons that release norepinephrine. The majority of brain norepinephrine is produced by the locus coeruleus, a collection of cells situated in the pons with major projections to both the septum and hippocampal formation. In animals, it has been observed that higher levels of locus coeruleus activity are associated with vigilance and attention to fear-provoking stimuli. It receives substantial afferent input from the viscera. Suggestions have been made that there is pathological dysregulation of the locus coeruleus in patients with anxiety disorder. However, it is also evident that such mechanisms alone, even if proven to operate in a hyperexcitable state, cannot fully explain anxiety proneness.

BIOPSYCHOSOCIAL APPROACHES

Unidimensional efforts to explain the richness of emotional experience in terms of physiological structures have been matched by similar efforts to explain emotional experience solely or largely in terms of psychological or cognitive variables. The cognitive approach was made popular by Schachter and Singer (1962), who viewed emotion as beginning with the appraisal of one's own emotional state in the context of a particular situation. In the classic Schachter and Singer experiment, subjects were deceived into thinking that they had been given a vitamin drug while in fact they were given injections of epinephrine, a drug which mimics the effects of the sympathetic nervous system. The drug would produce common sympathetic symptoms associated with arousal (palpitation, flushing, tremor) and a consequent need on the part of the subject to interpret or evaluate what was happening. The exact experience, according to Schachter and Singer (1962) would depend on the individual's context or situation. After the injection, subjects were escorted to a waiting room, where, depending on the group assignment, they were presented with varying degrees of information regarding the origins of the sympathetic symptoms. They were also confronted with confederates of the experimenters who created an atmosphere of euphoria or anger/hostility, the expectation being that the unknowing subject would "label" his bodily symptoms in terms of the contextual events taking place (i.e., experience euphoria or anger). Group differences in terms of the emotion experienced were found but the differences were weak and the experiment has not been replicated.

In spite of difficulties in replicating the original experiment, the Schachter and Singer "cognitive label" model proved valuable in emphasizing the contribution of situational context toward determining emotional experience. Ambiguous bodily arousal does lead to a search for an appropriate emotion label and arousal alone will not necessarily lead to emotional experience. For example, the presence of rapid heart rate, oxygen debt, and muscle weakness does not lead to emotion if one has just completed a weekly aerobic workout at the gym. However, the same physical state would be differently appraised, and fear experienced, if it occurred immediately after a pistol-brandishing mugger emerged from the gloom of a deserted alley. (Lang, 1988) The difficulty with the cognitive approach is that it fosters the notion that physiological changes are unidimensional or reflective only of arousal and do not have "quality of emotion" properties.

Biopsychosocial theorists like Izard (1990) and Lang (1985) have attempted to bring together the unique physiological and cognitive aspects of each emotion state. Thus, specific autonomic and somatic processes remain important for understanding the sensory aspects of feeling while cognitive concepts based on appraisal and attribution also remain important. These theorists emphasize that emotion can occur in the absence of cognitive mediation or "labeling." Izard (1990), for example, views emotion as the integration of three interdependent components: experiential, expressive, and physiological. He argues that the experience of an emotion is a feeling state that can exist in consciousness and influence thought and action without being articulated. Izard used both neuroscience and developmental research to suggest that there may be two pathways that activate emotions: one automatic and subconscious, activated through the subcortical pathway; and one mediated by cognition and relayed from the thalamus to the amygdala and neocortex. Izard believes that developmentally the subcortical pathway is primary during infancy, and that, with maturation, the corticolimbic pathway becomes dominant.

Lang (1985) explained the different dimensions of emotional experience in terms of "a network of functionally organized ideas or propositions surrounding the emotion." Termed the bioinformational model, emotions are represented in long-term memory as a network of coded information. Information is organized into three categories: (a) information about the stimulus characteristics of an emotional situation ("that is a snake coming toward me"); (b) information about verbal ("I am going to be attacked"), physiological ("my heart is pounding") and overt behavioral responses ("I had better run away"); and (c) information about the meaning of stimulus and response elements ("I'm doomed"). Activation of any one of these components evokes the other parts of the network. Lang proposed that the network is *processed* when a critical number of propositions is accessed. Accessing of propositions occurs when there is a match between environmental stimuli and information contained in the emotion network, or when prototype-matching information is internally generated, such as through imagery.

In order to treat phobias and emotional problems, within the bioinformational model, it is best to activate, as realistically as possible, the full associative network which is to be dismantled. Processing of a phobia network, for example, would occur relatively consistently when *in vivo* or real-life exposure methods are used, since there would be a near-perfect match between the stimulus information available to the client and the stimulus elements of the network. Processing of the phobia network is likely to be less consistent when imaginal exposure methods are used. In a similar formulation, Foa and Kozak (1986) offered *emotional processing* as the mechanism by which the phobic memory structure is modified. Two conditions are required for the reduction of fear. First, information relevant to the phobia must be made available in order to activate the fear network. Second, additional information must be made available as the phobia network is being processed—information that is incompatible with some of the information in the fear structure—so that a new memory is formed. Emotional processing, then, refers to changes in the fear structure that occur when there is exposure to phobia-relevant information, and information incompatible with the fear network is incorporated into the memory structure. Subjects who show autonomic changes during imagery are assumed to be processing fear-network information, including the response elements. There is some evidence that phobics who rate themselves as good imagers tend to be able to generate fear-relevant physiological changes during imagery. Also, activation of response elements is facilitated by instructions that explicitly direct subjects to experience fear physiologically. Similarly, fear treatment is more effective when treatment leads to activation of verbal, behavioral, and physiological propositions. Lang's model is especially attractive because of its effort to integrate the different dimensions of emotion (verbal, behavioral, physiological) into a single unified subjective experience. Primacy is not given to cognitions but rather cognitions are viewed as one component of a complex memory network that is maintaining the fear or emotion in question. Bodily sensations resulting from physiological change are an equal partner in determining the emotional experience.

Anger has been described within a biopsychosocial framework (Berkowitz, 1990). At the "bio" level, anger is viewed as a basic emotion, with a physiologic substrate that can occur as a primitive response in the absence of threat. Thus, people often become angry when they are exposed to foul odors, high temperatures, or even when they are not feeling well. Anger also often occurs alongside sadness, depression, and pain. Associative networks operate to connect specific types of feelings with particular thoughts and memories and also with specific expressive-motor and physiological reactions. The key assumption is a postulated associative connection between negative affect and anger-related feelings, ideas, and memories. Negative affect of any kind first activates anger-related feelings, action tendencies, and thoughts and memories:

> It is because of these associations that persons who feel bad for one reason or another—whether they have a toothache, are very hot, are exposed to foul smells or an unpleasant noise, or are just very sad or depressed—are likely to be angry, have hostile ideas and memories, and to be aggressively disposed. (p. 496)

People do not, of course, become angry every time an unpleasant event takes place. At the point of stimulus presentation, according to the model, only the rudiments or more primitive components of the anger experience might occur. A fraction of time later, however, higher order cognitive processes begin to operate and the person makes appraisals and causal attributions and considers what feelings and behaviors are appropriate:

> If the afflicted persons' arousal level is weak, for example, they may decide at this time that they are irritated or annoyed rather than angry. Or, as cognitive/ attributional theorizing proposes, afflicted persons may come to believe that they are, for example, sad and not angry, because they believe that one does not feel anger in this particular situation. They may even develop relatively complicated emotional experiences such as anxiety, contempt, guilt, and even depression. The present formulation maintains that these later, more developed emotional experiences are essentially constructed as the mind brings together various sensory, ideational, and memorial inputs from all those available, . . .
> Another important assumption in this model is that the higher order cognitive processing governing the full development of the anger experience does not necessarily always go into operation. The aversively stimulated persons may have to be motivated to think more extensively and deeper about the various kinds of information they have received. . . . (p. 497)

In differentiating anger and sadness, Berkowitz pointed to research which has found greater levels of muscular tension being observed under anger than under fear. In one experiment, women undergraduates were asked to recall and talk about an incident in which they were either angry, sad, happy, or neutral. While speaking they had to generate fist tension by squeezing a hand dynamometer at a weak level or with greater force. After four minutes, they were asked to rate their feelings at the time. As expected, the women recalling the anger-provoking incident while contracting their hand muscles with considerable tension reported the strongest angry feelings, while the greatest ratings on sadness were made by women who were talking about a sad event and not squeezing hard on the hand dynamometer. These findings are consistent with the early James-Lange formulations concerning the importance of motor feedback and also demonstrate the importance of activating cognitive-ideational components in determining the nature and degree of feeling experienced. In the clinical setting, patients with chronic pain conditions often exhibit evidence of considerable muscle activity in the head, face, neck, and jaw when discussing anger-related personal issues. Other investigators (Flor & Turk, 1989) have noted that the mere discussion or imagination of negative feelings produces increases in heart rate, skin conductance, and frontalis EMG in all subjects and very pronounced increases in EMG levels at the affected site of pain patients. Thus activation of a memory of an emotional event elicits bodily responses that are part of the propositional network of the event.

The biopsychosocial approach offers the promise of providing more complete descriptions of the human emotional experience than can be attained with purely biological or psychological formulations. We can see that emotions, although having a biological component, are seldom, if ever, totally determined by biologic variables. This is an important observation, especially for many individuals who are having emotional difficulties and who may believe that their origin is due to some biological "imbalance" or "abnormality." By better recognizing the primitive associative origins of emotions, the connections to other thoughts and feelings, as well as the peripheral physiological components, we are better able to understand emotions within ourselves and to assist those in need.

The biopsychosocial model also has direct relevance to understanding violence in the world at large. In 1986, a large number of scholars met at the University of Seville in Spain and, with the support of UNESCO, drafted the Seville Statement on Violence. The purpose of the statement was to challenge "unfounded sterotypic thinking on the inevitability of war" (American Psychological Association, 1990). The Seville Statement consisted of five propositions challenging the assumption that aggression and violence are genetically determined and that we are biologically programmed vis-a-vis our "violent brain" to engage in aggressive behavior. From our discussion, it is clear that while we do have the neural apparatus for aggression and violence, these behaviors are not automatically activated in true instinctive fashion. Instead, we have high-order brain processes based on conditioning and socialization which ultimately determine how we act.

CLINICAL ANXIETY AND PANIC

Individuals often present to medical and emergency clinics seeking treatment for physical symptoms which have their origins in anxiety. The most frightening anxiety experience is the panic attack. Some individuals are so troubled by this condition that it becomes a clinical problem. As defined by the American Psychiatric Association (1987), panic is viewed as a distinct anxiety condition and the attack is characterized by the sudden onset of intense apprehension, fear, or terror, often associated with feelings of impending doom. The symptoms most commonly reported during panic attacks are listed in Table 2-1.

Panic sufferers often associate the physical symptoms with impending heart attacks and because of the uncertain origins of the symptoms, especially the associated chest pain accompanying the attack, many panic patients seek help from cardiologists. These patients may undergo an angiogram to determine if their coronary arteries are occluded. The difficulty facing the patient is that chest pain symptoms associated with coronary artery disease are similar to chest pain symptoms reported by patients with normal angiograms. In patients where there is no evidence of occlusion or

TABLE 2.1 Somatic and Cognitive Symptoms of Panic

Somatic Symptoms
    Shortness of breath (dyspnea) or smothering sensations
    Choking
    Palpitations or accelerated heart rate (tachycardia)
    Chest pain or discomfort
    Sweating
    Faintness, dizziness, lightheadedness, or unsteady feelings
    Nausea or abdominal distress
    Numbness
    Trembling or shaking
    Flushes (hot flashes) or chills

Cognitive symptoms
    Fear of dying
    Fear of going crazy or doing something uncontrolled
    Depersonalization or derealization

Note: From American Psychiatric Association (1987). Diagnostic amd statistical manual of mental disorders (3rd ed., rev.). Washington, DC: Author. Copyright by the American Psychiatric Association. Reprinted by permission.

stenosis, the suspicion is that their chest pain may be resulting from panic-related anxiety (Mukerji et al., 1987).

Panic attacks are surprisingly frequent in the population, with studies showing that approximately 35% of the individuals sampled reported one or more attacks during the previous year (Barlow, 1988). Situations in which the attacks are commonly reported to occur include public speaking, interpersonal conflict, and tests and exams. Many individuals report experiencing panic attacks without any cause whatsoever. These "spontaneous" panic attacks have been observed to awake individuals from sleep and occur independently from recalled nightmares or environmental sleep interruptions (Craske & Barlow, 1990). Common symptoms experienced by those with nocturnal episodes are: rapid and/or irregular heart rate, shortness of breath, choking or smothering sensations, trembling and fear of dying. Shortness of breath is also one of the most frequent and intense symptoms of individuals experiencing a daytime panic attack.

For the panic sufferer, the most mysterious and frightening aspect of the panic attack is its sudden onset in the absence of apparent provocation. The anxiety is experienced as a "rush" that seems to develop without "cognitive" cause. This attribute of panic is illustrated in a short story by M.F.K. Fisher entitled "The Wind Chill Factor" (cited in Barlow, 1988). The story begins with the description of a woman who has been staying alone in a friend's cottage during a severe winter blizzard that has been raging for several days. In spite of the storm, the woman is warm, comfortable, unconcerned about the storm, and falls asleep. The onset of panic is described as follows:

> A little after four, an extraordinary thing happened to her. From deep and comfortable dreamings she was wrenched into the conscious world, as cruelly as if she had been grabbed by the long hairs of her head. Her heart had changed its slow, quiet beat and bumped in her rib cage like a rabbit's. Her breath was caught in a kind of net in her throat, not going in and down fast enough. She touched her body and it was hot, but her palms felt clammy and stuck to her.
>
> Within a few seconds, she knew that she was in a state—perhaps dangerous—of pure panic. It had nothing to do with physical fear, as far as she could tell. She was not afraid of being alone, or of being on the dunes in a storm. She was not afraid of bodily attack, rape, all that. She was simply in panic, or what Frenchmen home from the Sahara used to call le cafard affolé. . . . (Barlow, 1988, p. 2)

The only trigger to the panic that seemed possible was the unrelenting wind. The story character tried to manage her feelings with aspirin, warm milk, brushing her hair, reading nursery rhymes, and praying. Some success came when she decided to listen to her breathing and repeat "you are not badly hurt, soon you will feel alright." After a few hours, the panic episode passed. Throughout this period, she was not aware of thoughts of danger or dying; it was more a question of sound, it was simply the storm. Why the attack occurred is unknown. Barlow (1988) hypothesized that the answer has more to do with subtle *anxious apprehension* than identifiable fears. Her condition, he stated, is captured by the German word *angst,* a powerful state of anxiety that has its origins deep within the individual. For existential writers, pervasive anxiety of this nature is set off by a threat to a core value or characteristic of the person, a threat which challenges one's existence (e.g., loss of freedom, meaninglessness). For Freud, angst is elicited by the activation of unconscious childhood threats:

> Anxiety functions to warn of a potential danger situation and triggers the recruitment of internal psychological and/or external protective mechanisms. Freud would view the raging storm and incessant noise of [the] blizzard as providing sensory stimuli of real threat. Anxiety occurs in reaction to the possibility of being overwhelmed by this threat and rendered helpless. The sense of ultimate separation and isolation one can only experience alone in a blizzard may also elicit childhood memories of childhood fears of separation. (Barlow, 1988, p. 11)

Why do some individuals interpret bodily arousal with such apprehension and fear and others do not? According to Barlow (1988), the difference may lie in the degree to which the body arousal is experienced as unpredictable and/or uncontrollable. Most people who experience occasional fear or anxiety generally view the event as predictable and controllable. Thus, a fight with one's employer or a period of stress may lead to arousal which is understandable and to the view that such events are "water under the bridge." Persons, however, who have a deep sense of lacking control over events in their lives may feel less able to cope with such events.

The physiological substrate of panic remains poorly understood. Beck (1988) described panic as having a prehistoric origin, as part of a "flight-freeze-faint" reaction. In ancient times, "freezing" allowed the organism to buy time in order to prepare for possible physical assault. In modern life, the threat is now largely social or evaluative in nature. We are not afraid of physical harm but rather of appearing stupid or making a fool of oneself. Unfortunately, the freezing response, rather than serving to protect us, interferes with rational thinking and confident actions.

There has been considerable speculation that the physical symptoms of panic resemble respiratory symptoms produced by hyperventilation (e.g., dizziness, shortness of breath, pounding heart). Hyperventilation, both acute and chronic, is associated with characteristic blood gas and acid-base changes. The physiologic basis of hyperventilation is that rapid breathing "blows off" carbon dioxide (CO_2) from the lungs faster than it can be produced by the body. A certain level of CO_2 is normally maintained in the blood and only part of the CO_2 is passed in exhalation. The remaining blood level of CO_2 is measured in terms of CO_2 pressure (pCO_2) and is about 40 mmHg in the arteries. This action decreases the pCO_2 in the lungs and blood, which then leads to a rise in the blood pH (respiratory alkalosis). The increase in blood pH then contributes to cerebral vasoconstriction, leading to symptoms of dizziness, lightheadedness, confusion, nausea, and tremor. The traditional treatment for acute hyperventilation has been rebreathing using a paper bag (subject rebreathes his own CO_2), which quickly leads to increases in pCO_2 (hypercapnia).

A relatively consistent finding in those susceptible to panic episodes is that they do have lower resting pCO_2 levels (Gorman, et al., 1989). The suspicion is that this lower level may increase their sensitivity to increased ventilation. That is, small increases in breathing may be more likely to initiate symptoms of hyperventilation in panickers than nonpanickers. Panic attacks can also be reliably induced by having susceptible subjects hyper-ventilate in a lab setting. Normal room air contains nearly no CO_2. Having subjects take one or two gulps of air with 35% CO_2 and 65% CO_2 causes instant hypercapnia, and activation of chemoreceptors, followed by a very intense urge to ventilate. Panic-prone individuals are more likely than normals to experience a panic attack under such circumstances.

Some researchers believe that it is not the CO_2-induced changes but the subject's reactions to the accompanying interoceptive bodily changes which determine whether or not panic develops following gas inhalation. This argument receives support from the fact that panic attacks can be induced in the lab using a number of forms of biologic stimulation and each kind has served, at one time or another, as a theory of the condition. In 1967, Pitts and McClure noted that standard exercise was capable of producing some of the symptoms of anxiety. They hypothesized that anxiety symptoms associated with exercise may result from the rapid rise of blood lactate occurring as a consequence of the exercise. A series of studies using in-fusions of sodium lactate were able to induce panic episodes in between 60% and 80% of panic disorder patients and in about 10% of controls. It is not clear how sodium lactate generates panic. A number of other substances will also precipitate anxiety in patients with panic disorder. These sub-stances include caffeine, which is why many panic patients routinely avoid caffeine. Thus, the common denominator in these studies may have little to do with properties of the biologic agents used. Instead, it has been proposed that panic sufferers have acquired a high degree of *interoceptive sensitivity* to a number of bodily sensations. That is, panic-prone individuals attribute excessive fear or catastrophic ideation to otherwise benign bodily sensa-tions. In one study (van den Hout et al., 1987), panic patients, anxiety patients, and controls were required to indicate how fearful they were of the

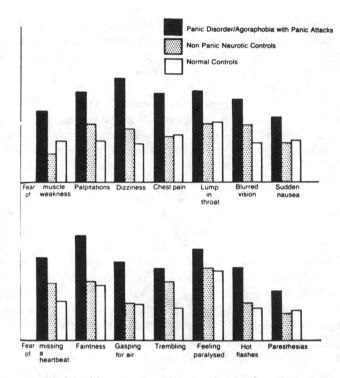

Figure 2.1. Fear of bodily sensations: mean scores of panic patients, nonpanic anxiety controls, and normal controls. (van den Hout, van der Molen, Griez, & Lousberg, 1987). Reprinted by permission.

bodily sensations that are part of the anxiety response. As shown in Figure 2.1, panic disorder patients associated the symptoms with significantly more fear than the other two groups.

The interoceptive sensitivity model begs the question of whether panic patients are making misattributions in their dealing with normal bodily sensations or in fact are experiencing bodily sensations which are at least partially consistent with their interpretations of impending doom and heart attacks. Lang (1988) rejected the misattribution approach as being too simplistic. If the approach were correct, he stated, then treatment should be as simple as providing panic sufferers with more accurate explanations for their symptoms. With tongue in cheek, he proposed that physicians tell their worried patients the following:

> Mr. Doe, our physical examination reveals that you have no heart ailment.
> However, you do have a tendency to hyperventilate when life gets tough.
> In the future, just breathe into this brown paper bag whenever you get ner-

vous. That will help balance the gases in your respiratory system and reduce these symptoms. But in any event, remember if they do occur that they are normal physical responses and have no implications for your physical health. (pp. 220-221)

The explanation contained in this quotation is in actuality quite close to the truth. However, it minimizes the role of underlying physiologic processes which are contributing to panic anxiety.

Recall, at the beginning of this discussion, the suggestion that panic may represent a primitive psychobiologic freezing response. There is some evidence that the physiologic substrate of the freezing response may be musculoskeletal in nature. (Lynch et al., 1991). As part of an ongoing study of the ventilatory response of panic sufferers to CO_2 inhalation, muscle activity was recorded from the sternum area. Chest pain, tightness in chest, and/or pressure in chest are often noted by panic sufferers as triggering/ accompanying the attack and in fact are largely responsible for the patient's view that he/she is having an angina or heart attack. These symptoms are more often noted by patients who are at home or alone during the panic attack. Figure 2.2 contains electromyographic and other physiologic data recorded from the sternum of patients and controls in the lab who were undergoing CO_2 provocation for panic. The panic disorder patients were divided on the basis of their subjective reports into those who were high anxious or "panicky" during the course of the study and those who were less anxious or "non-panicky." Observe that the sole physiologic variable which differentiated the groups was chest wall muscle activity. Because of anticipatory anxiety these subjects were in a state of high anxiety during the baseline phase and it could not be determined whether the elevated EMG activity was a general trait or specific to the situation. We suspect the latter interpretation is closer to the truth, as panic subjects who showed little or no anxiety during the course of the study exhibited low levels of chest EMG acitivity and were similar to the controls on this measure.

These data illustrate that, at least for some of the physiologic symptoms (chest pain, tightness, pressure), there is likely major activity in underlying chest wall muscles. The activity was sustained throughout the breathing cycle, suggesting that these muscles were holding the chest, in a tonic fashion, at a volume higher than its relaxed volume and serving no physiological purpose. Such activity could be potentially quite tiring and painful. It is not surprising that such sensations are often misunderstood as the beginnings of a heart attack. Convincing anxiety-prone individuals otherwise is not an easy task, partly because of the intensity of the sensations and the difficulty in bringing these sensations under control. For middle-aged and elderly individuals in particular, chest sensations are often catastrophically interpreted as the beginning of a heart attack:

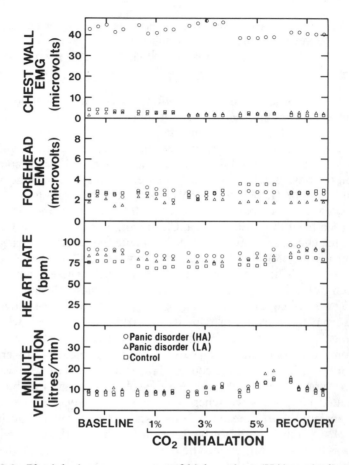

Figure 2.2. Physiologic average scores of high anxious (HA) panic disorder subjects, low anxious (LA) panic disorder subjects, and controls (P. Lynch, D. A. Bakal, W. Whitelaw, & T. Fung. Chest muscle activity and panic anxiety: A preliminary investigation. Psychosomatic Medicine, 53, 1, 80–89, 1991). Copyright by American Psychosomatic Society. Reprinted by permission.

A 72-year-old woman was admitted to medical clinic suffering from benzodiazepine (Valium) dependence. She was experiencing difficulty with her balance, hypertension, chest pain, back pain, and constipation. The patient underwent extensive laboratory investigation, including CT scan of the brain. All investigations were normal. A 24-hour monitor of her heart revealed no significant abnormalities. Eventually, it was determined that her symptoms were likely the result of panic disorder and drug dependence. She had been using benzodiazepines for anxiety management for a period of 16 years.

The patient's primary fear was of having a heart attack while alone, with no one available to call for help. She experienced nocturnal panic and would often awaken in the middle of the night with palpitations and chest pain. Her mind would immediately be filled with thoughts such as, "I am having a heart attack," "Here I am alone," "This is it, I am dying," "How the deuce will I ever survive this?", "I'm out of control." Similar thoughts would occur during daytime panic episodes. A familar pattern would be for her to rise in the morning, eat a light breakfast, and then "without reason begin to feel wobbly and weak."

The patient described herself as being anxious as far back as she could remember. Although experiencing a pleasant childhood and never abandoned, she had a deep fear of being left alone and of being separated from family members. Both her mother and husband died from heart failure. She exhibited a very high dependence on others for maintaining feelings of self-worth, although in later years the dependency seemed specific to her fears of having a heart attack with no one around to help. One hypothesis holds that panic sufferers fear losing control and any threat to that control is anxiety-provoking (this would explain why they panic in response to almost any stimulus in the lab, as placing oneself in the hands of a research team means giving up control and prevents easy escape).

Anxiety and panic are generally treated with anxiolytic medications such as diazepam. These drugs can be highly effective in reducing anxiety on a short-term basis but their long-term use is problematic, not only because of dangerous side effects but also because of developing tolerance. Behavioral treatments are generally multimodal in nature, consisting of relaxation/ breathing retraining, exposure to somatic cues and panic-inducing situations, and cognitive reinterpretation of somatic symptoms. Most individuals are helped in these programs. In the case of the patient example provided, treatment consisted of relaxation training as well as having her reinterpret the chest sensations as arising from muscle tightness rather than heart attack, and encouragement in using coping-related thoughts, such as "Relax, I will survive this—my heart is okay." Progress was very slow for a number of reasons. She remained very frightened of having to function without diazepam. Tremendous pressure had to be brought to bear by her physicians and family to have her agree to discontinue the diazepam. Although understanding that the chest symptoms were not indicative of heart failure, she admitted that a part of her mind was not convinced and questioned how she would know the difference. Also the patient had little or no awareness of contextual reasons for developing somatic symptoms (e.g., chest pressure), even though such symptoms would often appear in association with thoughts/events involving separation from family, friends, and being alone. On a positive note, she continued to improve following treatment and showed no evidence of returning to drug use.

SOMATIC AWARENESS

Somatic awareness may be defined as the processes by which we perceive. interpret, and act on the information from our bodies (Cioffi, 1991). The bodily changes accompanying emotionality are not normally perceived, unless of course the person experiencing the changes is frightened by their presence. Accurate perception of bodily events is not an activity that is either encouraged or practiced in children or adults. Psychologists have preferred to emphasize how poor we are at recognizing internal events and have designed studies/theories to reflect this position. The classic Schachter and Singer (1962) study discussed previously is a good example of this line of thinking, as efforts were made to have the subjects misinterpret drug-produced bodily sensations. A significant dimension of health promotion that remains to be tapped, however, is the degree to which individuals can monitor and regulate bodily sensations which are relevant to symptom prevention and management. Hanna (1988), in a book titled *Somatics,* made a useful distinction between the words soma and body:

> There are two ways in which a human being can be viewed: from the outside in, or from the inside out. Looked at from the outside, by a physiologist or a physician, human beings are very different from the beings they appear to be when they view themselves from the inside out. . . .
>
> When one looks at another human being, one sees a "body" with a certain external shape and size. . . . But when the human being looks at himself or herself from the inside, he or she is aware of feelings and movements and intentions—a quite different, fuller being. To view a body from the outside is a third-person view: One sees a "he" or a "she" or an "it." But when the human views himself or herself from the inside, it is a first-person view. . . .
>
> What physiologists [and physicians] see from their externalized, third-person view is always a "body." What the individual sees from his or her internalized, first-person view is always a "soma." *Soma* is a Greek word that, from Hesiod onward, has meant "living body." This living, self-sensing, internalized, perception of oneself is radically different from the externalized perception of what we call a "body". . . . (p. 20)

Hanna's central thesis is that many health problems develop as a result of individuals' failing to maintain somatic awareness throughout the course of life. He coined the term "sensory-motor amnesia" (SMA) to describe the lack of somatic awareness that characterizes many patients with varied chronic health problems:

> For example, while a client with a chronically sore shoulder is lying on my padded worktable, I lift her arm in the air and tell her to relax. Then, when I let go of her arm, it stays in the air. . . . Or a person who constantly has a sore neck will be on the table, lying on his back, while I try to lift his head. I cannot

lift it because the posterior muscles of the neck are rigid. All day, every day, he tightly contracts the muscles in the back of his neck, totally unaware of them, and comes to me wondering why he has constant neck pain. (p. 26)

In day-to-day functioning, most people exhibit little awareness of somatic sensations. Studies which require subjects to indicate level of heart rate, muscle tension, and sexual arousal have found little correlation between subjective ratings of bodily activity and actual bodily activity. Fisher (1986) made the following observation:

> The puzzling aspect of most of the visceral perception literature is that it portrays average people as having little better than chance ability in the quiescent state to identify their own visceral experiences, yet, paradoxically as becoming highly accurate after receiving corrective feedback information. . . . It seems to be incredibly maladaptive for the average person to be so out of touch with his or her visceral events. If, as the literature suggests, practice and feedback in the laboratory context can so quickly transform people into expert visceral perceivers, why would the infinite body experiences people have not provide them with comparable opportunities to learn? (p. 35)

Some of the literature reviewed by Fisher involved studies of subjects tracking their heart rates and having to report in which of two time periods their heart rates had reached the highest level. Initially, their judgments were at chance level but with feedback training their accuracy improved dramatically. Apparently, with instruction, subjects are able to identify internal sensations which covary with cardiovascular changes. It is often assumed that distance runners are more aware of their heart rate, even at rest. An early study found support for this hypothesis (Jones & Hollandsworth, 1981); however, it was only true for male distance runners. In a review of the heart perception literature, Katkin, Blascovich, and Koenigsberg (1984) concluded that the average person does little better than chance at perceiving heart rate at rest. Accuracy improves with activation and improves even further with training, with the greatest improvement occurring for males.

There has been considerable research examining the link between feelings of sexual arousal and body change. Studies in this area have used a vaginal or penile plethysmograph to measure respective genital organ activation in women and men. The recordings are obtained while the subjects are exposed to various kinds of erotic stimuli such as film recordings of sexual intercourse or sound recordings of sexual activity. Most of the subjects were college students without sexual problems. In general, the majority of these studies reported negative or unstable results. Correlations between sexual arousal and actual measures of physiological arousal have been low, especially in studies with women. Interestingly, the correlations become much higher when the subjects are encouraged to focus on the body regions that are likely to show the effects of the erotic stimuli. In a study by Korff and Geer (1983), for example, female college students were exposed to erotic slides while vaginal activation was recorded with a plethysmograph. Some of the students were instructed to specifically focus on genital and somatic sensations (lubrication, pelvic warmth, muscular tension, heart rate increase, breast swelling) while others were not given any instructions to body focus. The correlations of subjective arousal with the plethysmograph measure were very high for the women instructed to somatic focus.

Monitoring internal events involves the use of proprioceptive and visceral sensors. Proprioceptive sensors detect signals arising from the muscles, tendons, and joints while visceral sensors detect signals from the interior organs, including the lungs, heart, stomach, and intestines. Normally, we are unaware of this internal information, especially if the brain is preoccupied with processing information from exteroceptive sensors (eyes, ears, nose, skin). Only a relatively small area of the brain is devoted to analyzing visceral functions. In addition, signals from the viscera share afferent pathways with other sensory systems. The spinothalamic tract, which is part of the anterolateral system, for example, transmits information related to pain, touch, warmth, and cold as well as sexual and itch sensations. These sensory signals originate from visceral receptors as well as exteroceptive and proprioceptive receptors, making fine discriminations difficult. Contrast this form of diffuse transmission with the more direct transmission that occurs from the special senses (e.g., vision). Signals are sent directly to highly specialized areas in the brain.

The potential for sensory awareness of feedback from proprioceptors, although less than from exteroreceptors, is better than what might be expected from visceroreceptors. Exteroreceptive and proprioceptive sensory impulses reach the brain via the dorsal column pathway. This pathway tends to send very discrete signals to the brain and because of heavy myelinated fibers, exhibits far less cross-talk than the spinothalamic pathway. Exteroreceptive sensation, such as occurs when sensing an object with a hand, is very detailed and exact, because a large area of the cortex is devoted to detecting sensations of touch. Proprioceptive sensations, although much less precise and difficult to localize than exteroceptive sensations, are capable of being monitored. There are programs which are based on teaching "a better feel of oneself" and there is some evidence that this skill can be developed to a high level.

Usually we have better things to do than scan our bodies for proprioceptive sensations and this may account in large part for why we seldom bother to monitor our bodies proprioceptively. According to Shapiro (1974), absence of somatic focus may have been adaptive in an evolutionary sense as human functioning would become inefficient if people had to constantly shift attention from external to internal stimuli. This may have been more true when flight-or-fight responses were relatively immediate and straightforward. The situation is obviously now much more difficult as much of ongoing threat is generated by worry within ourselves. Barlow (1988) hypothesized that part of the problem is simply due to limited capacities of attention. If we are busily attending to events outside ourselves, it becomes difficult to attend to events within ourselves. There is, in his words, a mutual antagonism between a focus on the self and a focus on the environment. Our brain may simply not be designed to simultaneously monitor both internal and external events.

Self-defensiveness may also contribute to lack of somatic awareness. Fisher (1986) maintains that many people do not like to be confronted with their own external physical attributes. Most of the literature on this topic deals with the above-mentioned attributes or body image. Persons often become uncomfortable when made aware of one or more physical attributes. Such increased awareness may result from looking in a mirror, hearing a recording of one's voice, or being exposed to an audience. Apparently, self-representations contain information that is ordinarily shut out, but that becomes threatening when it cannot be avoided. Young women suffering from bulimia have a persistent concern with body shape and weight and it is this concern which leads to many of their symptoms, including depression, purging, and self-deprecating thoughts. According to Fisher, people have problems correcting distorted presentations of their own faces, of recognizing their faces in unfamiliar contexts, and of recognizing their own voices. "If people have difficulty correctly identifying their exterior, visible features, is it surprising that they should inaccurately perceive inner, less visible aspects of their bodies?"

Directing individuals to physiological sensations may cause them to reflect more intensely about themselves in general. In a simple demonstration of this effect, Wegner and Giuliano (1980) manipulated physiological arousal by having subjects lie down, relax, sit in a chair, or run in place. They then presented subjects with a form containing a series of sentences with words missing. Subjects who had experienced marked arousal from running in place chose more self-relevant words to complete the sentences. Thus, if someone has a negative self-image, focusing on heart rate or some other somatic sensation could trigger negative thoughts and feelings associated with anxiety. Fisher gave an example of college students with low grade point averages having less awareness of body sensations during an examination than students with high grade point averages. A second example involved religious individuals with a tendency to experience guilt. These individuals had difficulty monitoring their heart rate in the presence of guilt stimuli.

The effects of anxiety on sexual activity present an interesting description of the impact of self-esteem factors on performance. Anxiety is usually seen as hampering sexual performance and yet emotional situations are capable of facilitating sexual responses. Barlow (1988) cited some comparisons of the effects of anxiety on functional and dysfunctional males. In a series of studies, it was observed that threat of mild electric shock actually increases sexual arousal in males, even in males that were told that they "would receive a shock if they did not achieve at least as large an erection as the average male" in the lab. The shock was never administered but, rather than decrease the sexual response, it actually gave an overall "boost" to the magnitude of the penile response. In sexually dysfunctional males, however, the threat of shock led to a decrease in penile response. For dysfunctional males, attending to sexual sensations has acquired a degree of performance anxiety. Presenting these individuals with a video of a highly aroused woman seemed to cue in the dysfunctional males a chain of negative thoughts associated with lack of control and inability to obtain the desired results. If distraction were added, by having the subjects listen to a nonsexual audiotape while viewing erotic films, the normals showed a reduction in sexual response while the dysfunctional males showed a slight increase.

Psychodynamic writers view lack of somatic awareness in terms of an "unwillingness to self-soothe." That is, if somatic awareness is equated with physical discomfort or pain and therefore a sign of personal weakness, persons may feel that they should be able to ignore the presence of somatic sensations and "push on." Young children were found to feel that they must become more Spartan-like as they become older (Campbell, 1978) and to experience guilt in the face of illness. The degree of Spartan orientation was also found to positively correlate with the mother's educational level. The value system of mothers with higher education apparently emphasizes self-control and keeping a stiff upper lip in the face of adversity. There is no doubt that many adults believe that attending to one's body, or taking time to relax and pamper oneself, is a sign of laziness and something that is to be avoided. These individuals will often describe having very success-oriented parents. A case in mind involved a 60-year-old executive who remarked that the only time she noticed tension in her face was when she saw herself in a photo which was taken at her daughter's wedding!

Unwillingness to self-soothe is at the basis of a clinical condition called alexithymia. Alexithymia is a term which was coined by Sifneos (1973) to refer to a specific disturbance in psychobiologic functioning characterized by difficulties in the capacity to experience and verbalize affect. The difficulty goes beyond non-expressiveness as these individuals have difficulty identifying and describing their own feelings. Their thinking has been described as "literal," utilitarian," and "concerned with minutiae of external events," a characteristic that has been called la pensée opératoire (operative thinking). (Marty & de M'Uzan, 1963, cited in Nemiah, 1972) These individuals report few dreams and tend to have little or no awareness of body sensations which accompany emotional and stressful experiences.

They do, however, focus on physical sensations, once a symptom develops. Chronic pain patients, for example, are often described as having alexithymic characteristics. An example of the thinking of a patient which could be characterized as alexithymic is the following self-observation material provided by a pain patient who was asked to monitor her thoughts and feelings during the course of the day:

> "Saturday: Sore back this morning, very foggy out, other than that feel not too bad, very foggy out, rain and snow predicted, when will the sun shine? . . . Oat and bran flakes for breakfast with sliced bananas and milk . . . Later in the day went for a walk with a friend . . . had difficulty keeping up because of pain . . . Later in day my sciatic nerve really hurt . . . had difficulty walking because my right side hurt. Walked to grocery store . . . had breast of chicken, tomato and watermelon for dinner . . . pain now worse in hands, neck, lower back . . . started new blood pressure medication . . . my doctor suggested that I may have a rare neurologic disease, something like Parkinson's."

In summary, not thinking about oneself vis-a-vis somatic sensations may occur for a number of reasons. Ultimately, developing somatic awareness may require disrupting whatever internal psychobiologic equilibrium the individual had previously attained. The fact that we cope much of the time without awareness may allow us to go about daily living without experiencing too much threat of disequilibrium. To become aware may necessitate a change in personal life style and other events that are beyond our control. In the end, it might feel easier to say to hell with it and concern oneself with other matters. Developing such an awareness, however, represents an extremely powerful health promotion factor, especially if one is prevented from leading a healthy life by physiologic symptoms or conditions which require internal attention.

REGULATING INTERNAL STATES

Chronic tension is a suspected precursor of many medical conditions that have a psychological component. Almost all hospital-based self-regulation programs advocate reducing tension levels through a number of self-control strategies. In this section, we examine the techniques of progressive muscle relaxation, autogenic training procedures, biofeedback, qi gong, and mindful meditation.

Progressive Muscle Relaxation

Progressive muscle relaxation may be the best known and most widely used method for increasing somatic awareness in the clinical situation. Progressive muscle relaxation was devised by Edmund Jacobson (1938), who was both a psychologist and physician. As used today, progressive muscle relaxation is based on a "pendulum effect" in which individuals are asked to tense several muscle groups simultaneously with maximal effort and then to release them. The sudden release of extreme tension is theorized to produce a decrease in resting muscle tension, much as a pendulum swings back past its resting point after it has been raised and released.

In a clinical setting, progressive muscle relaxation begins with the patient comfortably seated or reclined with eyes closed in a dimly litroom. Once comfortable, the person is guided through the technique of alternating tension and relaxation in 16 muscle groups of the body. Each muscle-group cycle is composed of a muscle tension phase lasting about 7 seconds, followed by a 45-second relaxation phase. The entire procedure takes approximately 20 minutes. Following is a sample of the procedure as described by Lichstein (1988):

> When I say "now," go ahead and tense the muscles of your right hand and forearm by clenching your fist. Now. Keep it tight, feel the strain, the tension, the muscles are working so hard, and relax (7 seconds). Relax completely, relax immediately. Just give up control of the muscles and let them lie there quietly. Compare in your mind the feelings of tension you were feeling just a few seconds ago in your right hand and forearm to the restful relaxation that is emerging now. The more carefully you focus your attention on the feelings of serenity and tranquility, the greater the relaxation effect you will enjoy. Feel the peaceful, calm sensations growing more and more (45 seconds). (p. 120)

The next muscle group to be trained is the upper arm or biceps. While working on these muscles, the patient is also encouraged to monitor tension in the right hand and arm, the goal being to optimize the patient's ability to discriminate body phenomena and to minimize total muscle tension. The goal is to learn to tense only those muscles that one is instructed to tense. Other muscle groups include the left hand, forearm and biceps, forehead, nose, lower face, and neck. The neck is a difficult region to both tense and relax. Lichstein provided the following instruction for tensing the neck:

> There are many muscles there that act to pull your neck in different directions. You can tense all of these at the same time by trying to move your neck in four different directions simultaneously. Doing this, your neck will not be able to move in any direction, although you may feel a shaking tremor there since all the muscles are tugging against each other. (p. 121)

After the neck muscles, the patient is guided through the muscles of the upper back ("Pull your shoulders back as though you were trying to touch them behind you."), muscles of the chest and abdomen, muscles of the leg and ankle. In a clinical setting, the training is often revised to accommodate specific patient problems and needs, such as avoiding injured areas and/or providing added practice in problem areas.

Jacobson used the emotion theory of Gellhorn (1958) to explain the positive benefits of relaxation. The term ergotrophic is used to collectively describe the excitatory processes of the autonomic nervous system (e.g., heart rate acceleration, increased blood pressure), and the term "trophotropic" is used to describe the quiescent state defined by parasympathetic functioning. Gellhorn proposed that trophotropic processes are activated by the anterior hypothalamus and that the repeated practice of relaxation strategies is associated with trophotropic tuning. He noted that a high proportion of the innervation of the ascending reticular system emanates from skeletal muscle proprioceptors. The ascending reticular system innervates the posterior division of the hypothalamus which itself is associated with autonomic reactivity.

Jacobson intended relaxation training more as a skill than as a therapeutic procedure (Lehrer, Woolfolk, & Goldman, 1986). Furthermore, he did not encourage prolonged use of the severe tensing followed by relaxing. Instead, he used the "method of diminishing tensions" in which the person tenses a particular muscle group as little as possible while at the same time maintaining awareness of control sensations. During each training session, the person tenses a muscle a few times and spends the majority of time "switching off" the muscle, the goal being to require less and less tension to precede perceived control sensations. With continued practice, the person would develop a degree of "virtuoso" control over his muscles such that he would be able to switch off without any tensing at all.

Although Jacobson did not devise the technique as a therapeutic tool per se, he believed that repeated practice of relaxation would be accompanied by cognitive changes. He viewed the relationship between the peripheral physiology and brain as bi-directional in nature, whereby the level of activity in each of these systems is controlled, in part, by the amount of signal received from the other. Thus, the brain can be quieted by diminishing sensory input to it. So influenced, the brain in turn tranquilizes the autonomic nervous system. He believed very strongly that experiential anxiety varies directly as a function of muscle tension levels. He demonstrated in a series of studies that thoughts associated with movement led to increases in muscle activity from the appropriate limb and further that deep relaxation of a particular limb "blocked" or prevented production of an image of that limb in movement. His theory has even been tested with curare. Curare is a drug that blocks neural impulses to the muscles, thus temporarily rendering the subject totally paralyzed. Jacobson emphasized the role of afferent messages from the muscles to the brain, which are indirectly reduced to zero by curare. Under these conditions, Jacobson would predict parallel nullification of cognitive activity. Davison (1966) reviewed the relevant curare literature and concluded that this is often not the case, that subjects report anxiety while curarized. Still Jacobson demonstrated that muscle relaxation is an important concomitant of mental relaxation. Curare does not block efferent activity at its source (the brain), it merely blocks its muscle effect. Clinical studies using relaxation place less emphasis on the skill aspect and more on the experience of feeling relaxed. Also Jacobson's exact method involved over 20 sessions, extending over six months or longer, of working through specific muscle groups; whereas current clinical exposure is often limited to five to seven sessions (Lehrer, Woolfolk, & Goldman, 1986).

Autogenic Training and Biofeedback

Autogenic training, unlike progressive muscle relaxation, does not require the subject to tense muscle groups. Instead it achieves relaxation largely through an imaginal method. The procedure as devised by Schultz and Luthe (1969) depends on having the subject adopt a passive attitude by using imagery exercises to produce relaxing bodily sensations. There are six relaxation exercises, involving sensations of heaviness, warmth, cardiac regulation, respiration, abdominal warmth, and cooling of the forehead. The six exercises were based on early observations of subjects under hypnosis. Schultz observed that his subjects regularly experienced sensations of heaviness and warmth as well as calming of the heart and cooling of the forehead. The first two exercises require the subject to generate the sensations of heaviness and warmth, first in the right arm, then the left arm, followed by both arms, right leg, left leg, both legs, and finally arms and legs. The required *passive* attitude is suggested as follows:

> It is important that throughout this procedure you adopt a relaxed, passive, and casual attitude. You cannot force relaxation to occur. Just give up conscious control over your body, and allow your bodily processes to flow naturally. If the relaxation experience does not evolve exactly as you wish, do not become concerned but rather maintain your passive attitude. . . . (p. 109)

An example of autogenic relaxation utilizes the sensations of heaviness and warmth to achieve relaxation of the arms and legs (Budzynski, 1974):

> Okay let yourself go. Get deeply relaxed all over right now . . . Let's start out by having you take a very deep breath, inhale so that the air flows into your lungs and feel as though it is flowing way down to your lower abdominal region . . . inhale very deeply down into your abdominal region . . . Now exhale slowly and as you do so feel yourself floating down through the chair or the bed . . . Continue to breathe very slowly and regularly . . . Make your breathing very regular and slow, like waves slowly washing in on a shore and then back

out again . . . very quietly, slowly, regularly . . . This is your time . . . do not waste it on any thoughts of things that you are going to be doing later or thoughts of things you should have done earlier . . . focus only on what the tape is saying and what your body is feeling at this moment. . . .

Now direct your attention to your right hand and arm . . . make mental contact with your right hand and arm . . . feel it, be aware of it, notice where it contacts the chair or the bed and as you maintain this rather passive concentration just be aware of the arm and let it become heavy and warm . . . just let it become heavy and warm as you maintain contact with it and as you repeat this phrase, 'My right arm is heavy, my right arm is heavy and limp, my right arm is letting go and as you maintain contact with that arm and continue to breathe regularly and slowly say those three phrases to yourself right now, 'My right arm is heavy, my right arm is heavy and limp, my right arm is letting go . . .'

The autogenic relaxation session, as with progressive muscle relaxation, takes approximately 20 minutes. Patients are often amazed at the intensity of the initial sensations and experiences which take place when listening to the tape. These include: heaviness, soreness, aching, and the experience of one or both arms actually disappearing. Appropriate phrases such as "Heartbeat calm and regular," "My forehead is cool" are added to the other exercises. In addition, it is possible to tailor the standard phrases involving heaviness, warmth, and coolness to suit the particular clinic needs of a patient. For example, a patient with Raynaud's disease, which is associated with abnormal vasoconstriction to the extremities upon exposure to cold or stress, might find the phrase "My hands and feet are warm" useful. Many of these patients are surprised to discover that the sensation of warmth accompanying the silent repeating of such phrases is associated with actual skin temperature increases in their hands and/or feet. So convinced were Schultz and Luthe of the physiologic power of such imagery that they advised against using the formula of heaviness or warmth in relation to the head, for fear of causing excessive blood flow to that region.

Biofeedback can be used to enhance the effects of autogenic training and the two procedures are often used in combination in therapy. As a technique, biofeedback never became the magic cure that some promised. In the 1970s there was tremendous enthusiasm for the approach and entrepreneurs were establishing biofeedback clinics and marketing biofeedback boxes for home use. The entrepreneurs have long since disappeared and there is considerable skepticism regarding the necessity of using the technique. Reviewers have noted that biofeedback training is no more effective than relaxation training in the treatment of psychophysiological disorders. Chronic headache sufferers, for example, show similar reductions in headache activity following relaxation training or biofeedback training. Although group treatments yield similar results, biofeedback still constitutes a useful clinical tool for individual use. Patients with high muscle tension levels in specific regions (e.g., neck, shoulders, stomach) often find it impossible to relax relevant muscles by simply listening to a tape. The addition of electromyogram (EMG) or muscle biofeedback brings about a degree of somatic awareness and muscle relaxation in these muscle groups that would otherwise not be attainable. Similar clinical applications have been made for the Raynaud's symptoms of cold hands and feet where temperature biofeedback (along with relaxation) is used to warm the hands and feet and chest/abdominal breathing ratio is displayed to improve diaphrammatic breathing. In fact, biofeedback can be used on any symptom which is under neural control. The clinical application of biofeedback for controlling pain is discussed in Chapter 6.

Crane-Flying Qi Gong

"Qi gong" is a relaxation technique from China which has some followers in North America and which is also used for clinical purposes. It involves deep breathing exercises and has a very ancient origin. Hwa Tuo, a famous physician of the Han dynasty (206 B.C.–220 A.D.) established the idea that if humans imitated the actions of cranes, bears, tigers, deer, and apes, health would be promoted:

> Blowing and respiring, getting rid of the stale and taking in the fresh, performing the movement like a bear or a bird, then you may live longer. (Shan, 1988, p. 299)

Crane-flying qi gong is based on the Chinese concept of qi (sometimes spelled ch'i) which means vital energy, vital essence, or vital breath. Qi is considered important in the maintenance of all bodily functions and the obstruction of its circulation can lead to disease. The aim of the crane-flying exercise is to release obstructions to qi. People who participate often do so to seek relief from physical symptoms. The technique is associated with stylized body movements such as imitating a crane skimming over water and quiet motionless reflection. While the participant is standing still, the instructor provides relaxing suggestions such as, "the environment is tranquil and the air is fresh, spontaneous skill will emerge easily, don't be surprised if something touches you." During this period, the subject experiences the arrival of qi, which is often described as "a feeling of comfort, warmness, relaxation, a cool or hot sensation, numbness, or an aroused and inspired feeling." Since most practitioners using the technique for health reasons believe that their disease is caused by stagnant air in the body, it is not surprising that the arrival of qi is also associated with sensations of freely moving air within their bodies. Subsequently, the subject engages in a variety of spontaneous movements such as "a beautiful dance, rubbing or striking the diseased region, shouting or crying, venting of grievances, or giving rise to revolutionary songs." At this point in time, there is no solid evidence for the existence of qi as a special form of life energy.

Mindful Meditation

Kabat-Zinn (1990) developed an approach to relaxation based on the meditative notion of mindfulness. Our thoughts, according to Kabat-Zinn, are usually in the past or future and seldom in the present. When driving a car, for example, it is quite common to have very little awareness of what we saw on the journey as our thoughts wander to things that happened in the past or things that need to be done in the future. To demonstrate, he asked readers to conduct the following exercise:

> You can experience the pull of the thinking mind for yourself right now if you perform the following experiment: Close your eyes, sit so that your back is straight but not stiff, and become aware of your breathing. Don't try to control your breathing. Just let it happen and be aware of it, feeling how it feels, witnessing it as it flows in and out. Try being with your breath in this way for three minutes.
>
> If, at some point, you think that it is foolish or boring to just sit here and watch your breath go in and out, note to yourself that this is just a thought, a judgment that your mind is creating. Then simply let go of it and bring your attention back to your breathing. If the feeling is very strong, try the following additional experiment, which we sometimes suggest to our patients who feel simply bored with watching their breathing: Take the thumb and first finger of either hand, clamp them tightly over your nose, keep your mouth closed, and notice how long it takes before your breathing becomes very interesting to you!
>
> When you have completed three minutes of watching your breath go in and out, reflect on how you felt during this time and how much or how little your mind wandered away from your breathing. What do you think would have happened if you had continued for five or ten minutes, or for half an hour, or an hour? (pp. 22-23)

The point of this exercise is to demonstrate how difficult it can be to focus on body processes until we train ourselves to stabilize and calm the mind. Mindfulness involves allowing experiences to unfold from moment to moment and accepting them as they are. It does not involve trying to reject or avoid certain thoughts but rather paying attention to where the mind is from moment to moment throughout the day. By not paying attention, by allowing the mind to be dominated with day-to-day worries and concerns, we lose the ability to maintain contact with our bodies. This unawareness prevents us from being in touch with body signals and messages.

Being aware of what you are doing while you are doing it is the basis of mindfulness living. A significant aspect of mindfulness training is diaphragmatic breathing or breathing in a fashion which relaxes the stomach ("belly breathing"). The diaphragm is the sheet of muscle that is attached to the rib cage. During inhalation it moves downward, allowing the chest cavity to expand and air to flow inward. If the muscles of the abdomen are tense, however, the diaphragm will meet resistance as it pushes downward and result in shallow "chest breathing." By becoming mindful of breathing, a person learns not only to relax the abdomen but the mind as well. As the technique strengthens, the person is then able to be more aware of thoughts and feelings which are relevant to healthy living.

A form of mindfulness recommended for the control of somatic symptoms is body-scan meditation. The technique involves having the person lie on his back and then use the mind to move through different regions of the body. That is, the person is instructed to direct his breathing, say, to his toes and then directing or "channeling" his breathing in to the toes and out from the toes. The objective is to develop an awareness of sensations from regions throughout the body and eventually breathing through an imaginary "hole" in the very top of the head. The key to the success of the technique, according to Kabat-Zinn (1990), is the maintenance of mindfulness throughout the practice period:

> The quality of your attention and your willingness just to feel what is there, and be with it no matter what, is much more important than imagining the tension leaving your body or the inbreath revitalizing your body. If you just work at getting rid of tension, you may or may not succeed, but you are not practicing mindfulness. But if you are practicing being present in each moment and at the same time you are *allowing* your breathing and your attention to purify the body within this context of awareness and with a willingness to accept whatever happens, then you are truly practicing mindfulness and tapping its power to heal. (p. 89)

"Letting Go" and Psychological Control

The greatest difficulty with all body awareness techniques is that the active ingredients must become assimilated into the person's psychobiologic makeup. This is a tall order and is often not understood. In fact, many hard-working and high-achieving people resent the need for such drastic change as they prefer to be "pumped up" and do not feel alive without a degree of tension within their system. Such individuals might listen to one or two playings of a relaxation or meditation tape and secretly leave the tape some place so that they will not have to listen to it again. Listening to relaxation tapes, using biofeedback, or any of a number of other strategies represents only the first step in a difficult process of change which can often go against the person's preferred way of relating to himself and the larger world.

All body awareness techniques, to be successful in the promotion of health, require cultivation of an attitude of letting go or nonattachment (Kabat-Zinn, 1990). The letting-go state is so unnatural for some individuals that their first experiences with the technique are stressful rather than soothing. *Relaxation-induced anxiety* (Heide & Borkovec, 1984) has long been observed to occur with both progressive muscle relaxation and autogenic training. According to Schultz and Luthe (1969), a fair percentage of individuals experience apprehension, panic, and anxiety at the beginning of autogenic training. They coined the term "autogenic discharge" to describe the phenomenon and saw it as a first step toward normalization of underlying brain processes. They interpreted the unsettling sensations as a positive sign that relaxation is beginning to impact on an individual unaccustomed to the relaxation experience. There are also isolated reports of individuals developing similar "complications" during the practice of crane-flying qi-gong.

Psychological control and effort are believed to contribute to relaxation-induced anxiety. Both of these states also run counter to developing an awareness of one's internal functioning. Control is defined as the ability to modify outcomes by voluntary responding, whereas effort, in contrast, refers to active or applied force or the intensity of the individual's active attempts to affect the world. Thus, someone susceptible to relaxation-induced anxiety might have a strong need to remain in control and an equally strong belief in the importance of active, effortful strategies as a means to that end. Many patients with physical symptoms do find it difficult to relax for fear of losing control. Bodily sensations associated with "letting go" are themselves experienced as frightening and to be avoided at all costs. Consequently, they will maintain a degree of bodily tension in order to avoid the onset of particular unpleasant sensations.

A life approach characterized by control and effort also goes against incorporating relaxation into one's philosophy of life:

> What is passively required in relaxation is opposite to virtually every active coping procedure used to adapt to stress. As such, it is the antithesis of the person's conception of adaptive functioning. To relinquish efforts to control to maintain adjustment or to resolve one's difficulties is to leave oneself without known strategies and with a feeling of unpreparedness. (Heide & Borkovec, 1984, p. 9)

In Eastern cultures, by way of contrast, meditation/relaxation become an inseparable part of a person's values and religious beliefs. In our culture, relaxation is something that one does as an isolated strategy to gain symptom relief and is not seen as part of an individual's normal lifestyle. Individuals who believe in the merit of sustained effort often report the mere thought of sitting still or "relaxing" as aversive and not likely to lead to accomplishment. These values are rapidly changing as people become more and more aware of the need to take care of themselves at all levels of human functioning. Kabat-Zinn (1990) provided two exercises that can be utilized to facilitate this awareness: (1) try to be mindful for one minute in every hour, (2) touch base with your breathing throughout the day wherever you are, as often as you can.

3
Understanding Stress

My life seems to be one pressure point after another . . .
my days are like tightropes, stretched really thin . . .

"Sleeping in the night is hard . . . I lay awake and can't
sleep . . . then I toss and turn all night on waves, up and
down, in and out of sleep . . . and in the day, I'm
constantly fatigued . . ."

No, I'm fine . . . just constantly fatigued . . .

School's O.K. If my folks would only leave me alone. I
feel they are constantly looking over my shoulder, judging me, expecting me to meet their standard . . . it's no
wonder I can't concentrate on school work.

These examples of personal distress, taken from Suinn (1990), demonstrate
the pervasiveness of stress and anxiety in modern life. The necessity of
reducing stress in our lives is regarded as one of the most significant aspects
of illness prevention and health promotion. Stress reduction techniques
have become an industry with countless workshops, tapes, and books
readily available which promise the consumer a formula for a healthier life
free of stress. This chapter examines current models of stress in the context
of some common disorders. The focus is how each of us needs to understand the complex interplay between stress-induced psychic and somatic
symptoms. Current psychophysiologic stress research is illustrated through
a look at hypertension. Sleep disorders, surgery, and trauma are also examined. In addition, the basics of stress management programs are reviewed.

INITIAL FORMULATIONS

Early theorists viewed stress as a bodily response that was generally caused
by physical rather than psychological stimuli. Walter Cannon (1929–1970)
was the first modern researcher to apply the concept of stress to humans in

these kinds of terms. Cannon was principally concerned with the effects of cold, lack of oxygen, and other environmental stressors on organisms. Cannon's emphasis on *stress as a response* was carried on by Hans Selye (1956). From his beginning days as a student in internal medicine, he was struck by the observation that patients with different diseases also shared many of the same symptoms: "They felt and looked ill, had a coated tongue, complained of more or less diffuse aches and pains in the joints, and of intestinal disturbances with loss of appetite" (p. 15). This thinking led Selye to the conception of a "general syndrome of disease" and eventually to depict stress as a general bodily response designed to protect the body from physical challenges associated with injury and illness. Specifically, he felt that there was a common reaction to outside stressors which followed the sequence of alarm response, resistance response, and exhaustion. He theorized that this general reaction of the body, which he called the *general adaptation syndrome,* occurred to all forms of physical stress and illness. That is, in addition to localized changes produced by specific damage such as a cut, burn, or an infection, the general adaptation syndrome was superimposed on the specific changes.

The physiological pathway underlying the general adaptation syndrome is called the *pituitary-adrenal axis.* The pituitary gland consists of two major subdivisions or lobes: the adenohypophysis, or anterior lobe, and the neurohypophysis, or posterior lobe. The pituitary gland is under the control of hormones, the hypothalamus, and the autonomic nervous system. The anterior portion of the pituitary gland secretes several hormones, called *trophic hormones,* because their function is to stimulate other glands to secrete their own hormones. Adrenocorticotrophic hormone or ACTH is the pituitary hormone that completes the pituitary-adrenal axis by stimulating the adrenal cortex to secrete cortical steroids.

Selye demonstrated, through a series of animal experiments, that the general adaptation syndrome occurs in three distinct phases: the alarm reaction, the stage of resistance, and the stage of exhaustion. During the alarm reaction, the anterior pituitary gland secretes ACTH, which then activates the adrenal cortex to secrete additional hormones. If the stress-producing stimulus continues, the alarm reaction is followed by a stage of resistance. During this period the physiological changes that occurred during the first phase cease. At this point the organism's tolerance to additional stress is increased. If the stressor is prolonged, however, the organism reaches a state in which it can no longer respond either with an alarm reaction or with resistance. The anterior pituitary and the adrenal cortex lose their capacity to secrete hormones, and the organism can no longer adapt to the stress. Exhaustion and even death are the outcome.

Selye's model has been difficult to apply to the human condition, because the majority of human stressors are psychological and not physical in nature. As a result, it is not possible to specify the parameters of stress involved or the person's tolerance for stress. Selye himself recognized the difficulties in being exact on these issues and likened the problem to measuring adaptation or life energy itself. It was as if, he said, all organisms possessed a finite amount of adaptation energy for dealing with life's demands and after years and years of repeated activation of the defense alarm reaction, the end result may be hypertension or heart failure.

The psychological rather than physical nature of stress was recognized as a difficulty with animal studies very early in the stress literature. Thus, it became questionable whether research based on physical stressors (cold, heat, shock) had any relevance for understanding the human condition. Even the animal's psyche had to be taken into account:

> In fasting, for example, little or no corticosteroid change occurs in monkeys, if fruit-flavored nonnutritive cellulose fiber, i.e., placebo food, is given in place of similarly flavored and shaped food pellets, in order to minimize discomfort from emptiness of the gastrointestinal tract and to avoid the psychosocial stimuli associated with sudden deprivation of routine food dispensation by the animal caretaker. (Mason, 1975, p.24)

Life Change Measurement

The concept of life change measurement (Holmes & Rahe, 1967) represented an effort, at the human level, to systematically measure events in a person's life that are stressful. The basic premise was that diverse aspects of life experience could be conceptualized and measured as relatively discrete events. Visits to the dentist, a woman awaiting breast biopsy, examinations for students, debilitating illness, and marital discord represent such events. They are considered stressful on the grounds that they normally lead to stress reactions. A scale was constructed that assesses life stress in terms of life changes or life change units. Each change, such as divorce or pregnancy, according to theory, requires some form of adaptation, and this in itself is stressful. An effort was even made to assign relative numerical values or "life change units" to the various items. Divorce was assigned 73 units while pregnancy was assigned 40 units. Variants of the scale included a device for measuring life change units specific to college students, in addition to scales which allowed for the monitoring of daily stressors or "hassles."

The approach came very close to Selye's concept of adaptation energy in that it shared the assumption that excessive life change exhausted the individual's ability to cope with additional stress and increased the likelihood of illness. Over the years a number of studies appeared which demonstrated weak relationships between the number of life change units persons reported during a specified period, ranging between three months and two years, and the frequency of reported illnesses and stress-related physical symptoms. Although a number of studies reported statistically significant relationships between life change units and symptom frequency, the observed relationships were generally weak in magnitude. Also, it has never been clear as to what to make of the relationships in terms of health and illness. A review of the literature (Cohen & Williamson, 1991) linking stressful life events and infectious diseases (upper respiratory infection, herpes virus infections, bacterial infections) concluded that stress, measured in terms of life change and/or daily hassles, is associated with increased onset and reactivation of infectious disease. These data point to the need for further study of the psychobiologic processes involved, in addition to potential moderators of the stressor-disease relationship.

There were many problems with attempting to measure stress in terms of life change. Both positive (e.g., promotion) and negative (e.g., dismissal) life changes were lumped together. The lumping together of both negative and positive life changes or events into single scales reflected the traditional negative view of arousal. Researchers have never found correlations between positive life events and illness. In addition, many of the studies were retrospective, having subjects who were currently ill recall life changes in their recent past. Subjects who are ill may be more likely to remember life changes than subjects who are not. Also some of the life events such as weight loss and change in sleeping can be seen as symptoms of illness rather than life changes per se. Another problem with this approach is the general tendency of individuals to underreport events as stressful or even happening, with the problem increasing proportionately to the length of the retrospective interval involved. In some of these studies, subjects were asked to rate events over past time periods as long ago as two years. The greater the time interval between the event and the rating, the greater the underreporting that occurs. Another difficulty is the variability across subjects in terms of the meaning of the items. Many items in the scale have quite general wording, such as "major change in health of family." It has also been suggested that individuals will lower their threshold for describing certain experiences as events, especially if they feel compelled to provide some responses for the researcher. Finally, there may be a reporting bias in those individuals who are experiencing a variety of somatic symptoms and/or psychological difficulties at the time of being asked to reflect on life changes. Individuals who are distressed may attempt to "explain away" their problems in terms of existing life stress. For example, someone who is currently experiencing acute distress may lower his or her threshold for defining certain events as being relevant (e.g., "troubles with boss," "difficulties at work." This point takes on even greater significance, given that a substantial proportion of individuals in the general population suffer from relatively chronic psychological problems.

TRANSACTIONAL MODEL

Psychological as well as physiological systems within the individual contribute to stress vulnerability. Eysenck (1988) noted that confusion surrounding the relationship between stress and the individual is in part due to confusion between the concepts of "stress" and "strain." In physics, stress is what is imposed upon the material in question by the outer world; strain is the reaction of the material to stress. In psychological terms, the loss of a wife is stress while the spouse's reactions are the strain. Identical stresses can result in quite different reactions depending on the psychological makeup and circumstances of the individual:

> The loss of a wife may be a devastating blow to a young husband who loves his wife, and is inconsolable about her loss. It may be a relief to the husband of a wife who has been ill with a painful malady for many years, and who regards her death as a deliverance from pain. It may be a joyous occasion for a philandering husband who inherits his wife's money, and is now free to spend it on his girlfriends. (pp. 57-58)

Individuals with similar life-threatening illness often exhibit remarkable differences in their reported level of stress. Dunkel-Schetter (1984) observed that cancer patients differ more from one another in level of reported subjective distress than cancer patients and noncancer patients. In her study, cancer patients were asked to rate how stressful it was to be diagnosed and treated for cancer. Thirty-six percent of the respondents endorsed "extremely or very stressful," 27% endorsed "moderately stressful," 18% endorsed "slightly stressful," and 19% endorsed "not at all stressful." The range of responses from a group of patients with cancer illustrates the great differences one can expect when assessing subjective stress reports.

Experimental research on stress has indicated that the physiologic, as well as the psychologic and behavioral effects of stressors depend strongly on cognitive factors. That is, if situations are not viewed or interpreted as harmful, threatening, or noxious they produce smaller physiologic responses. Lazarus and Folkman (1984) defined stress as a particular relationship or *transaction* between the person and the environment that is appraised by the person as taxing or exceeding his or her resources and endangering his or her well-being." (p. 19) The definition has been widely followed because of its emphasis on the individual and his or her ability to cope with external demands. It is not stress per se that is important in adaptation, it is the way we cope with it.

The term "transaction" has been used for some time in psychology. It was intended to bridge the distinction between the person and the environment.

A good example of the tight relationship between person and environment is the changing phases of being a university student (Wapner, 1987). Initially, campus life can be stressful because of overwhelming workloads, indifferent professors, absence of social support, loneliness, unfamiliar surroundings, etc. With experience, however, there is better organization, establishment of priorities, social contacts, familiarity with advisers and professors, and consequently less stress in the system. Similar transactional perspectives are being applied to the workplace. In the occupational stress literature, there has been a growing attention toward identifying the environmental conditions which both create and reduce stress. These conditions include job demands, job autonomy, and job satisfaction. Job demands are job conditions that tax or interfere with the worker's performance abilities, such as increased workloads, role conflicts, and excessive responsibilities. Nurses often experience difficulties in these areas. Job autonomy refers to the ability of the worker to control the speed, nature, and conditions of work. Job satisfaction includes gratifications of the worker's needs and aspirations that are derived from employment. High demands and low job autonomy are a particularly troublesome combination.

Clinical studies of stress have focused primarily on appraisal and coping factors within the individual. Appraisals are conscious or unconscious judgments about the nature of the environment and one's ability to respond to it. To quote Lazarus, "the appraisal of threat is not a simple perception of the elements of the situation, but a judgment, an inference in which the data are assimilated to a constellation of ideas and expectations." Primary appraisal refers to the initial perception that there is danger or threat, whereas secondary appraisal refers to what a person can do about the threat or to what extent any action will relieve the danger or threat. Lazarus and Folkman (1984) distinguished secondary appraisal from primary appraisal in order to emphasize the vast range of individual differences in responses to an event that is perceived as stressful. Secondary appraisal is intricately related to how an individual copes with the perceived stress. The transactional model emphasizes the importance of the individual's resources in dealing with stress and in this respect places the burden of stress management on the individual. Individual differences in ways of perceiving, appraising, and interacting with the environment are more important determinants of maladaptive response than the frequency and character of the potential stressor itself. Generally, coping is defined as "constantly changing cognitive and behavioral effects to manage specific external and/or internal demands that are appraised as taxing or exceeding the resources of the person" (Lazarus & Folkman, 1984, p. 141).

Coping involves both cognitive, emotional, and behavioral strategies designed to manage a stressful situation. Coping orientations are grouped into problem-focused and emotion-focused (Lazarus, 1990). Problem-focused coping consists of efforts to change the environment or oneself. It would be reflected in self-statements such as "I knew what had to be done, so I doubled my efforts to make things work" and "I made a plan of action and followed it." Emotion-focused coping involves mental strategies that do not directly alter the relationship with the environment but do alter how this relationship is cognized:

> thus, one can try to control what is attended to, say, by avoidance of certain facts or their implications, or one can attempt to reappraise these facts or their implications, for example, by denial or distancing. In other words, emotion-focused (cognitive) coping regulates emotional distress by affecting what is being attended to or by changing its meaning. When this process succeeds, there is little or no reason to experience emotional distress since the harmful or threatening relationship has been made subjectively benign. . . . (Lazarus, 1990, p.101)

Escape-avoidance is an emotion-focused factor that includes fantasies, day-dreaming, use of alcohol and drugs, sleeping more than usual, and avoiding other people. Minimization involves conscious coping efforts to refuse to dwell on the problem and to carry on as if nothing had happened.

There is no "correct" way to cope across all situations nor do individuals cope the same way throughout a situation. Prior to an exam, for example, students are likely to engage in problem-focused coping by seeking information from others and so forth; however, after the exam and prior to grades being announced the preferred strategy might be to distance oneself from exam-related thoughts. The strategy of coping employed by individuals depends on whether they believe that something can be done to change harmful or threatening conditions for the better. When little or nothing can be done, people are likely to engage in emotion-focused coping such as avoidance and distancing. If the person feels that there is a chance of change, he or she is more likely to engage in problem-focused coping. Some research suggests that optimists are more likely than pessimists to utilize problem-focused strategies in sustained efforts to deal with real problems, the implication being that problem-focused coping is functional and emotion-focused coping is dysfunctional. Lazarus (1990) cautioned against accepting this generalization as there are circumstances when individuals who persist with problem-focused efforts simply worsen their situation or condition. This notion is contained in the motto of Alcoholics Anonymous: "God grant me the serenity to accept things I cannot change, courage to change the things I can, and the wisdom to know the difference."

The transactional model has been applied to a wide range of emotional and physical conditions. For example, romantic jealousy, mentioned in the previous chapter, has been studied and treated as a stress reaction, involving both the appraisal and coping aspects of the transactional model. At the first sign of a rival, there is primary appraisal that the self or relationship is under threat or danger of harm. The threat might deal only with the potential for a rival relationship to develop, whether real or imaginary—the important point being that the person perceives the existence of a rival relationship. A person may become jealous of the advances of a rival even when it would seem to an outside observer (including the beloved) that the beloved has no interest in the rival. Secondary appraisals are judgments about what might and can be done to deal with the threat or harm. Coping strategies might include problem-solving efforts directed toward improving the relationship (reading books on how to make oneself sexier, going more often to entertainment the beloved likes, undergoing psychotherapy, developing alternatives), or emotion-focused efforts directed toward interfering with the rival (interrupting conversations between the rival and the beloved, verbally or physically assaulting the rival or beloved, derogating the partner and/or rival, or getting drunk).

BODILY RESPONSES AND INDIVIDUALITY

Cognitive models of stress present a very rational view of reality with little recognition of the individuality of stress reactions that is seen from one person to the next. This individuality is in large part biologically determined. There is tremendous physiological and biochemical variation from one individual to the next and such variation is at the basis of differences in both stress reactions and coping styles. Parents see these differences every day in their children, as one child may manifest stress-related bodily reactions in both play and school situations while a similar-aged sibling does not.

The diathesis-stress model of illness recognized bodily susceptibility to stress through genetic predisposition. The model depicted a genetic or physiological vulnerability factor which represented the predisposition (diathesis) to develop a specific disorder. Thus, individuals are not born with a disorder such as heart disease, migraine, or hypertension but with a predisposition toward one of these conditions. The factors which determine whether a disorder becomes manifest are largely psychologic in nature.

Knowledge of how psychobiologic variation from one individual to the next influences and interacts with life experience is needed. Most researchers assume that the majority of human attributes, whether psychological or biological in nature, follow a bell-shaped or "normal" distribution in the population. That is, although we all manifest considerable differences in physical properties, there is assumed to be a "normal" or average head size, foot size, heart rate, blood pressure, and so forth. Some years ago, Williams

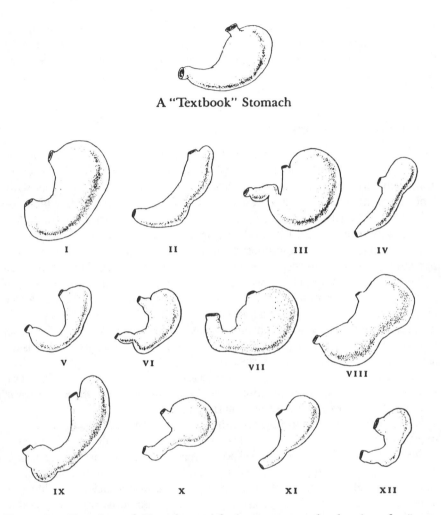

A "Textbook" Stomach

Figure 3.1. Drawings of 12 real stomachs in contrast to the drawing of a "textbook" stomach (Williams, 1967). Reprinted from R. J. Williams, *You are extraordinary.* New York: Random House, 1967. Illustration originally appeared in B. J. Anson (1963). *An atlas of human anatomy* (2nd ed.). Philadelphia: W. B. Saunders. Reprinted by permission.

(1967) entitled one of his books *You Are Extraordinary* to emphasize the individuality rather than the sameness which characterizes human anatomy and physiochemical attributes. One of his illustrations, presented in Figure 3.1, shows an "average" or "textbook" stomach followed by shapes of stomachs belonging to "normal" individuals. Some of the drawings do not even look like stomachs. He presented similar observations for a number of biochemical and physiological systems. People with no known stomach ailment were shown to exhibit variation in gastric-juice pepsin levels of 0 to 4,300 units. Some normal hearts were observed to beat more than twice as fast as others and some pumping capacities to be at least three times as great as others.

Physiological Response Specificity

The individuality known to exist at the anatomical and biochemical levels continues to be identifiable at the physiological response level. An early approach to cataloging this variability involved confronting subjects with laboratory stressors and studying the individuality in responses which resulted from the exposure (Lacey, 1959). The different "stressors" included the cold-pressor test and mental arithmetic. The physiological responses examined ranged across a number of modalities, including heart rate, blood pressure, galvanic skin response, and hand temperature. Initially, there was evidence that individuals showed a characteristic response profile across stressors (known as individual response stereotypy) and maximal activation in one particular response modality (known as individual response specificity). Examine the data from Fahrenberg (1986) presented in Figure 3.2. The figures show the physiological activation in heart rate and forehead muscle activity elicited by laboratory stressors during a typical psychophysiological experiment. There are systematic increases associated with the different stressors (mental arithmetic, interview, blood taking) but there are even greater differences in individual reactivity.

Does such variability in normal individuals set the stage for the development of a particular disorder or disease? Years ago, Malmo and Shagass (1949) extended the concept of response specificity to symptom specificity. The principle of symptom specificity stated that for individuals with a physical symptom (headache, hypertension), the physiological mechanism underlying the symptom is specifically responsive to activation by stressful stimuli. Malmo and Shagass examined the responses to stress stimuli of patients with a history of cardiovascular complaints and of patients with a history of head and neck pains. Consistent with the specificity concept, they found that heart rate, heart-rate variability, and respiratory variability were greater for the group of patients with cardiovascular complaints, whereas muscle potential scores were greater for patients with a history of head and neck pains. The concepts of response specificity and symptom specificity faded in popularity over the years, mainly because of difficulties in demonstrating consistency across repeated testing occasions. A subject may show specificity on a particular variable on one occasion and another variable on a second occasion. Approximately one-third of subjects, however, are believed to exhibit consistent response patterns across occasions.

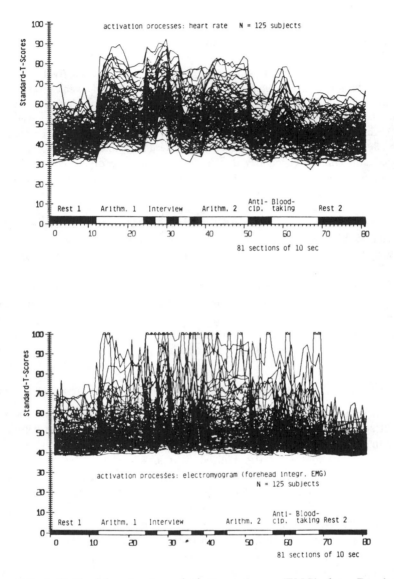

Figure 3.2. Individual heart rate and electromyogram (EMG) data. Reprinted with permission from Advances in Behaviour Research and Therapy, 8, J. Fahrenberg, Psychophysiological individuality: A pattern analytic approach to personality research and psychosomatic medicine. Copyright 1986, Pergamon Press.

The notion of symptom specificity has its origins in ancient ideas regarding constitutional or organ vulnerability:

> The constitutional vulnerability concept postulates that the individual has a characteristic *"locus minoris resistentiae"* or even several "weak links." The most vulnerable organ system is especially predisposed to deviations from homeostatic processes and under emotional, stressful, or otherwise exerting conditions will exhibit physiologically inappropriate, exaggerated, or abnormally weak reactions that are labile or persistent in character. When a generalized and chronic regulatory deficiency develops, the organ system finally becomes malfunctional, symptomatic, and, perhaps, irreversibly damaged. (Fahrenberg, 1986, p. 82)

Although the vulnerability concept has intuitive appeal, it is nearly impossible to test. Examining reactivity in individuals that already have a symptom, as was the case in the Malmo and Shagass study, begs the question of whether the reactivity is at the basis of the disorder or vice versa. In addition, some studies have found no evidence for symptom specificity. For example, patients with irritable bowel syndrome show no clear evidence of a characteristic gastrointestinal response that differentiates them from normal controls. The concept of response specificity continues to be explored, with some of the strongest support coming from cardiovascular research.

Psychophysiologic Reactivity, Hypertension, and Coronary Disease

Researchers are exploring the possibility that a form of individual response specificity is partially responsible for essential hypertension and/or coronary heart disease (CHD). Hypertension and CHD still account for more than half the deaths in the United States. Close to 30% of the adult population is hypertensive and approximately 85% of cases are classed as primary or essential hypertension, in which the exact cause of the elevated blood pressure is unknown (Schneiderman, Chesney, & Krantz, 1989). CHD begins with the symptomless development and progression of atherosclerosis, followed by clinical manifestations such as angina, heart attack, and sudden death. Epidemiologic research has identified a set of physical risk factors for CHD, and many of these have implicated elements of lifestyle and habits of living (e.g., high blood pressure, smoking, high serum cholesterol, excessive intake of dietary fat). And yet a large percentage of cases of CHD occur in absence of one or more of these risk factors. The hypothesis has been advanced that cardiovascular reactivity to naturally occurring stressors (competitive situations, time constraints, exams) varies across individuals and that individuals high in reactivity, so-called "hot reactors," may be more susceptible to the development of both hypertension and CHD. The behavior pattern may be associated with both vasoconstriction in the peripheral vessels and accelerated heart rate, leading to eventual heart damage. Another explanation focuses on the development of atherosclerotic lesions produced through adrenaline and noradrenaline. It is possible, for example, that adrenaline discharged under conditions for which it was intended (fight/flight) is metabolized differently than adrenaline discharged when no large muscle response is possible. A series of elevations in blood pressure and heart rate are thought to damage the inner layer of the coronary arteries which contribute to atherosclerosis and subsequent CHD. Also, the elevation in circulating catecholamines plays a role in cholesterol mobilization, which is a culprit in the formation of plaque.

A variety of laboratory stressors have been used to study cardiovascular reactivity in humans, the most common being some form of cognitive challenge such as the mental arithmetic task and the anagram task. In the mental arithmetic task, subjects may be asked to perform serial subtraction by 17s, aloud, from each of three four-digit numbers, with a new four-digit number being introduced at the end of each minute. Subjects are generally pressured to "work as quickly as possible" and told that they will be "evaluated on the basis of speed and accuracy of performance." In the anagram task, subjects are generally presented with a series of five-letter anagrams (e.g., rieee), with each anagram being presented on a screen for a few seconds. The anagrams are solvable (e.g., eerie). In some experiments, a "harassment" condition is added in order to activate feelings of anger and hostility. While the subject struggles with finding anagram solutions, the technician might be instructed to make comments such as "I told you these are five-letter words" or "Stop mumbling, I can't understand your answers."

Studying the concept of cardiovascular reactivity outside the laboratory is difficult and it is unknown whether a person's responses to laboratory stimuli resemble in any fashion the responses which may occur to everyday life stressors. It remains unknown whether persons who show the most pronounced responses to acute stressors are more likely to suffer coronary pathology. It is unknown whether individual differences in cardiovascular reactivity measured in the lab mirror differences in reactivity in the natural situation. Some investigators believe that the relationship between a person's responsiveness to standardized stress tests and responsiveness to the stresses of everyday living is minimal. In a direct test of the relationship, Van Egeren and Sparrow (1989) compared the blood pressure responses of subjects to laboratory stimuli with the blood pressure responses to everyday stressors. Subjects wore an ambulatory blood pressure monitor which was programmed to read blood pressure every 30 minutes from from 6 A.M. to 12 P.M. and every 60 minutes from 12 P.M. to 6 A.M. Activities and mood states were recorded by the subjects using a behavioral diary. There was very little correlation between the responses obtained under laboratory and naturalistic conditions, suggesting that laboratory tests are not valid for estimating real-life reactivity in the individual. A significant difficulty with the laboratory model is that the observed cardiovascular responses represent an acute response to an artificial challenge or provocation whereas life stress involving work, relationships, and other aspects of daily life is more continuous in influence.

Alexander Revisited

The Type A Behavior Pattern (TABP) is frequently cited as a clear example of the relationship between personality and disease. As conceived by its originators (Friedman & Rosenman, 1974), the TABP describes a person who is competitive, achievement-oriented, possesses a sense of time urgency, and is often hostile or angry. The term "time urgency" often refers to concern over very small amounts of time, as illustrated by the person who changes lanes to make up a car length or two. Williams (Suarez & Williams, 1989) hypothesized that hostility/anger is the major coronary-prone element and may account for agitation apparent in these individuals when caught in traffic or delayed in a shopping line. Some theorists believe that the competitiveness of the Type A person is largely a function of low self-esteem and the decision to remedy this low esteem by doing as much as possible in as short a time period as possible. Their remedy, however, is doomed to fail and simply increases their need to push themselves harder in order to "catch up." A common attribute of these individuals is to feel very uncomfortable if not doing something all the time.

In the 1960s and 1970s a number of studies found a positive relationship between Type A attributes and CHD. The Western Collaborative Group Study (WCGS) began in 1960 and examined approximately 3,200 initially healthy men for eight and a half years. The final report showed that those men assessed as Type A were more than twice as likely to develop clinical CHD than those assessed as Type B (Rosenman et al.). Later studies, however, failed to find strong relationships between TABP and heart disease (Matthews, 1988). A major study that failed to confirm the Western Collaborative Group studies and other findings about the risk of Type A in CHD was the Multiple Risk Factor Intervention Trial (MRFIT) study (Shekelle et al., 1985). A population of 12,700 men who were CHD-free at entry were followed for an average of seven years. The data indicated that the TABP was unrelated to the seven-year incidence of CHD.

Matthews pointed out that evidence of risk factor might disappear with disease onset. For example, in most angiography studies of risk factors and extent of occlusion of the coronary arteries, blood pressure at the time of the study is not a risk factor for coronary artery disease, although blood pressure is a risk factor in prospective studies of coronary artery disease. This nonassociation is thought to occur because most hypertensives are under treatment and their study blood pressure is not a valid indicator of their pretreatment levels. The same may happen with Type A correlations; once diagnosed with CHD, patients may alter their Type A behaviors to increase the probability of survival such that their study classification may not reflect their previous Type A classification.

There is limited evidence that Type A subjects compared with Type B subjects display larger acute increases in blood pressure, heart rate, catecholamines, and cortisol when confronted by appropriately challenging or stressful tasks. Two studies have even shown that Type A patients, when under general anesthesia for coronary bypass surgery, showed increased systolic blood pressure responses during the surgical procedure. Reactivity differences measured in the natural environment, however, have not been that great. Type A and Type B subjects participating in the naturalistic ambulatory blood pressure monitoring study reviewed earlier (Van Egeren & Sparrow, 1990), showed some differences in the direction of greater reactivity for the Type A group. As shown in Figure 3.3, the Type As had higher blood pressures across all the situations and activities recorded but the differences may or may not have clinical significance. The greatest activity differences occurred with walking, talking, drinking a caffeinated beverage, drinking an alcoholic beverage, and relaxing.

The key behavioral characteristics of the TABP are becoming less and less important in understanding the connection between personality and hypertension. What is taking place is a return to the classical formulations of Alexander (1950) which posited hostility as the primary emotional precursor of both hypertension and CHD. Current researchers are finding relationships between CHD and measures of hostility, anger-in (difficulty expressing angry feelings), and certain speech characteristics. Dembrowski and colleagues, for example, took a second look at two coronary angiography samples in which there was no reliable association between atherosclerosis and globally defined Type A behavior. They found that potential for hostility was a significant correlate of coronary atherosclerosis as was a measure of anger-in. Some investigators believe that basic mistrust of others not only relates to heart disease mortality but to mortality from all causes. A specific psychological inventory, the Cook-Medley Hostility Scale, has been used to study the link between hostility and CHD. The scale was originally designed to identify teachers who had difficulty getting along with students. The items reflect traits of hostile attributions, cynicism, hostile affect, aggressive responding, and social avoidance. In a prospective study (Barefoot et al., 1989), the scale was administered as part of a larger test to 128 law students at the University of North Carolina during the years 1956 and 1957. The test was administered to compare the psychological profiles of law students with those of other students. A mortality follow-up of the students took place in 1985. Alumni records and legal directories were the

Diastolic Blood Pressure

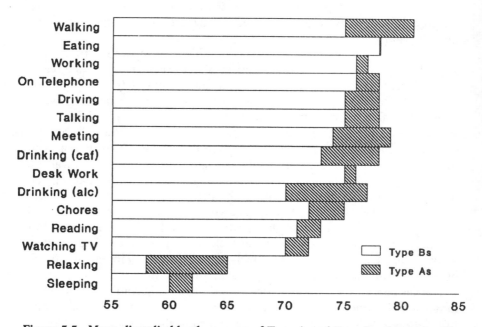

Figure 3.3. Mean diastolic blood pressure of Type A and Type B subjects for 15 activities. (L. F. Van Egeren & A. W. Sparrow, Ambulatory monitoring to assess real-life cardiovascular reactivity in Type A and Type B subjects, Psychosomatic Medicine, 52, 3, 297–306, 1990). Copyright by American Psychosomatic Society.

primary sources of the follow-up information. Thirteen individuals were identified as deceased—six of these were attributed to CHD, cancer accounted for four deaths, and two were due to thrombosis associated with diabetes mellitus. The researchers reported that hostile item subsets were predictive of mortality (e.g., "I often have to take advice from others who know less," "I don't like being interrupted," "Some of my family members do things that really irk me.").

Both the psychodynamic formulations of Alexander and ongoing research attest to the importance of understanding the cardiovascular system in psychobiologic terms. Clinicians have long recognized the importance of this approach in assessing their cardiovascular patients. Shapiro (1988) cited a study which examined 25 patients entering 2 hospitals with acute pulmonary edema. Although the patients all had heart disease, the precipitating event of the attack in the majority of cases was a "profound emotional event occurring within the previous few days." Shapiro believes very strongly in the connection between behavioral events and heart disease and encourages medical students to watch for these connections in the clinical situation:

[Asking] a patient who has recently incurred a myocardial infarction the simple question, "What were you doing during the day before the pain developed?" provides incidents, often elicited by the students, such as the illness of a family member, an impending breakup with a loved one, a job crisis, etc. An example of one dramatic incident was a man who was our orchestra's assistant conductor and who was scheduled for his first venture in leading the local orchestra himself the next day, in the presence of scouts from a prestigious orchestra who were looking for a new conductor. He developed chest pain while sitting in the barber chair the afternoon before the concert. When he was brought to the emergency room, an EKG revealed a newly developed inferior infarct. When he was informed of this, he said, "Oh no, it can't happen today; I've got too much to do," at which point he promptly went into ventricular fibrillation. (p. 201)

Self-regulation of Hypertension

Relaxation is a commonly used technique for lowering hypertension. Interest in this procedure is partly the result of concern with possible side effects of antihypertensive medication. Antihypertensive medication, although effective in controlling blood pressure, can be accompanied by both behavioral and medical side effects. Views as to how effective relaxation training is in lowering blood pressure vary. The technique has been associated with clinically significant reductions in blood pressure (Agras, 1988). Reductions occur with treatment and the magnitude of reduction appears to correlate highly with initial blood pressure levels (i.e., the higher the initial level, the greater the change). The treatment gains also appear to be maintained across time, even though there is little evidence that subjects actually maintain their practice of relaxation across time. Although there is considerable variability in who responds to relaxation therapy, it has not been easy to identify subject characteristics that predict magnitude of response. Relaxation training may be best suited for patients who respond poorly to pharmacologic treatment, either for reasons of poor adherence or inability to tolerate the side effects of the medication. In such patients, relaxation training leads to lowering of blood pressure, "with some two-thirds of such patients showing diastolic blood pressures below 90 mmHg following training." The best predictor is apparently pretreatment blood pressure level. Whether this is simply a physiological or psychobiological parameter deserves study. There is some evidence that mild hypertensives with higher baseline heart rates and norepinephrine levels respond better to relaxation training than hypertensives lower on these sympathetic nervous system parameters, which would suggest that pretreatment anxiety levels might be a predictor of treatment responsiveness.

Agras also reviewed several studies showing that simple monitoring of blood pressure results in blood pressure decreases which, in some instances, match those observed following relaxation training. Most programs go beyond relaxation training and include a stress-management component to treatment. The stress-management consists of identifying each patient's reaction to stressful events, altering cognitions accompanying or leading to stress, and teaching coping strategies to better deal with stressful situations. Lynch (Lynch et al., 1982) developed a psychophysiologic approach to blood pressure regulation which involves having the patient discuss personally relevant information while his/her blood pressure is being monitored. The approach emphasizes "not only feedback to patients of minute-to-minute blood pressure changes, but one linking changes in pressure to the ebb and flow of human dialogue within the psychotherapeutic context." Lynch noted that hypertensive patients in clinic exhibited the greatest increases in blood pressure while they were talking and that the magnitude of the increases was linked to emotion-laden topics. Initially, they were quite unaware of the connection between bodily changes and the verbalization of emotional topics. The strategy for increasing their awareness of this relationship consisted of having them become more aware of respiratory patterns during speech. Many of these patients would change, outside of awareness, their respiratory pattern by breath holding or hyperventilation. A case study from Lynch et al. illustrates the treatment approach:

> Patient B was a 50-year-old single professional male who was referred to us with a diagnosis of hypertension by a neurologist. . . . Psychological testing showed no significant psychological disturbance, except high denial. . . . At the onset of therapy, the patient was on hydrochlorathiazide, 250 mg b.i.d.
>
> In the initial sessions the patient discussed his problems in becoming close to others, although he described himself as a "happy person, lucky and well contented with his lot". . . . his initial mean BP in the clinic was 170/100, and it ranged from a high of 180/106 to a low of 160/100 in that session. . . . the patient's BP was always lower at home than in our clinic. . . .
>
> During the initial sessions the patient was reluctant to discuss personal material, but agreed that certain stresses might be involved in high BP, stresses such as worries about his BP and excessive weight. We began by probing the patient as to why he thought his BP was always higher in our presence than when he took it at home alone. He specifically denied that interpersonal factors were involved in BP changes, but did acknowledge that he found such differences "most curious." The subsequent psychophysiological therapy focused on the relationship between the rapid shifts in BP and the content of communications during the feedback sessions, and his inability to breathe regularly while speaking. We eventually focused on his inability to relate to others in a close, personal manner.
>
> In the next eight months the patient's pressure gradually decreased to 155/80. Home reports also showed reductions in pressure to 130/70. During this time he was taken off all medications. He gradually became more willing

to discuss interpersonal issues, and showed increasing ability to accurately estimate his own pressures. He also began to relate the changes in his BP to various interpersonal situations. (Lynch et al., 1982, pp. 149-150)

Lynch's patient example illustrates that self-regulation can be achieved in a very simple fashion, once the person becomes aware of the connection between thoughts, feelings, speaking style, and bodily reactions. This condition of mind-body awareness can be attained a number of ways and often without formal training. Having individuals recognize these psychobiological mechanisms is important both for prevention and treatment. At a psychological level, it is likely to involve the ability to self-focus in a number of ways and to varying degrees. Certainly distancing of self from the stressful world—the passive state of meditation—would be effective as would diminishing negative affect in oneself, including anxiety and anger. Aggressive and competitive individuals, because of their strong need for control over the environment, have little awareness of internal body events accompanying this need. Because they are always concentrating on events outside of themselves, they have little or no attention left to identify internal events. They also have difficulty with relaxation training. The fact that their hard-driving style often results in advancement and achievements is an obvious reason why they may resist any attempt to modify or change their behavior patterns. There are signs, however, that, as with smoking and other physical risk factors, the populace is beginning to reject the values associated with aggressiveness and competition. Indeed, the suggestion has been made that industrial nations are now having difficulty finding people who are not lazy! The slowing down of life and finding greater enjoyment in what one is doing will undoubtedly lead to large-scale reductions in both hypertension and coronary heart disease.

Fitness and Cardiovascular Response to Stress

Fitness may be one of the most widely employed techniques for combating the stress and strain of modern living. The link between increased aerobic exercise and a reduction in CHD risk is established (Biddle & Fox, 1989). Claims are also made that exercise can reduce back pain, anxiety, and depression and delay the debilitating effects of aging. It is assumed that aerobically fit persons meet the same physical demands with less sympathetic activation than persons with a lower level of aerobic fitness (van Doornen, & de Geus, 1989). In comparison to "low fit" persons, aerobically fit persons have been found to show less catecholamine secretion, heart rate acceleration, and peripheral vasoconstriction at the same physical workload. This difference in physiological responses between high and low fit persons disappears when the two groups exercise at a fraction of their maximal aerobic power. In other words, the physiological adaptations to aerobic exercise are a function of the *relative* physical load: since the maximum aerobic capacity of fit persons is larger, they show smaller physiological responses to the same absolute workload. Several authors have hypothesized that, in accordance with the reaction to aerobic exercise, the sympathetic response of fit persons to psychological stress would be reduced as well because the same neurogenic and endocrine response systems are involved in both types of reactions.

How can sympathetic reactivity have negative effects during stress, when at the same time it is the driving force behind the adaptive response to physical exercise? Blix, Stromme, and Ursin (1974) discovered that the normal relationship between oxygen consumption (VO2) and heart rate as determined during several levels of exercise does not apply in stress situations. They observed aircraft pilots during flight operations and found heart rates that were about 30 bpm faster than the heart rates predicted from oxygen consumption values. They called this difference between actual and predicted heart rate, "additional heart rate." Physiological reactions to stress are, at least to a certain extent, "metabolically inappropriate." During exercise, changes in cardiac output vary directly with workload and oxygen consumption, whereas during psychological stress cardiac output may increase considerably, while oxygen consumption may change very little. This creates a state of overperfusion of the peripheral vessels during stress (more blood supply than dictated by metabolic needs). Autoregulatory reactions to the overperfusion might be the first step toward stress-induced hypertension. In view of the possible pathological consequences of this cardiovascular stress response, any reduction in sympathetic reactivity seems advantageous.

It is possible that aerobic fitness is capable of producing a direct reduction in sympathetic reactivity to stress. Although a few studies have observed smaller heart rate responses to stress in aerobically fit persons, the differences have not always been demonstrable. The same is true of systolic blood pressure. van Doornen and de Geus (1989) suggested that heart rate is too simple a measure; that it is important to also measure other cardiovascular indices such as stroke volume and peripheral resistance. Also the interaction between heart activity and peripheral resistance is important because increasing the resistance adds to the "afterload" of the heart which leads to a decrement in stroke volume by shortening the ejection time. Their study compared the aerobic fitness (defined as the maximum oxygen consumption [VO2max] that can be reached during aerobic exercise) and "stress" fitness of eight long-distance runners and seven sedentary individuals. The experiment consisted of two sessions on separate days. On Day 1, their oxygen consumption was assessed in response to 10 minutes of pedaling on a bicycle ergometer. The two groups were, not surprisingly, quite different in V02max. On the second day, subjects participated in a reaction time coping task chosen to evoke sympathetic responses:

> Two light bulbs were positioned on a small panel in front of the subject. A push-button was mounted on each of the handgrips. After a random foreperiod of 0.5-1.5 s, either the right or the left light bulb would come on. The subjects had to press the opposite button within a certain criterion time. Incorrect or too slow responses were punished with a loud noise burst. In addition to noise there was a financial penalty.

The authors found some evidence for the hypothesis that fit persons show diminished sympathetic response. They obtained the difference primarily in terms of peripheral resistance, as measured by diastolic blood pressure. Low fit subjects showed a stronger blood pressure response than the high fit subjects.

People active in sports can differ from inactive people in several respects other than their fitness level: for example, they may differ in psychological traits, such as hostility, that modulate stress sensitivity (e.g., people living in New York compared to people living in California). At the same time. we should not conclude that such differences are purely psychological as it is also possible that physiologic differences in fitness may account for observed psychological differences. Dienstbier (1989) hypothesized that exercise leads to *physiological toughness,* a bodily condition characterized by lower arousal levels, quicker return to resting levels after stress, better glucose utilization, as well as relative increases in high density lipoprotein ("good" cholesterol). Exercise is also useful for reducing muscle tension and self-reports of anxiety. Recall Jacobson's (1938) hypothesis that, in the absence of muscle tension, anxious thoughts are not possible.

SOCIAL SUPPORT: CAUSE OR CONSEQUENCE?

Social support is widely believed to reduce the impact of stress. Two models of the effects of social support have been proposed: the buffering model, which holds that social support has beneficial effects on health only or chiefly when individuals are exposed to stress, and the direct or main effects model, which holds that social support is health promoting irrespective of whether individuals are exposed to stress. Findings supportive of the main effects model would be those which have found that individuals with strong social networks, defined in terms of marital status, number of close family and friends, church membership, and group affiliation are less likely to die than individuals with weak social networks. Within this framework, social relationships "may provide a sense of identity, a source of positive evaluation, or a sense of self-efficacy" and contribute to a general state of health (Kaplan & Toshima, 1990). Social relationships might be associated with diminished death rates due to cancers and respiratory diseases—conditions the immune system defends against. Studies have linked reduced lymphocyte proliferation to both bereavement, which could be seen as a loss of social support, and self-reported loneliness which could reflect low social support.

Within the buffering model, social support is believed to operate by reducing the health-threatening impact of stress. An example of research supporting the buffering effect of social support was provided by Theorell, Orth-Gomér, and Eneroth (1990). They studied changes in serum immunoglobulin G (IgG) across several weeks of changing levels of job stress. IgG has a long turnover rate and takes several days or weeks to change in level. They examined self-reported job strain on several occasions across three to four months in 50 individuals. Job strain as well as perceived social support were assessed by questionnaire. Blood was sampled at the beginning of the working day. The researchers found that progressively more IgG was utilized when job strain increased. In addition, individuals with increasing job strain and low social support reported greater increases in IgG than individuals with adequate social support.

A number of studies have found that a combination of high stress and low social support are strong predictors of illness (Kaplan & Toshima, 1990). The Framington Heart Study (Kannel, 1987), for example, found that women who worked in clerk or clerical roles and had unsupportive spouses had a higher incidence of cardiovascular disease. Others studies have reported a relationship between cardiovascular disease and perceived low social support and control over the work environment. Not all studies, however, have shown a relationship between social support and health outcomes.

The difference in prediction between the buffering hypothesis and the direct effects hypothesis is shown in Table 3.1. The buffering hypothesis predicts an interaction between stress/strain and social support and predicts

TABLE 3.1. Hypothetical Levels of Disorder as a Function of Life Events and Social Support According to Buffer Hypothesis (adapted from Depue & Monroe, 1986).

Life events	Social support	
	Low	High
Low	Slight-to-moderate disorder	Minimal disorder (normals)
High	Highest disorder	Slight-to-moderate disorder

the greatest illness for persons under high life stress and low social support. The direct effects model predicts the greatest incidence for individuals receiving low social support, regardless of life stressors present.

There is a problem in knowing what is leading to what in this design and it has been dubbed the "person-environment covariance problem" (Depue & Monroe, 1986). The fourfold table assumes that life events and social support are independent events and can be studied separately from the person. Depue and Monroe noted that environmental variables associated with life demands and presence/absence of social support do not happen to the person independent of attributes of the person. Job strain, for example, is as much determined by personal attributes as situational attributes. An example of the importance of personal attributes comes from a study which explored the relationship between social support and mortality in Type A and Type B cardiac patients (Orth-Gomér & Undén, 1990). Social integration and its opposite, social isolation, were measured with a scale that assessed frequency of attending movies or plays or concerts, of entertaining friends or attending parties, of visiting social clubs, and of attending sporting events. Ten-year mortality was higher in individuals who scored high on social isolation but the effect was statistically significant only for Type A men (Figure 3.4). In socially isolated Type A men, the mortality rate was 69%, whereas in socially integrated men, the mortality rate was 17%. The social support variable did not statistically discriminate the Type B subjects, although social isolation was again associated with a higher mortality rate than social integration. Personal attributes associated with Type A appeared to have determined the health-impairing effects of social isolation.

Personal attributes often contribute to how much or how little support one receives from significant others. Lonely college students, for example, were observed to have greater difficulty than nonlonely students in introducing themselves to others, making phone calls to initiate social contact, participating in groups, asserting themselves, and taking social risks. Lonely college students also evaluated themselves negatively and expected others to reject them, although they were not differentially evaluated by non-lonely students (Rook, 1984). One hypothesis holds that lonely people avoid social interaction to protect their fragile self-esteem. Withdrawal from interpersonal situations minimizes the threat of rejection by eliminating the possibility altogether. Those who work with the lonely need to be sensitive to the possibility that these individuals' fear of rejection may override their motivation to establish supportive relationships.

Another example of how personal attributes might be the key factor comes from the study of marital status. Marital status or marriage is often used as an index of social support. However, the psychological and social advantages of marriage may be restricted to happily married persons. Unhappily married persons are under considerable debilitating stress. Even

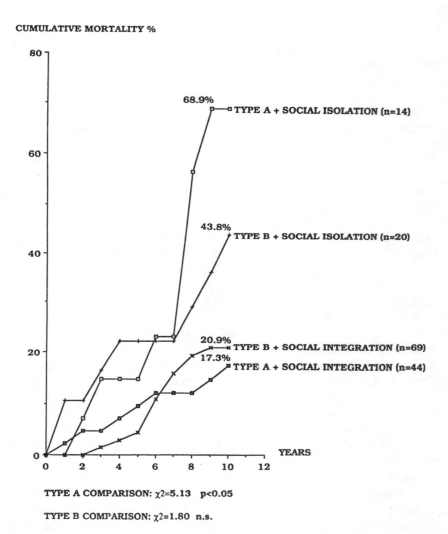

CUMULATIVE MORTALITY %

80

68.9%
▫—▫ TYPE A + SOCIAL ISOLATION (n=14)

60

43.8%
✶ TYPE B + SOCIAL ISOLATION (n=20)

40

20.9%
✶—✶ TYPE B + SOCIAL INTEGRATION (n=69)
17.3%
▫ TYPE A + SOCIAL INTEGRATION (n=44)

20

0   YEARS

0   2   4   6   8   10   12

TYPE A COMPARISON: χ^2=5.13   p<0.05

TYPE B COMPARISON: χ^2=1.80   n.s.

Figure 3.4. Cumulative mortality for Type A and Type B individuals. (K. Orth-Gomér & A. Undén, Type A behavior, social support, and coronary risk: Interaction and significance for mortality in cardiac patients, Psychosomatic Medicine, 52, 1, 59–72, 1990). Copyright by American Psychosomatic Society.

claims that marital satisfaction is predictive of indices of health is not proof of a causal relationship. It is possible that "persons who are physically healthy, psychologically adjusted, and interpersonally skilled are more likely to get married, remain married, and be maritally satisfied."

It is quite possible, according to Depue and Monroe (1986), that chronic personal conditions associated with hostility and depression and/or anxiety, generate stressful life events as well as loss of social supports. Personality attributes of individuals which involve moodiness, inadequate functioning, excess illness behavior, and dependency may alienate friends and family and lead to their withdrawal. The life stress measure of "increased arguments with spouse" may result from the dependency accompanying a chronic illness condition and contribute to further life stress associated with separation and divorce. In this example, the stress and lack of social support are both the result rather than the cause of the person's illness. Depue and Monroe observed that suicide attempts associated with depression are often associated with loss of support, "but that in every case the loss was generated by the consequences of the already-present episode or of the combined effects of previous and current episodes." The bias contained in Table 3.1 is that chronically disordered individuals would be the most likely to end up in the cell represented by high life events and low social support, but this placement might well be largely determined by stable person attributes rather than environmental variables. Social support measures are best used in the presence of an understanding of their interaction with characteristics of the individuals under study.

SLEEP DISTURBANCE: INSOMNIA

Insomnia is an example of a stress disorder that is very troublesome for the individuals afflicted. Insomnia is defined as the perception by individuals that their sleep is inadequate or abnormal. The perception includes difficulty falling asleep, frequent awakenings from sleep, short sleep periods, and nonrestorative sleep. Some insomnias are transient conditions while others are persistent (Roehrs, Zorick, & Roth, 1989). Central nervous system arousal, specifically brainstem reticular activating system (RAS) arousal, is believed to be largely responsible for transient insomnia. Thus, almost any condition or situation that produces arousal, whether a psychological or environmental factor, can potentially disturb sleep.

A second factor contributing to insomnia is the misalignment of the sleep-wake schedule with the underlying circadian rhythms. Unfamiliar sleep environments and shift work represent conditions that might promote such misalignments. Shift work is especially disruptive because the environmental cues are completely out of phase with the sleep-wake cycle. Shift workers have been reported to have shortened and disrupted sleep and increased daytime sleepiness. They also exhibit patterns of reduced sleep efficiency, as evidenced by greater amounts of stage 1 sleep and reduced amounts of stage 3-4 sleep. Stage 1 is considered the lightest stage of sleep and is characterized by low-voltage desynchronized EEG activity (Figure 3.5). Stage 2 is characterized by low-voltage, regular activity at 4 to 6 cycles

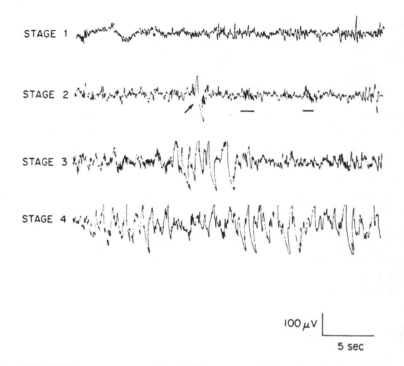

Figure 3.5. EEG patterns associated with stages of sleep (Carskadon & Dement, 1989). Reprinted by permission.

per second and the appearance of K complex or sleep spindle which some investigators take as the onset of "sleep." Later, in stage 3, low frequency (0.5 to 2.5 cycles per second) high voltage delta waves begin to appear. When the delta activity increases and dominates the tracing (over 50%), the individual has entered stage 4 sleep. The four stages roughly parallel a "depth of sleep" continuum, with arousal thresholds generally lowest in stage 1 and highest in stage 4 sleep. It is extremely difficult to awaken a person during stage 4 sleep.

Psychobiological patterns of sleep and wakefulness which persist under constant environmental conditions and in the absence of environmental cues are said to "free-run." Free-running rhythms usually have a periodicity (the time required for one complete rhythm cycle) which is approximately, not exactly, 24 hours; hence, they are termed "circadian" (circa = about, dies = a day). When humans are kept in isolation, without access to light or a clock, they continue to show a daily sleep-wake cycle of approximately 25 hours. In most organisms, circadian rhythms are generated by one or more master circadian oscillators, or pacemakers which, in turn, are synchronized by one or more environmental cues or zeitgebers. Although rhythms are endogenously (internally) generated, there are also mechanisms for ensuring that the rhythms maintain a correct phase relationship to the environment, such as following the light-dark cycle and seasonal fluctuations in light. The process of phase and period control of an oscillator by an environmental cycle is called *entrainment*. Light is a powerful zeitgeber for the circadian rest-activity rhythms displayed by most organisms. Light pulses will cause phase shifts of free-running rhythms, the direction of which depends on when the light pulse is presented. In nocturnal rodents, light pulses presented at the beginning of the daily active period produce phase delays, whereas pulses produced toward the end of the active period produce phase advances. A phase delay means that running activity begins/ends later than usual, whereas a phase advance means that activity begins/ends earlier than usual. Light pulses presented during middle portions of the active period have no systematic effects.

There are 24-hour rhythms in a number of biological processes, including body temperature, hormone production, and brain metabolism, which are systematically organized in synchrony with sleep-and-wake behavior and the light-dark cycle. The physiological mechanism controlling circadian rhythms is believed to lie in the suprachiasmatic nuclei (SCN), a group of cells located in the ventromedial area of the hypothalamus. These cells receive projections from the retina via the optic chiasm. Surgical destruction of this area eliminates circadian rhythms and electrical/chemical stimulation of the area produces phase shifts similar in nature to the shifts produced by light pulses.

Sleep-onset insomnia is the most common form of insomnia. It is characterized by frequent difficulty initiating sleep with less difficulty maintaining sleep once it is initiated. The sleep architecture of these individuals is relatively normal, except for an increase in percentage of stage 1 sleep. There are adequate percentages of stage 2, delta, and REM sleep. Elderly individuals often have difficulty with insomnia and it is not clear whether these difficulties originate from age-related changes in sleep architecture or other factors. Periodic leg movements (PLM), characterized by rhythmic extensions of the big toe and dorsiflexions of the ankle, as well as flexions of the knee and hip, increase in frequency with the elderly and are a common cause of insomnia. Breathing difficulties are another source of insomnia in the elderly. The primary age-related change in the EEG is a decrease in the percentage of slow wave (stages 3 and 4) sleep. Some REM reductions have also been observed but the reductions are of questionable significance.

There are some data which suggest that sleep-onset insomnia is associated with a disruption in circadian rhythms. One hypothesis is related to the concept of "wake maintenance zones," defined as phases of the body's circadian temperature rhythm during which sleep onsets were not selected

in free-running studies. Body temperature is higher during wake maintenance zones and subjects choose not to go to bed during these times.
Shortest sleep-onset latencies and maximum sleep times occurred when
bedtime was close to the body temperature minimum. One study (Morris,
Lack, & Dawson, 1990) observed insomniacs to exhibit a phase delay in
body temperature when compared to normal sleepers (Figure 3.6). The
body temperature of normals began falling several hours before their chosen
lights-out times. The temperature pattern for the insomniac was delayed an
average of 2.5 hours, which resulted in their attempting to fall asleep during
a wake maintenance zone. One solution for these individuals would be to
delay their bedtime by three or four hours; the problem initially would be
that they would get even less sleep, assuming that they had to rise at the
same time.

Severe occurrences of sleep-onset insomnia are called the delayed sleep
syndrome (Roehrs, Zorick, & Roth, 1989). Sleep onset may be delayed until
early morning (3:00 A.M. to 6:00 A.M.), and if the person ignores the
demands of waking life, he/she may not rise until midday-early afternoon
(11:00 A.M. to 2:00 P.M.). The individual has no difficulty maintaining sleep.
The condition is treated by systematically delaying bedtime by three-hour
steps, which in effect establishes a 27-hour day. The procedure is maintained until the desired bedtime of 11:00 P.M. or midnight is reached and a

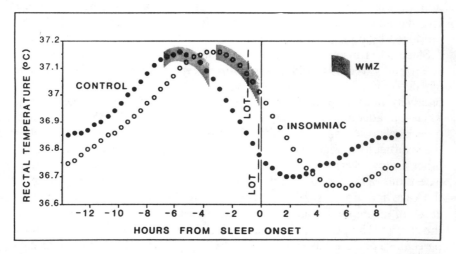

Figure 3.6. Group 24-hour temperature data for insomniacs and controls. The
usual mean lights-out time (LOT) for each group are indicated as vertical dashed
lines. The estimated mean wake maintenance zone (WMZ) for each group is
indicated as a shaded area. (Sleep, Sleep-onset insomniacs have delayed temperature rhythms, by M. Morris, L. Lack, & D. Dawson, 13, 1990, 1–14.). Reprinted by
permission.

24-hour day can be maintained. With less severe sleep-onset insomnia, it may only be necessary to alter a late life style, particularly on weekends. Consistent early waketimes may be adequate to phase advance their temperature rhythms and decrease the sleep-onset difficulty.

Sleep-onset insomnia also has a large psychological component which may ultimately account for observed circadian rhythm deviations. The condition is also called persistent psychophysiological insomnia (PPI) (Hauri, 1989). A case study provided by Hauri is reported at length:

Mr. R, a 32-year-old laboratory technician, was referred to the sleep disorders center for an evaluation of his insomnia after he had twice fallen asleep at the wheel and had nearly caused an accident. On interview, it developed that Mr. R had been a light sleeper for most of his life, with sporadic nights of serious insomnia during tense life situations, such as before important examinations. After working as an electronics technician most of his life, four years ago he had tried to establish his own manufacturing firm. He was only lightly insured when soon thereafter an accidental fire destroyed his plant. Bankruptcy ensued, serious depression followed, and Mr. R was treated with psychotherapy and antidepressants. Depression lifted three months later, but insomnia remained. A second course of psychotherapy three years later, undertaken expressly to treat the insomnia, ended in his referral to the sleep disorders center because his psychiatrist came to feel more and more that Mr. R's insomnia was not secondary to psychopathology, even though he did admit that Mr. R was a somewhat rigid, obsessive, and hard-driving man.

Polysomnographic recordings on two consecutive nights in the laboratory confirmed serious sleep latency problems: 2 h on the first night and 4 1/2 h on the second night. Once asleep, Mr. R first slept fitfully both nights for 1 to 3 hs, with increased stage 1 sleep and little delta or rapid eye movement (REM) sleep. About 2 h before he had to get up on both nights, he finally fell first into a 45-min stage 4 episode, followed by a REM period lasting over 1 h. There was no evidence of any respiratory disturbances, and although Mr. R was restless on both nights, there was no evidence of periodic leg movements. In the morning, Mr. R rated his night 1 as "better than my average" and his night 2 as "average."

After a diagnosis of persistent psychophysiological insomnia was made, Mr. R's bedtime behavior was examined in detail. Because he was typically worrying about small everyday matters and rehearsing speeches and letters when he could not sleep, he was advised to schedule a 30-min "worry time" immediately after supper each day in which he would free-associate and write down his worries and the possible solutions to them. During that time, he might also put down on paper the types of letters and speeches that he had previously rehearsed at night. At bedtime, he was then asked to read until he fell asleep reading. He was prescribed a few hypnotics, to be taken no more than twice per week after particularly poor nights. An increase in exercise was also recommended. These measures gradually reduced Mr. R's sleep latency to an average of about 1 h per night. However, because Mr. R still felt quite tense when going to bed, a course of frontalis electromyographic (EMG) biofeed-back and some stress management training were then prescribed, with the result that Mr. R regained his prebankruptcy sleep patterns. He now typically fell asleep in 15 to 20 min. Occasionally, no more than four to six times per month, he would still find that he had to read for 1 to 2 h before feeling sleepy, and on some rare occasions, he then took a short-acting benzodiazepine to help with sleep. He professed total satisfaction with this regimen. (p. 442)

This case study illustrates how an individual's waking thoughts and feelings continue into the presleep period as well as the sleep cycle itself. Patients seldom recognize this connection and if anything become harder on themselves for being unable to fall asleep. After a number of poor nights of sleep, they become increasingly concerned about their inability to sleep and try even harder on subsequent nights. The most common thoughts reported by chronic insomniacs are: "I find it hard to let go and relax," "My mind keeps turning things over," "I can't get my sleep into a proper routine" and "I am unable to empty my mind." (Espie, Brooks, & Lindsay, 1989). Patients showing a pattern of "trying too hard to sleep" often fall asleep easily when they are distracted—for example, when they are watching television or reading. However, when they try to fall asleep, they often cannot. Or, if they are being bothered by certain thoughts or even symptoms, they may begin to feel dominated by thoughts of self-doubt, worry, and general panic about not being able to cope.

PSYCHOLOGICAL STRESS AND SURGERY

The psychological experience of surgery can be one of life's most stressful events. Many clinicians believe that the cognitive appraisal processes of individuals undergoing surgery may affect the success of the operation both in terms of recovery and postsurgical symptoms. Presurgical psychological interventions designed to improve psychological adjustment to and recovery from surgery are routinely administered in many hospitals. A key determinant in understanding how patients receive and react to this information is their way of coping with the threat of surgery.

Irving Janis (1958) found that a moderate amount of fear expressed prior to surgery facilitated postsurgical recovery. Patients who showed extreme fear reactions or who showed little or no fear before the surgery coped less well during the recovery period. Patients who showed the least preoperative anticipatory fear were presumably employing denial defenses. Janis hypothesized that the group that showed moderate fear used their fear constructively to engage in a cognitive process that he labeled *work of worrying.* These patients apparently used their fear to prepare themselves for the discomforts and frustrations that they were to experience later. Janis hypothesized that the absence of cognitive preparation in the form of work of worrying characterizes patients who fail to cope adequately with surgery. Because the patient has failed to cognitively rehearse the outcome, he/she may be overwhelmed when the danger materializes.

According to Janis and Mann (1977), successful coping with the threat of surgery is a three-step process. First, exposure to surgery-related information generates fear and begins the work of worry. Second, the patient mentally rehearses the upcoming event and, finally, the patient draws upon his or her coping techniques in order to get through the event. The literature supporting the usefulness of efforts to assist patients in dealing with the stress of surgical intervention is generally favorable. Studies have found that patients given instruction in self-help physical activities such as deep breathing and coughing had a quicker recovery and required less analgesic medication than those not given similar training (Alberts et al., 1989). Not all studies have found positive benefits; some studies have observed reports of increased pain following information about surgery. It is safe to say that the effectiveness of information before surgery depends on a host of factors, including how the information is presented, characteristics of the communicator, and the coping mechanisms in use by the patient receiving the communication. These factors all interact, making outcome predictions extremely difficult. For example, an early study (Williams et al., 1975) manipulated the kind of preoperative visit given to patients. One kind of visit was brief and only of sufficient duration to provide patients with a brief explanation of the forthcoming procedures. Another kind of visit was more supportive and it included enough time for patients to ask all the questions they wished. Both types of interviews were successful in decreasing the levels of anxiety in highly anxious patients. In low-anxiety patients, however, the supportive interview had no effect on anxiety levels, whereas the brief interview actually increased anxiety levels. Thus, straightforward staff communications may not always be effective or may even be disruptive for patients that are prone to using denial.

The individuality of reactions to surgery makes it difficult, if not impossible, to isolate effective coping strategies that apply to all persons. A reviewer of a book titled "The Psychological Experience of Surgery" commented:

Having lived by the rule of "for a long happy life, stay away from the knife," for most of my years following a traumatic tonsillectomy at age 5 1/2, I found myself undergoing three surgical procedures in two years: a vasectomy (it was downhill after the prep), a hernia repair (I was not going to cough postop no matter what they did to me), and a total hip replacement (the postop pain was minimal, but my helplessness in terms of mobility was more profound than I' had anticipated). Whatever my pre- and postsurgical experiences were, they were too complex and ambiguous to be encompassed by terms such as denial, regression, and depression. For example, I could not get to sleep at night. My usual pattern of relative insomnia was greatly accentuated. I also think that I was hyperemotional. I am not sure about this, but I cried during a Tarzan movie at 3 A.M. The memory stands out in my postsurgical experience. (Kroll, 1989, p. 467)

Our scientific understanding of the psychology of surgery is limited but based on what is known it is important that members of the health team remain sensitive to individual differences in coping styles and not present communications that overwhelm the patient or that prevent recognition of the anxiety and fear that accompany the experience.

Trauma and Stress

Posttraumatic stress refers to a clinical condition seen in a small number of individuals who have been exposed and survived major catastrophes such as natural disasters, combat, and accidents. The condition is discussed at some length to illustrate the overwhelming effect severe trauma may have on the individual's psychobiology. It is also important that health professionals have a good understanding of the condition. Recognition of both psychologic and physiologic aspects of posttraumatic stress were evident in the original naming of the condition as *physioneurosis.* The major symptoms of posttraumatic stress are: intrusive reexperiencing the traumatic event, emotional numbing, and hyperarousal. Horowitz (1976) suggested that these symptoms represent an ongoing oscillation between the states of *intrusion* and *denial/numbing* until the experience is resolved. The intrusion state represents a conscious reaction to memories of the traumatic event while the denial/numbing state is believed to represent an unconscious coping reaction to the pain.

Intrusive reexperiencing. Painful recollections of the traumatic event are often observed in victims of trauma. Rape victims report reliving the experience, particularly during sexual activity when the woman may suddenly feel that her present partner is the rapist. Other intrusive symptoms include sleep disturbances, the most frequent being nightmares and waking at night with an inability fall asleep. Survival guilt is another symptom, with the victim feeling that he/she "should have done things differently." With rape, societal expectations cause many victims to believe that they should have been more active in preventing the incident (Burge, 1988).

Psychic Numbing

Psychic numbing is the second major symptom of posttraumatic stress. Trauma victims often feel detached or estranged from other people, or they may lose interest in significant activities that they previously enjoyed. Interpersonal emotions involving intimacy and tenderness in particular may decrease dramatically. Rape victims often have difficulty with sexual activities, because of reduced affect and fear of intrusive thoughts during sexual activity. Psychic numbing may also be experienced as a sense of alienation, isolation, and problems with intimacy and interpersonal relations. With respect to alienation, the victim may feel outside of mainstream society and sometimes feel tainted or unworthy of participation in society. This may lead to a lifestyle characterized by isolation, a tendency to maintain self-control through avoidance of contact with others. Problems with intimacy are also present in which the individual becomes emotionally distant, which is often expressed through fears of loss and explosive fits. This loss of feeling may explain their tendency to place themselves in highly dependent or highly independent interpersonal situations. Not trusting their inner feelings, they either become fully dependent on someone else or find it difficult to share intimacy with another person.

Hyperarousal

Hyperarousal appears to alternate with numbing in persons who have experienced trauma under a variety of circumstances, including combat, kidnapping, spouse abuse, incest, and child abuse. These individuals often report a general nervousness, trembling, and apprehension, as well as a tendency to be "on guard." The pervasive nature of the hyperarousal has been documented in presence of sounds, symbols, and visual stimuli reminiscent of the trauma. The intensity of the posttraumatic physiological response may be the best predictor of long-term outcome (van der Kolk, 1988). In addition to hyperarousal, traumatized people have a tendency to respond in emotional situations in an all-or-nothing fashion; they have an impaired capacity to modulate the intensity of their emotional responses, regardless of the nature of the emotion. This emotional style is especially maladaptive in interpersonal situations, especially if such situations involve stress and conflict. The increased physiological arousal interferes with their ability to make calm and rational decisions as well as to grow emotionally from such confrontations. Their characteristic way of dealing with emotional conflict is by action rather than thought, leading to excessive use of alcohol, drugs, sensation seeking, and emotional constriction.

van der Kolk (1988) noted a similarity between the hyperarousal seen in traumatized individuals and the biobehavioral changes observed in animals exposed to inescapable shock. Animals in this situation demonstrate both behavioral helplessness and biochemical alterations in norepinephrine, dopamine, serotonin, and endogenous opioid. With the initial stress, there is a massive release of these amines followed by depletion. The depletion is believed to result in receptor hypersensitivity which itself can lead to excessive responsiveness at times of emotional stress. Whereas the depletion can account for the numbing attributes of these individuals, receptor hypersensitivity may explain the startle responses, explosive outbursts, nightmares, and intrusive recollections. The chronic noradrenergic hypersensitivity combined with the chronic low serotonin may contribute to the decreased capacity of many trauma victims to feel in control of their lives.

Physical and/or emotional stress in childhood is far more devastating in impact than acute stress in adulthood. Freud maintained that traumatic mental events in childhood are seldom recalled in full detail because the accompanying anxiety elicits defenses to protect the psyche. Another possibility is that the traumatic event, having occurred at an early age, is not fully represented in memory. The portion of the brain (hippocampus) which serves as a mapping function for locating memories for experiences in space and time does not mature until the third or fourth year of life. However, the maturation of the system, which subserves memories related to the quality (feel and sound) of things occurs much earlier. Thus, in the first few years of life only the quality of events but not their context can be remembered. Early traumatic experiences may be encoded at a sensorimotor form and therefore not easily translated into symbolic language necessary for linguistic retrieval. The victim continues to experience, long into adulthood, affective and somatic reactions that are largely without context. A clinical case serves to illustrate the dissociation that can occur.

> This individual presented at clinic suffering from severe facial pain. At the time of therapy, Susan was a 37-year-old housewife with a professional husband and three teenage children. At the age of 31, she began experiencing extremely severe pain in the jaw region. After repeated conservative treatments failed to provide relief, she underwent surgery to disks in the joints. This surgical action also failed, the pain became more severe, and the patient began to use more and more alcohol and narcotic medication for relief. Although the drugs and alcohol helped, the pain often became unbearable. The patient began using a coping style that she had developed as a young child. She would mentally block the pain from awareness. Although effective, the cognitive strategy had two unforeseen consequences: the ability to experience other feelings (happiness, sadness, anger) while blocking the pain was impossible, and the prolonged use of the strategy led to periodic rise in suicidal thoughts and actions. Thus, she would "get by" for

several months and then suddenly notice that on occasion she would tempt fate by skiing or driving in a reckless fashion. During a suicidal phase, her activity level would also become very high and she would do everything, from shopping to driving, in an intense fashion. During these activities, she would have very little or no awareness of her environment (people, places) and experience no pleasure from the activities engaged in. At times, she would develop a sense of trembling and dizziness, and on rare occasions, would simply black out.

Her discussion of suicide was most often matter-of-fact, with no apparent emotional concern. During therapy, repeated efforts were made to link pain to feeling. She would reply that such a hypothesis might make sense if she knew what a feeling was. In her words:

> It is hard for me to understand why, when you use a word like resentment, you have no difficulty and yet I do. I think I can feel resentment, but I don't have a direct link; first, I have to go back and recall the situation and decide if others in similar circumstances are likely to feel that way . . . It is easier for me to first identify it in somebody else. Some time ago, the hope and aspiration was knocked out of me—I feel that I am just putting in time. Simply using words like "love" are difficult not because of the expression but because of the experience. I am quite capable of expressing love but feeling is another matter . . . that is something different . . . it is something that threatens to put me out of control . . . it is the experience that threatens me. . . . this is different stuff . . . I can't operate this way. . . . it threatens to destroy my independence.

Susan experienced a very traumatic childhood and has very little memory of all the traumatic events that may have taken place. In fact she has no recall of the first 10 years of life, other than fragmented memories of being beaten and locked in closets. As a teenager, her father would hide in the dark waiting for her to come home and then beat her about. There was much more darkness to her past: during the course of therapy, it was discovered that the patient could not look at herself in a mirror, because of intense fear of what she would see. Looking at her own self-reflection caused feelings of terror and accompanying shaking and trembling. The reflected mirror image of her face consisted of two faces, made up of each side of her face. The left-sided image was her social face, the face she presented to others which in her mind created the impression of a person in control and confident in herself. The right-sided image represented her inner self, the self in pain and suffering. She preferred to block this self from awareness, as acknowledging this self created inner confusion and activated self-destructive forces. Initially, there was no content or symbolization associated with these forces.

During therapy, an effort was made to identify the traumatic content which was initiating these feelings and impulses by having her spend a few minutes of each session looking into a mirror. This "mirror time" would cause fear and apprehension and also cause her to begin rubbing the right side of her head, as if in pain. She once remarked, "I guess there is a lot of emotion caught up in there somewhere." Eventually fragmented memories began to appear such as "arm with something wooden striking me in the head." Eventually her mother was seen as being attached to the arm. Other fragmented images also appeared which included sensations of being trapped, being caged, being inside locked closets.

Posttraumatic experiences are responsive to therapy. However, such individuals are often difficult to engage in therapy because of their reluctance to believe that what may have happened to them actually did happen. Often victims of abuse simply cannot accept that their parent(s) could have treated them in such a horrible fashion. To acknowledge emotionally that the abuse occurred might lead to guilt as well as violence toward oneself and and/or parents. These individuals, however, cannot develop a healthy sense of self, trust, and intimacy until they integrate past traumatic experiences into a reformed sense of self. Therapy needs to provide a context which allows the trauma victim to reestablish a sense of self, an understanding of the event, and a new assumptive world that successfully integrates the traumatic experience. The trauma material must be approached very gradually, otherwise there will be an intensification of both affect and physiological arousal. In severe cases, too rapid confrontation might lead to a worsening of the individual's psychological condition, or what psychiatrists term decompensation. Whether through therapy, or in the presence of peer/ family support, disclosure of trauma is important for improvement in both psychological and physical health.

STRESS MANAGEMENT TRAINING

There are a number of effective therapeutic programs available for stress management. These programs are in widespread use for assisting with conditions which include chronic headache, hypertension, heart disease, and cancer. Although the programs vary somewhat in technique and emphasis, they share similar philosophies. Two of the most popular programs are Meichenbaum's (Meichenbaum & Deffenbacher, 1988) Stress Inoculation Training and Suinn's (1990) Anxiety Management Training Program. Both programs emphasize the skill rationale to their therapies and present stress management as something that clients must learn to do. That is, clients must learn coping strategies that not only have immediate use but also future applications for dealing with the various stressors in their lives.

A complete description of these procedures requires reading the respective authors. An important aspect of the initial assessment is determining how persons experience their anxiety. Suinn suggested that a presenting anxiety complaint be analyzed in terms of three response subsystems: affective-autonomic, somatic-behavioral, and cognitive. The following, taken from Suinn, are verbal examples of each subsystem.

Affective/Autonomic-Dominant Stress Response

"I feel that my nerves are breaking up inside of me; I'm just one nervous wreck all the time. . . ."

"My hands suddenly get cold; it's like all the blood drained out of me and along with it, the heat . . . I shake my arms, put on extra clothes, but I'm still cold."

Somatic/Behavioral-Dominant Stress Response

"Yes, I knew in my head that there was nothing to fear and that I was completely safe, but my head was listening and my knees were not paying attention . . . they were wobbling and shaking. . . ."

"I can't sit still . . . I wind up pacing . . . moving around . . . not with anything in mind, just to be moving . . . I guess you would say aimlessly, but it's like my motor is wound up. . . ."

Cognitive-Dominant Stress Response

"I just know the worst thing is happening to me . . . I'm not going to survive the experience . . . I'm sure my whole life is going to fall apart right now, and I can't do anything about it—I know these thoughts are not rational, but I can't stop them. . . ."

"I worry, I just worry . . . I think about all the things that could go wrong . . . I'm not ready . . . or maybe I'll forget something . . . I know I shouldn't worry, because it makes things seem worse, but I can't stop." (Suinn, 1990, pp. 183–184)

Initially clients receive training in progressive muscle relaxation and the identification of a real life situation that is associated with being relaxed. The relaxation scene needs to be very concrete and include both scene-setting elements (e.g., "on the sand alone, with a breeze") and feeling-setting elements (e.g., "I'm comfortably warm, I can feel my body completely relaxed"). An example of a scene with both these elements is the following:

> My boyfriend and I had been on this picnic in the meadow part of the state
> park . . . it was just starting to be the Fall, so the air was getting cool, but not
> uncomfortably so since I was dressed warmly . . . Jon had left to walk to the
> creek to see if there were any fish . . . and I was sitting with my back to a tree
> . . . I was just letting my eyes gaze at this broad expanse of green, and up on
> the hills at a distance the beginning of some yellow and orange colors mixed
> with the green forest . . . it felt like one of those paintings you see with
> everything peaceful . . . occasionally some birds would be singing . . . (Suinn,
> 1990, p. 225)

Clients are given guided instruction in how to "turn on" such scenes in order
to strengthen the relaxation response. In a later session, clients are also
required to provide an anxiety scene which is capable of generating considerable moderately high anxiety (approximately 60 on a scale of 0–100).
An example of such a scene is as follows:

> I'm listening to my spouse who is angrily blaming me for something that is not
> quite clear yet . . . it turns out that I had forgotten to meet her for lunch and
> she had been waiting, alone and embarrassed. I can never handle her anger,
> even when she's wrong, and this time the anxiety washed over me . . . I'm
> thinking 'Good God, how could I do that, will she ever forgive me' . . . my
> stomach is knotting up and I want to leave and run away . . . I keep thinking
> 'She doesn't love me anymore, I'm going to have a terrible evening . . . I can't
> stand it . . . I have this crushed feeling inside, like bile in my stomach and
> inside I'm shaking . . . (Suinn, 1990, p. 233)

The next step is to have the client relax in session, induce anxiety arousal
with the appropriate scene, and then switch back to relaxation. Each time
the anxiety-relaxation cycle is repeated, the client is learning to use the
anxiety scene as a cue to switch off the anxiety and initiate further anxiety
reduction by using relaxation. In following sessions, the client learns to
self-initiate relaxation, identify bodily and cognitive cues associated with
anxiety onset, and to utilize his or her anxiety management skills in everyday
situations.

Stress Inoculation Training (Meichenbaum & Deffenbacher, 1988) also
emphasizes relaxation and skill acquisition as the means of coping with
anxiety. The approach appears to place greater emphasis than Anxiety
Management Training on the cognitive as opposed to the autonomic and
somatic dimensions of anxiety. The key to therapy is having patients recognize their stress-related thoughts and then, through a collaborative cognitive restructuring process, develop alternate coping styles for dealing with
stress and anxiety. Examples of self-statements that might be utilized in
therapy are "Just stay cool," "It's not a disaster, just a problem to be solved,"
and "Keep my thoughts straight and focus on how to handle it."

Stress management techniques are also being used outside the clinical setting to help individuals cope with day-to-day stressors as well as to enhance human artistic and athletic performance. Both Stress Inoculation Training and Anxiety Management Training have been successfully used in nonclinical situations to enhance performance of athletes, musicians, and artists. There are some data which suggest that strategies which focus on body monitoring are more effective than strategies which ignore or distract the individual from body sensations. Silva and Appelbaum (1989) examined the cognitive coping strategies used by Olympic marathon contestants. The elite or top 50 runners were more likely to use flexible associative strategies and not dissociate themselves completely from the pain and fatigue. They were more likely to pay attention to bodily sensations throughout the race. Less successful contestants adopted a dissociative strategy early in the race and maintained the strategy throughout the race. As a result, these individuals were "less attuned to the perceptual feedback available from their bodies." Body or somatic awareness is an important component of stress management, especially when the individual is faced with managing physical symptoms.

In closing this chapter, mention is made of the stress management program of Kabat-Zinn (1990), which is based on mindfulness meditation. He believes the majority of stress and anxiety management programs focus on "doing and getting somewhere" whereas his approach provides individuals with a philosophy of life and experiences which extend beyond such methods (i.e., "nondoing and being"). The essence of mindfulness in daily living is to make every moment one's own. Even when excessive demands are being made, a person needs to be aware of the mounting mental and physical tension and focus on what is really important. Whether one wishes to fully embrace the meditative philosophy or not, attitudes and values associated with nonjudgment, patience, trust, experience, nonstriving, acceptance, and letting go are essential to a healthy synergistic mind-body state.

4
Mind and the Immune System

A NOTE OF CAUTION

This chapter examines a controversial and sensitive area within behavioral medicine: the relationship between mind and immune system. Can the mind influence the immune system and thereby in some way be utilized to deal with diseases which attack the body? There is a very strong belief that with cancer in particular, a patient's mind might play a role in the onset, course, and recovery from the disease. A similar belief exists for AIDS; not all individuals exposed to the human immunodeficiency virus (HIV) become infected and, in addition, HIV-infected individuals do not necessarily develop clinical symptoms (Kiecolt-Glaser & Glaser, 1988). Whether or not psychological status can hinder or enhance immune system function is a question that is being explored in a number of research centers. The number of popular books and testimonials on the topic would indicate that the matter is proven, that with the correct state of mind an individual can overcome any illness. With cancer in particular, there is very strong public sentiment that cancer can be controlled by a particular psychological frame of mind. Unfortunately, these "mind-over-immunity" books have far outstripped the supporting facts and provide the reader with little in the way of evidence to support the claims being made.

We agree with those medical specialists (Angell, 1985) who believe that there is a need to proceed cautiously in this area. Quite often evidence supporting the link between psychological variables and cancer outcome is flawed by some undetected organic factor related to severity of the disease or nature of treatment. At the same time, there is growing proof that a person's mental state does make a difference in disease onset, progression, and outcome. At a more basic level, there is considerable evidence that the immune system and the central nervous system interact and this observation alone means that the pursuit of knowledge in this area will continue.

THE IMMUNE SYSTEM

The discussion begins with an overview of the immune system. A parallel has been made between the immune system and the central nervous system.

Both systems discriminate between self and nonself and incorporate principles of recognition, learning, memory, and transmission of information. The immune system has been called the "liquid nervous system" as it operates as a sensory system for stimuli that cannot be detected by the central nervous system (bacteria, viruses, tumor cells). It is an amazingly sophisticated system given that this capacity to respond to foreign antigens generally occurs without disrupting central nervous system homeostatic mechanisms.

There are two major arms to the immune system: cellular and humoral. Cellular immunity is believed to be mediated by lymphocytes (subfraction of white blood cells) acting directly on an invading antigen, while humoral immunity is thought to be rendered by lymphocytes which produce antibodies that circulate systemically. The cellular immune system is important to the defense against intracellular viruses such as the HIV virus responsible for AIDS, and cellular immunity refers to immunological activities that do not produce antibodies. Other immunologic functions are ascribed to phagocytic cells (cells that are able to ingest and often to digest other cells), such as neutrophils, monocytes, and macrophages.

Lymphoid stem cells give rise to two major subdivisions of lymphocytes, depending on which lymphoid organ serves as the site in which they mature (Figure 4.1; Calabrese, Kling, & Gold, 1987). The cells of one major

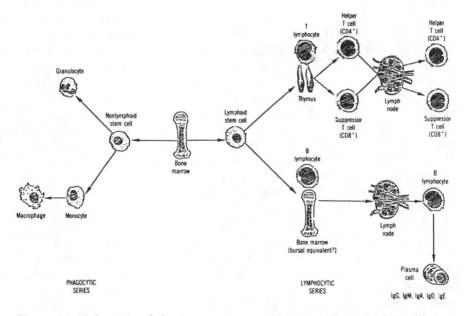

Figure 4.1. Schematic of the immune system. (American Journal of Psychiatry, 144, 1123–1134, 1987.) Copyright 1987, the American Psychiatric Association. Reprinted by permission.

subdivision, the T lymphocytes, mature in the thymus, where they differentiate into at least two major functional subsets, helper T cells and suppressor T cells. The T lymphocytes mediate cell-mediated immunity (i.e., confer immunity directly by cell-antigen interaction). It has also been learned, however, that T cells also produce humoral mediators of immunity known as lymphokines (interferon, interleukin-2, B cell differentiation factor). Lymphoid stem cells that mature in the bone marrow are called B lymphocytes. B cells confer immunity humorally (i.e., by secretion of antibodies).

With maturation, T and B cells make their way to various secondary lymphoid organs in the body, the lymph nodes, spleen, and tonsils, where they remain until confronted with health-threatening pathogens such as viruses, bacteria, and organic pollutants. Approximately 60% to 70% of the lymphocytes in the circulating blood are T cells and 10% to 20% are B cells. There are also T natural killer or NK cells (approximately 10% to 15% of lymphocytes) which directly attack tumors and virus-infected cells. B cells respond to a pathogen by producing a clone of lymphocytes which themselves release protein antibodies designed to destroy the particular pathogen. Antibodies attach themselves to pathogens and mark them for destruction or prevent them from infecting healthy cells.

T cells work in a number of specialized ways. T helper cells, which constitute the majority of all T cells, release lymphokines which enhance the ability of B cells to produce antibodies. Helper T cells also produce the lymphokine interleukin-2 which assists in the development of cytotoxic T and suppressor T cells. AIDS represents a specific defect in helper T cell function. In fact, it is when the virus moves from the latent stage and begins to destroy the T cells that the individual develops AIDS. With reduced presence of helper T cells, the infected individual becomes increasingly unable to combat disease-causing pathogens. The extreme suppression of the immune system that is characteristic of AIDS leaves the individual vulnerable to "opportunistic" infections, diseases that are generally not a threat to healthy individuals. An opportunistic infection that is considered diagnostic of AIDS is *Pneumocystis carinii* pneumonia which is often carried in the lungs of healthy individuals but rarely results in pneumonia in individuals with a normal immune system.

Suppressor T cells are believed to block the differentiation of B cells into plasma cells and the activity of helper T cells. Suppressor T cells can turn off antibody-mediated immunity and thereby serve as counterregulatory immune modulators. A proper balance between help and suppression appears necessary. Although suppressor T cells do not have cytotoxic properties, a second major subset of T lymphocytes, cytotoxic T cells, exists and does have direct killing potential. Cytotoxic T cells constitute the effector cells that respond to specific antigens to confer antiviral, antitumor protection and to mediate the transplant rejection phenomena, They are the targets of immunosuppressive agents used after transplant surgery.

The activation of B lymphocytes results in their growth and differentiation into two cell lineages: plasma cells and memory B cells. Mature plasma cells are antibody-secreting and they become mature under the influence of helper T cells. This illustrates the interdependence between B and T lymphocyte systems. Some activated B cells, however, do not undergo plasma cell differentiation; instead they turn into resting memory B cells, which upon second exposure to the same antigen rapidly differentiate into antigen-specific plasma cells.

Classically, immunologic functions mediated by B lymphocytes (humoral or antibody-mediated immunity) have been thought to confer protection against bacteria and viral reinfection, and to carry out immediate allergic reactions. Antibodies are typically unable to penetrate cells, so intracellular bacteria and viruses are not susceptible to their effects. Although antibody-mediated immunity has not been thought to play a primary role in conferring protection against intracellular viruses and fungal agents or in tumor cell surveillance, it plays an adjunctive role.

Plasma cells produce five classes of antibodies or immunoglobulins (Ig): IgG, IgM, IgA, IgE, and IgD. These classes differ in structure, in their sites of origin, and in some instances, in their mode of conferring immunocompetence. For instance, IgG, the major circulating antibody, enters most tissue spaces and functions by coating microorganisms, a process called opsonization. This makes it possible for phagocytic cells (e.g., neutrophils, macrophages) to recognize, engulf, and destroy foreign antigens such as bacteria.

IgA is the predominant antibody class in bodily secretions. IgA concentrates in body fluids like tears, saliva, and secretions of the respiratory and gastrointestinal tracts, functioning to protect these mucosal entrances to the body. Most infectious agents enter the body through mucosal surfaces, and the presence of IgA antibodies in the secretions that bathe these surfaces provide a first line of defense against infections, particularly those of the upper respiratory, gastrointestinal, and urogenital systems. Although their mechanism of action is unknown, they are thought to act as a barrier, denying microorganisms access to mucosa rather than being involved in direct killing.

NK cells are a subpopulation of non-B, non-T lymphoid cells. They are naturally occurring cells and appear as large, granular lymphocytes. NK cells are thought to provide an important defense against virus-infected cells and cancer cells. Unlike cytotoxic T cells, NK cells can attack tumor cells directly, without prior antigen interaction. NK cells comprise a defense system in which the effectors appear to have an innate ability to recognize and kill neoplastic cells. Interferon, one of the lymphokines or chemical mediators, is a potent enhancer of NK cell activity. There is suggestion that the NK cell lymphocytes have neuropeptide receptors and in this way may communicate with the central nervous system.

The phagoyctic series illustrated in Figure 4.1 represents another arm of the immune system. It contributes to both cellular and humoral immunity and consists of granulocytes, monocytes, and macrophages. Granulocytes are circulating cells that recognize, ingest, and destroy foreign antigens. They are called granulocytes because they contain granules filled with potent enzymes that enable them to digest microorganisms and contribute to inflammatory and allergic reactions. Monocytes and macrophages are antigen-presenting cells that display fragments of the alien antigens on their surfaces. The macrophage is a scavenger cell that destroys antigens. Macrophages operate to enhance the immune system in several ways. The first of these is to kill pathogens directly and the second is to recognize, process, and present antigens to helper T cells.

Macrophages accomplish this task by ingesting the antigens and then incorporating the antigenic determinants of the pathogen into the structure of their own cell surface for presentation to helper T cells. Macrophages are believed to be a primary target of the human immunodeficiency virus (HIV) and may be the first cells to become infected by HIV. The cells are not destroyed by the virus and at this stage the virus is dormant. There may be no warning signs or symptoms that it is present. Some individuals at this stage are known to experience somatic symptoms such as unexplained weight loss, night sweats, chronic diarrhea, fatigue, fevers, or viral and yeast infections, especially in the mouth. The virus may operate in this fashion for years.

Current research is increasing our knowledge of the relationships between the immune system and the central and peripheral nervous systems. Anatomical and functional relationships between the central nervous system and the immune system are generally accepted as being bidirectional in nature (Felten & Felten, 1988). The central nervous system is viewed as influencing the immune system through (a) neuroendocrine release of neurohormones that travel via the circulatory system to immune effector organs, and (b) direct innervation of lymphoid organs. The sympathetic noradrenergic system is known to have close contact with lymphocytes as noradrenergic fibers accompany the vasculature that supplies both primary and secondary lymphatic organs.

BEHAVIORAL IMMUNOLOGY

Robert Ader (Ader & Cohen, 1975) is credited with demonstrating a behavioral link between the central nervous system and the immune system.

For a long time it was believed in the scientific community that systems within the body do not interact with one another. Thus the immune system was viewed as an automaton of the body, with no relationship to the brain and accompanying conscious experience. Studies in the behavioral area have typically used the classical conditioning paradigm. The paradigm consists of presenting a "meaningless" or neutral sensory stimulus with an unconditioned stimulus. The unconditioned stimulus (e.g., sight of food) is known to elicit a physiological response, termed the unconditioned response (e.g., salivation). With repeated pairings, the neutral stimulus, now the conditioned stimulus, comes to evoke the unconditioned response in the absence of the unconditioned stimulus. Because this response was not previously manifested in the presence of the conditioned stimulus, it is called a conditioned response.

Demonstrations of the behavioral responsivity of the immune system have involved the use of the conditioned taste aversion paradigm. Conditioned taste aversion is a form of classical conditioning in which consumption of a novel taste stimulus (e.g., vanilla solution) is paired with an aversive unconditioned physiological stimulus (e.g., mild food poison), with the outcome that the taste stimulus elicits an avoidance response when presented alone. In the immune system studies, the unconditioned stimulus often used is cyclophosphamide, which is a cytotoxic agent with potent immunosuppressive effects. Cyclophosphamide also causes gastrointestinal distress, making it an ideal agent for taste-conditioning research.

In their original research, Ader and Cohen (1975) were studying conditioned taste aversion using saccharin as the conditioned stimulus and an injection of 50 mg/kg of cyclophosphamide as the unconditioned stimulus. Rats, in one trial, received saccharin-flavored water to drink, followed by an injection of cyclophosphamide. To see if the rats' subsequent taste aversion depended on the strength of the conditioned stimulus, some rats received more saccharin flavoring than others in the conditioning trial. Over the next several weeks, the saccharin-flavored water was presented without the cyclophosphamide. During this period, the researchers observed an unexpected finding: a number of animals had fallen ill and died and these tended to be the ones that had been given the greatest amount of saccharin during the conditioning trial. They speculated that the saccharin had become a powerful conditioned stimulus for immunosuppression. To test the hypothesis, they paired the saccharin solution with an injection of 50 mg/kg of cyclophosphamide and three days later injected the rats with foreign blood cells and reexposed the animals to saccharin without further cyclophosphamide. The rats showed decreased saccharin consumption upon reexposure, indicating the presence of taste aversion. Six and/or nine days after receiving antigen and saccharin CS reexposure, the rats were sacrificed and the amount of serum antibody determined. The animals showed lower amounts of serum antibody compared to controls, which was taken as evidence of immunosuppression.

Ader and Cohen (1982) also examined the therapeutic impact of conditioned immunosuppression on the spontaneous development of an autoimmune disease—systemic lupus erythematosus in New Zealand mice. These particular mice develop lethal renal complications of this illness by 12 months of age. By pairing cyclophosphamide (the unconditioned stimulus) with saccharin (the conditioned stimulus), and then later reexposing these mice to saccharin alone, Ader and Cohen were able to demonstrate that the conditioned stimulus had developed therapeutic immunosuppressant properties, as these mice lived longer and had a reduced morbidity.

The conditioned immunosuppressive effect has been replicated and there is some evidence of an effect on suppressor T cells. There is also some evidence for conditioned immunoenhancement (Kusnecov, King, & Husband, 1989). For example, the use of levamisole, an immunopotentiating drug, in the taste aversion paradigm not only produced taste aversion but also led to a conditioned increase in the helper/suppressor T cell subset ratio.

Animal models provide some of the best precision and control over the hypothetical variables involved. Yet, even with such control, it has often proved difficult to replicate initially positive findings. A good illustration of this difficulty is cited by Maier and Laudenslager (1988). In initial research, they demonstrated a relationship between stress and immunosuppression using an inescapable-escapable electric shock paradigm. Separate groups of rats were exposed to either a series of escapable electric tailshocks, yoked inescapable tailshocks, restraint, or no treatment, followed by a footshock one day later. Mitogens (substances foreign to the body) were used to stimulate the proliferation of lymphocytes. Lymphocyte proliferation in response to mitogen stimulation is thought to model the immune system's proliferative response when challenged by naturally occurring infectious agents. Poorer proliferative responses following mitogen exposure suggest that lymphocytes may be less efficient in their ability to respond to foreign invaders. The researchers initially discovered that rats exposed to inescapable shock, when compared to rats exposed to escapable shock, had reduced proliferative responses. The results were exciting because the failure of escapable shock to have any impact suggested that the reduction in proliferation in the inescapably shocked subjects was not produced by the physical stressor per se, but rather by the psychological stressor of inescapability of shock. The finding suggested that psychological control was an important determinant of whether a stressor would have an influence on immune function.

Although an exciting initial finding, the researchers noted the difficulty in replicating the effect. On occasion the effect has been reproduced but on many other occasions the effect has been minimal, absent, or even opposite to the initial finding, that is, studies in which proliferation in both escapable and inescapable subjects exceeded that of home cage controls. Maier and Laudenslager commented on a number of significant difficulties associated with this type of research. Mitogen proliferation is highly variable across animals, making it difficult to detect the effects of stressors when superimposed on such large individual differences. Also the use of in vitro assay may be artificial as the effector cells are removed from their natural neural and endocrine environment. It is these neural and endocrine influences, possibly long lasting in origin, that are removed with in vitro assays. Other problems include sampling biases associated with the collection of cells from a particular lymphocyte site such as peripheral blood or spleen. Activity from one site may not be similar to activity from another site. It is also unknown whether the changes observed in these studies are of sufficient magnitude to increase the risk of disease.

In spite of difficulties finding consistent results, there is a strong sense that "something is happening" between the mind and the immune system. Structurally, there is no question of the flow of information between the immune system and the central nervous system. The neuroendocrine system is believed to be the link between the two systems. A lymphocyte-pituitary axis-adrenal axis has been identified, with virtually all peptides released by the pituitary, including ACTH, B-endorphin, growth hormone, oxytocin, and vasopressin having been linked to alterations in immune responsiveness. Conversely, lymphocytes are known to lead to releases in a large number of peptides. For instance lymphocytes have been shown to contain ACTH for direct stimulation of the adrenal cortex. The endocrine gland hormones also influence immunity: cortisol, for example, is known to suppress immune responses. The glucocorticoids are believed to suppress the immune system in order to quickly terminate the inflammatory and/or immune response to injury that is expected during stressful fight-or-flight situations.

Autonomic nervous system signals influence the immune system through nerve fibers that innervate the lymphoid organs and the adrenal medulla. Several neurotransmitters and peptides released by autonomic nerve fibers have been found to modulate immune system through specific leukocyte membrane receptors. The hypothalamus is the likely site of the very extensive neural-immune-endocrine integration (Daruna & Morgan, 1990). The immunologic apparatus not only receives signals from the brain but transmits signals as well. For instance, such soluble products of the immune system as thymosins not only regulate immunity directly but in addition serve as "immunotransmitters" by modulating the hypothalamic-pituitary-adrenal axis. It is thought that this lymphoid/endocrine information provides the brain with data derived from contact between immunocytes and various antigens or tumors. In this regard, circulating lymphocytes can be seen as "sensory organs" converting information derived from contact with pathogens to useful endocrine information for the brain. Given the very complex biologic links between the central and immune systems, it seems more than reasonable to assume that a person's mind contributes in some way to the day-to-day status of the immune system.

PSYCHOIMMUNOLOGY

The first study which reported a relationship between psychological state and immune function was reported by Bartrop et al. (1977). The subjects who participated in that study were 26 men and women whose spouses were seriously ill. Clinic subjects provided a blood sample one–three weeks and six weeks after the death of his/her spouse; a group of 26 age- and sex-matched control subjects provided similarly spaced blood samples. Bartrop et al. studied immune system reactivity in vitro through mitogen stimulation and in vivo by challenging the system with several specific antigens known to produce a characteristic delayed hypersensitivity reaction that is apparent on routine skin testing. In this study, some evidence was found for reduced proliferative response to mitogen stimulation in bereaved spouses but no in vivo differences were found, suggesting that the cellular interactions required for delayed hypersensitivity were intact. Differences at cellular level indicate a more profound change in immunologic mechanisms.

Psychological depression has been examined in relation to immunosuppression and the findings have been mixed. Some studies have found blunted responses to mitogen stimulation in drug-free depressed subjects and others have not, making it impossible to draw conclusions (Calabrese, Kling, & Gold, 1987). There are methodological difficulties in attempting to link immunosuppression to depression, as the groups in question typically differ in physical as well as psychological factors, such as weight, medication, sleep and exercise patterns, and malnutrition. Also there is no clinical evidence that depressed individuals are more susceptible to immunodeficiency-based diseases.

Kiecolt-Glaser and Glaser (1988) studied immunocompetence in individuals undergoing marital separation through divorce, poor marital relationships, and bereavement, which are all forms of potentially chronic stress. They presented data indicating that these conditions are generally associated with decreased immunologic response. They have also examined the more acute effects of examination stress in medical students and determined a degree of immunosuppression, at least on some of the measures. In one of their studies, medical students showed a short-term decrement in blastogenesis during an examination period. Blastogenesis is a commomly used assay procedure in which lymphocytes are cultured for several days with a mitogen, a chemical that mimics infectious agents such as bacteria or viruses and stimulates cell growth and division. Their lab examined the immunological correlates of psychological distress in first- and second-year medical students during academic examinations. They compared data from blood samples drawn during an examination period with similar "baseline" data obtained four weeks before examinations. They found some evidence for lowered activity by NK cells. Also they observed higher antibody titres (a measure of amount of antibody in an antiserum per unit volume of serum) to Epstein-Barr virus (EBV) relative to the levels found on the students' return from summer vacation. EBV is the human herpesvirus which is responsible for infectious mononucleosis. Higher antibody titers to EBV and other herpesviruses indicate that the cellular immune response is less competent in controlling EBV latency. Once a person is infected with the virus, he or she will carry for life the virus in latently infected cells. It may be reactivated from these cells under a variety of circumstances, particularly if an individual is immunosuppressed. Reactivation of latent herpesviruses is thought to reflect poorer control of these viruses by the cellular immune response.

Of particular interest was the finding that those students who described themselves as lonelier had lower NK activity and higher EBV antibody titres than did those students who described themselves as less lonely. Loneliness is associated with unsatisfactory interpersonal relationships and is generally perceived by individuals as distressing. The same investigators examined immunologic data from women who have been separated/divorced for 12 months or less with married comparison women and again found lower percentages of NK cells. In addition, a positive immune system response occurred in several of the students who underwent relaxation training. Other studies have failed to demonstrate improvements in immune functioning following relaxation/stress management training. In summarizing these studies together, there can be no conclusion concerning the clinical implication of reduced lymphocyte responses to mitogenic stimulation. "These responses merely suggest that in an artificial, in vitro, situation, lymphocytes are less capable of undergoing mitosis, a finding that need not translate into clinically relevant immunocompromise."

There is growing interest in the possibility that personality/family interaction patterns (or absence thereof) may influence immunocompetence. Kasl, Evans, and Neiderman (1979) examined the relationship between psychosocial and immune data collected from West Point cadets. The cadets were part of a prospective study of the development of infectious mononucleosis. Those cadets who were EBV negative on arrival at West Point (i.e., had no prior exposure to the virus and thus were not latently affected) and who had a triad of psychological risk factors (high motivation for military career, poor academic performance, and a father who was an "over-achiever") were more likely to become infected with EBV. Moreover, anti-body titres to the latent virus showed a similar relationship among those cadets who did not develop clinical symptoms. These data were among the first to show significant relationships among psychological stressors, im-munological indices, and actual health outcomes. Levy and Wise (1988) noted that in healthy individuals, those at risk for severe infectious diseases had persistently low levels of NK activity over repeated testing. They also cited the work of Aoki and colleagues who believe that they have identified a new immunological disorder called the "Low NK Syndrome." The key phenomenologic characteristics of this condition are persistent complaints of fatigue and depressed mood.

PSYCHOLOGICAL SUSCEPTIBILITY AND CANCER

The immune system may or may not be directly involved in the development of cancer. The immune explanation is derived from the hypothesis of immune surveillance. Within this theory, neoplastic cells are regularly formed in the body, but the immune system, through killer cells and other mechanisms, regularly controls their presence. If the immune system is suppressed, more neoplastic cells escape destruction and the risk for de-velopment of cancer increases. Individuals with immunodeficiency do have higher rates of malignancy but not necessarily for common cancers such as breast cancer. Recent findings on the role of oncogenes in carcinogenesis make it unlikely that the immune system could recognize such small quan-titative changes or that immune surveillance is involved in the detection of the earliest malignant changes. Cancer development and progression is also under the control of local processes at the site of tumor development. Researchers are now seeking to understand the role of "switch mechanisms" involving biochemical signaling pathways in the cell environment itself. It has been shown, for example, that local growth factors are the local mech-anism determining whether or not a cell behaves in a malignant manner. It is believed that human cancers produce growth factors which act on their own cell receptors to maintain the growth of cancer.

Psychological factors, if present, are likely to be nonspecific in nature. One suggestion of more local effects is based on a study which dealt with hypnotic control of warts. A wart is actually a benign tumor which is caused by a virus. Warts have been controlled by hypnosis, and some writers have argued that since warts could be removed by suggestion on one side of the body and left unchanged on the other, this constitutes evidence for a possible specific relationship between mind and cancer control mech-anisms. This phenomenon of wart control, even if reproducible, is not necessarily proof for a high degree of localization. Endocrine changes associated with stress and emotion, as we saw in a previous chapter, have generally been nonspecific and highly individualistic in nature.

In searching for clues for the mediating factor(s) between psychology and cancer, it is instructive to begin with the psychological breast cancer literature. Cancer of the breast is the most common malignancy in women and afflicts approximately 8% of women living in North America. The notion that breast cancer victims have a distinctive personality/emotional style has a very long history. Galen observed, in the second century A.D. for example, that cancer was more frequent in melancholic women (Stolbach & Brandt, 1988). Clinicians throughout modern time have remarked on the connection between depression and feelings of hopelessness which seem to precede the onset and progression of cancer. A series of studies beginning in the 1950s found support for such notions but these studies were generally retrospective in design and thus confounded by the effect of the knowledge of having cancer on the responses to the psychological tests and interviews. There are now much better controlled studies, but at the same time, it remains very difficult to determine what in a woman's psychology may render her susceptible to breast cancer. There are findings to contradict most any of the other reported results. Breast cancer patients or cancer patients generally may show increased presence of one trait, decreased presence of the same trait, or no difference from comparison groups. An example of the contradictory reports are the studies dealing with personal loss and depression, where approximately half the studies report a positive relationship and half the studies report a negative or no relationship (Hu & Silberfarb, 1988).

The strongest data continue to be in the area of decreased outward expression of negative emotions. Greer and Morris (1975), in a controlled study, interviewed and administered a series of psychological questionnaires to 160 women who were being admitted to a hospital for breast biopsy. The women with malignant disease were quite similar to the women with benign disease on the majority of psychological measures assessed, including sexual adjustment, frequency of psychiatric disorders, extraversion, neuroticism, and hostility. One difference appeared to be in terms of emotional expression, with the cancer patients reporting greater difficulty expressing emotions. Anger expression was mentioned as a particular emotion that differentiated the groups, with cancer patients having problems handling such feelings. No normal controls were used in the comparison.

Pennebaker (1988) advanced the hypothesis that an unwillingness to confide or share feelings with others requires "physiological work" and may lead to immunosuppression. Thus, inhibition of feelings associated with anger, trauma, or general dissatisfaction may lead to short-term bodily demands which, in the long run, might increase an individual's susceptibility to serious disease. Highly charged events associated with sexual trauma, divorce, and other events associated with humiliation are particularly likely to be denied expression.

In a test of the Pennebaker hypothesis (Esterling et al., 1990), a personality measure was initially used to classify college students into those who exhibited (a) a repressive coping style, (b) a sensitization coping style, and (c) neither repression or sensitization as a preferred coping style. All students were required to compose a letter to a close friend about an event which they had experienced and which had been highly stressful. A blood sample for immunologic assay was taken on the same day. The letters were scored for the number of emotional words used. The immune response studied was antibody response against the viral capsid antigen (VCA) and early antigen (EA) of the Epstein-Barr virus. The student letters dealt with a range of highly personal and upsetting experiences, including interpersonal conflicts, loss and loneliness associated with leaving home, illness, and parental problems. The letters showed a real range of responses from no emotional words to a few individuals who wrote up to 50 emotional words in a 400-word essay. The results showed a higher level of antibody titre for repressors than the other two groups. Low disclosers also had higher antibody titre levels. These results are consistent with the view that emotional suppression/repression is associated with reduced immunologic function. The findings, however, are also a long way from demonstrating differential effects on recurrent disease.

Temoshok (1990) summarized the various personality traits or coping proclivities associated with cancer progression and possible development under the rubric of "Type C." "Type C coping has been described as being 'nice,' stoic or self-sacrificing, cooperative and appeasing, unassertive, patient, compliant with external authorities, and unexpressive of negative emotions, particularly anger. . . ." The Type C personality itself may consist of both excessive rationality and antiemotionality. In a study of Dutch college students (van der Ploeg et al., 1989), these two attributes correlated negatively with a measure of emotional expressiveness. A rational/antiemotional approach to life would reflect endorsement of the following types of items:

I always try to do what is reasonable and logical.
I try to act rationally in all interpersonal situations.
I avoid interpersonal conflicts by using reason and logic, even if contrary to my feelings.
If someone hurts my feelings, I will still try and understand him rationally and not react purely emotionally.

Students who endorsed these types of items also exhibited higher scores on an anger-control scale. Thus, people who exhibit personality styles of "acting rational and reasonable" and "trying to understand other people in spite of negative feelings" suggest the suppression and repression of hostile feelings, irritation, and anger—or at least the control of anger by means of rational behavior and trying to be nice toward others. "Being nice" may not be effective in sufficiently defusing the impact troublesome situations have on the immune system.

In an earlier study (Grossarth-Maticek, Bastiaans, & Kanazir, 1985), the rational/antiemotional coping style was found to be a predictor of cancer of all types. In a prospective study conducted in Yugoslavia, over 1,000 elderly inhabitants between the ages of 59-65 were given a very detailed questionnaire which dealt with life stress, rationality, and antiemotionality, as well as other psychosocial issues. Ten years later, a physician assessed the occurrence of different diseases in the sample. In those who died of cancer, breast, uterine, and cervical cancer occurred in the majority of females, while cancer of the lung, prostate, and rectum predominated amongst the males. The rationality/antiemotionality factor was found in 158 of the 166 cancer deaths in the study (hypochondriasis showed a *negative* correlation with cancer). These observations are very strong in supporting a relationship between emotional control and cancer. The psychological dimension of rationality/antiemotionality remains the strongest bet for a relationship with breast cancer and with cancers in general. Extreme caution in reading these data remains essential and we should remember that cancer is a very complex disease and that there may be over a hundred distinct forms of the disease. The available data would support one process for the cancers studied, given that similar psychological variables seem to appear over and over from one study to the next. If and how these variables combine with immmune/cancer mechanisms is unknown.

Temoshok (1990) provided a model for integrating Type C personality formulations with a developmental disease framework. Rather than viewing personality as a direct cause of the onset of cancer, she proposed that these relationships be viewed in an ongoing dynamic fashion. There are two aspects to the model, depicted in Figure 4.2, which are significant. First, the concept of *neoplastic process* is substituted for cancer, the end point in the process, to emphasize the developmental nature of the disease. Second, psychosocial processes involving Type C, emotional expressiveness-nonexpressiveness, and stressor load play different roles at different times along the continuum of cancer development and progression. Understanding the model begins with an analysis of the impact of the Type C coping style:

In its extreme form, a Type C coping style is seen as a fragile accommodation to the stressors in the world. If a person can only respond to stressors by focusing on others, denying or minimizing one's own needs, not expressing one's true feelings, and keeping a "stiff upper lip" in the face of difficulties,

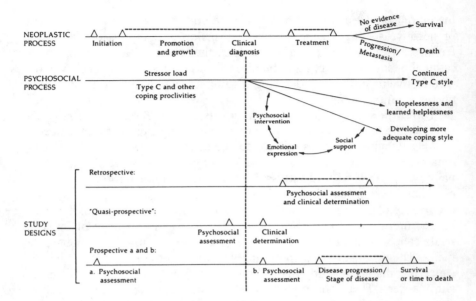

Figure 4.2. A process model for biopsychosocial cancer research. From Temoshok, L. (1990). On attempting to articulate the biopsychosocial model: Psychological-psychophysiological homeostasis. In H. S. Friedman (Ed.), Personality and disease. New York: John Wiley & Sons. Copyright © 1990. Adapted from Temoshok, 1987, Cancer Surveys, 6, 837-209. Reprinted by permission of John Wiley & Sons, Inc. and Oxford University Press.

adaptation to a number of challenging situations will be problematic. While this style may "work" in certain situations, if applied inflexibly to all situations, it will probably not result in satisfactory adaptation. Social equilibrium may be maintained at the expense of psychological and/or biological homeostasis. Problems are more likely to be pushed under or away than genuinely resolved. To the extent that this situation continues over time, and is perhaps even exacerbated by more demanding life stressors, the Type C coping style will become increasingly inadequate as a "stress buffer." (Temoshok, 1990, p. 213)

The model assumes that prolonged coping in this fashion, under some life circumstances and bodily conditions, may lead to a weakening of immune surveillance and allow the neoplastic process to take hold. There are three possible outcomes to this development: (a) the individual continues to cope with the same Type C style; (b) the Type C pattern begins to change, leading to feelings of helplessness and hopelessness; or (c) the individual becomes more internally aware and begins to develop a more adequate coping style. With the latter, the individual begins to "express needs and feelings, recruits more genuine social support in the process, and is believed to have a more positive mental health outcome as psychological and biological equilibrium is achieved. Whether there are any physical health consequences is an empirical question" (p. 214).

Temoshok's model also depicts the different research designs which researchers use in studying the psychosocial aspects of cancer. Retrospective studies, which involve obtaining psychological measures from patients who have already been diagnosed with cancer, were initially used to infer that the identified personality characteristics (e.g., depression) existed before disease onset. However, these characteristics could as likely be the result of being diagnosed with a life-threatening disease and/or psychological/physiological changes attributable to the treatment of the disease itself (surgery, chemotherapy, radiation). Quasi-prospective or discrimination studies involve assessing patients psychosocially just before cancer diagnosis (i.e., at biopsy) and then comparisons are made on psychosocial measures between benign and malignant patients. It is assumed that the cancer and noncancer patients will have similar levels of distress about the possibility of having cancer. Experts doubt that this is the case, however, as patients may pick up cues from themselves and physicians about the likely status of their biopsy. That is, subjects might have a subtle sense at this stage whether their tumor condition is malignant or benign. Thus, group differences on measures such as depression, anxiety, and hopelessness may reflect differential reactions to anticipated cancer diagnosis and are not premorbid.

Prospective studies are defined on the basis of the assessment of psychosocial variables before cancer diagnosis. A truly prospective study has a relatively long interval (e.g., 10 years) between the assessment of psychosocial variables and cancer outcome. The Grossarth-Maticek et al. (1985) study is a good example of such a design. The long interval between psychosocial assessment and cancer outcome tends to eliminate the possibility that the disease was the cause of the psychological change. The presence of a relationship, however, does not prove that the psychological variable(s) in question caused the cancer. A second category of prospective studies shown in Figure 4.2 are those which administer psychosocial studies at the time of clinical diagnosis and then attempt to predict the course of disease progression and/or survival time. The issue is whether coping styles have an impact on the course of cancer and is examined in the next section.

CANCER CONTROL AND THE "FIGHTING SPIRIT"

Cancer support groups openly advocate "taking charge" of the disease and becoming an active partner in the health care team in the struggle to return to health. The overwhelming public interest in the possibility of controlling cancer demands that a solid understanding be gained of the claims that an individual can make a difference in the course of and recovery from the disease.

Interest in hopelessness/helplessness as a coping style is often supported with a frequently cited clinical case study reported by Klopfer (1957). The case involved a patient with lymphosarcoma whose condition, thought to be preterminal, remitted almost totally for two months while he was receiving injections of Krebiozen, an experimental drug he thought would cure him. After learning from the news that the drug was useless, he relapsed. His physician cleverly reactivated the patient's faith in the medication by giving him water injections that were described as a refined and more potent form of the same drug. The patient once again recovered, only to relapse and die several months later after discovering from a nationwide announcement that Krebiozen had no therapeutic value. The concept of helplessness/hopelessness has had a long history in medicine and for a time represented the cornerstone of psychosomatic medicine. For example, it has been suggested for some time that persons who have psychologically "given up" are at increased risk for all severe or chronic physical disease (Engel, 1968).

Popular books like Norman Cousins' (1989) *Head First* offer readers hope. Cousins is credited with the following anecdote: While visiting a self-help group in Los Angeles, he met an attractive and proud-looking woman who appeared to him the essence of grace and dignity. The woman had gone to her physician years before and was told that she had only six months to live. What did she say to her doctor, Cousins inquired? "Go f . . . yourself" she said as she related this story six and one-half years after the doctor's pronouncement. Similar angry responses can be justifiably expected from patients who, with life-threatening cancer, are suddenly told by physicians or family members to take charge of their lives! At the same time, clinicians have long recognized that some patients seem to survive long after strict disease criteria indicate they should have succumbed.

The nonemotional coping style linked with cancer onset has been studied in relation to cancer progression and recovery. In a prospective study of women with early breast cancer (Greer, Morris & Pettingale, 1979), psychological coping style assessed three months postoperatively was related to outcome five years later. Recurrence-free survival was significantly more common among patients who reacted to cancer with "fighting spirit" than among patients who responded with "stoic acceptance" or "helplessness/hopelessness." A 10-year follow-up on the same group of patients indicated that a "fighting spirit" was still significantly associated with a better prognosis (Pettingale, et al., 1985).

Similar findings have been reported with another form of cancer, malignant melanoma. Melanoma is a tumor which has its origin in the melanocyte, a pigmented cell in the skin. It is treated by excision and does not respond to radiation or chemotherapy. The most common form of melanoma is the superficial spreading type. It has a biphasic evolution, with a relatively slow horizontal growth phase followed by a rapid vertical penetration. Metastasis coincides with the vertical phase. A disproportionate share of all cases of spontaneous regression have been reported for melanoma which suggests endogenous host factors affecting tumor control. Di Clemente and Temoshok (1985) assessed a group of melanoma patients in the early stages of the disease and followed their outcome for a period of 26 months. Two factors predicted disease recurrence: tumor thickness and feelings of helplessness/hopelessness. The major prognostic determinant remained the biology of the tumor.

An important negative finding in this area was reported by Cassileth, et al. (1985). They found that psychological responses were unrelated to survival in a group of patients with advanced cancers and a group in the early stages of breast cancer or melanoma. They used a wide range of measures which had been implicated in the literature, and based on a large sample, they found no evidence for the predictive value of psychosocial measures, either in terms of length of survival or time to relapse. They concluded that biological aspects of the cancer diseases predominate and override the potential influence of psychosocial processes once the disease is well established. Levy (Levy & Wise, 1988) has also stressed that biologic rather than psychologic factors are the strongest predictors of cancer progression. Levy initiated a prospective study of 34 breast cancer patients in 1979. A large percentage of the sample had died and she concluded that survival time was largely determined by biologic factors (number and location of metastic sites, number of lymph nodes positive for metasteses, disease-free interval). Of possible psychological predictors, a mood measure of well-being and happiness appeared to be the most promising as women who scored high on this parameter showed longer survival rates.

Given that there is not a known relationship between cancer recovery and coping style, we are in a difficult position in knowing how to help others and ourselves cope with this disease. Cancer patient expectations of needing to do something are very high. At the same time, there is no evidence that a literal application of the "fighting spirit" is advantageous. Families often expect, if not demand, that the afflicted member adopt an aggressive approach to the disease:

One of my students reported the following family situation: her aunt was in the end stage of cancer that had begun in the breast and had metasticized to several other sites. She had undergone several rounds of chemotherapy, without success, and was now experiencing severe pain and fatigue. The patient had accepted the terminal nature of her illness and asked that chemotherapy not be continued. Her family was angry with this decision and felt that she was not trying hard enough and should continue the fight.

Most cancer programs provide some instruction in both notions of coping and mastery with the expectation that certain mental techniques might retard the physical disease. Unfortunately, the research literature provides little support for these notions.

Norman Cousins (1989) in the book *Head First* argued for the power of hope and determination in bringing about therapeutic changes in the immune system:

The effectiveness of brain-spleen-immune interaction came to my mind when a dentist and a lawyer came to visit me at UCLA. . . . The dentist said he was going to die of AIDS—he was HIV-positive—and he wanted to leave a considerable sum of money to support our research at UCLA. . . . I told the dentist that I would not talk to him about the bequest but I would be glad to work with him if he wanted to mobilize his will to live and his determination to fight the disease. He accepted the challenge, I put him through some of the mind-body exercises developed by Dr. Elmer Green of the Menninger Foundation clinic. . . .

Three months later, the dentist returned, bearing medical documents showing that he was no longer HIV-positive. The look of incredulity on my face produced a wide smile on his.

'My doctor gets the same reaction when he talks about me to other doctors," he said. "Some of his friends say that it can't be, that it was a mistaken diagnosis, but my doctor knows better. He checked and double-checked the original tests and he knows it was no mistake.' (p. 77)

The mind-body exercise mentioned in this passage is a biofeedback technique designed to increase blood flow to the hands. Although designed for migraine management, Cousins argued that hand warming can be used in a nonspecific sense to enhance patients' sense of self-control over bodily functions. Temperature biofeedback, when combined with relaxation, can often bring about increases of body temperature of 10 degrees or more.

Cousins (1989) recognized that there is more to dealing with cancer than a combative spirit and a will to live. He also tackled the difficult question of guilt in patients who might feel that in some way they are not struggling hard enough. To the question of providing false hope in patients, he responds that no treatment should be held back that offers a chance of improvement, even if recovery seems impossible. Freeing patients of depression and despair increases their confidence in themselves as well as their confidence in the health care team. Even if the disease is irreversible, the extension of life by a few years or even months can have profound significance. At the same time, he acknowledged that attempting to provide a never-ending progression of patients in the terminal stages of illness with hope is itself associated with repeated frustration and defeat. The restorative energy, he stated, comes from "the occasional patient who does triumph—despite predictions based on the most sophisticated technology."

There are few scientific studies of the effects of psychological intervention upon survival from cancer. Linn, Linn, and Harris (1982) found no benefit to patients in terms of increased survival as a result of counseling. Five cancer groups were selected, all of which were clinical Stage IV with an estimated survival of 3–12 months. Although patients reported improved quality of life following therapy there were no changes in survival. The researchers concluded that "if the disease process is far advanced, intervention of any kind probably has little survival value." Additional studies which are based on specific therapeutic strategies are described in the next sections.

GUIDED IMAGERY AND VISUALIZATION

The systematic use of imagery and visualization in the treatment of cancer began with the work of Simonton and Mathews-Simonton. Known as the "Simonton method," cancer patients were asked to imagine their defense system and medical treatment "overcoming" their cancer (Simonton, Matthews-Simonton, & Creighton, 1978). Their visualization procedure incorporates four elements: (1) seeing the treatment destroying cancer cells that are too weak and confused to repair the damage; (2) seeing the white cells of the immune system swarming over the cancer, killing cancer cells and cleaning up the debris; (3) seeing the cancer shrinking; and (4) seeing a return to perfect health. The survival time for patients in the program was reported as twice the expected median. Unfortunately, the study provided no control condition and their patients may have done better than average simply because they represented highly selected individuals.

Green and Schellenberger (1991) argued that, at this point in time, it is impossible to scientifically verify the usefulness of visualization in the control of cancer. Based on their own clinical experiences and those of others, however, they believe that the techniques contribute to quality of life, enhanced well-being, and, occasionally, prolonged life. Their most dramatic example involved the case of Garrett Porter (Porter & Norris, 1985), who at the age of 12 was diagnosed with a brain tumor which was expected to take his life.

As with most children, it was easy for Garrett to believe that imagery and visualization can influence the body, and his success with biofeedback training proved this for him. Garrett's visualization centered on a "Star Trek" theme and space exploration:

In Garrett's visualization, his programming ego (the "self") is portrayed by Blue Leader, the leader of a squadron of fighter planes. His brain is represented by the solar system, and his tumor is an invading planetoid which is entering his solar system and threatening its existence. His white cells and other immune defenses are represented by the lasers and torpedoes with which the squadron of fighter planes is armed. (Porter & Norris, 1985, p. 28)

Using this theme, Pat and Garrett made a cassette tape in which Pat, as ground control, and Garrett, as Blue Leader, attack the planetoid and after a very dramatic battle, destroy it. As an aid to visualization, Garrett created sound effects for the battle with an electronic game, punctuating all the strikes and misses. . . .

Garrett also created a more "organic" visualization in which he took a journey across the brain, walking over the convolutions until he came to the tumor. The tumor looked like a meatball. He saw millions of white cells attacking and destroying the tumor. The white cells were balls with large mouths, sharp teeth, eyes, and radar antenna—competent and all-seeing.

Garrett used visualization at home before falling asleep every night for over a year. Then one night he could not find the tumor; he looked again, but it was gone. A victory party was held inside Garrett's brain in his next therapy session with Pat; two months later the CAT scan proved the tumor was gone. (p. 277)

Green and Schellenberger (1991) provided other examples of the success of visualization and they believe that the technique is often effective with patients who have a very poor prognosis and who would not have recovered "anyway." To their credit, they also provided evidence of a patient who, although a firm believer and practitioner of visualization techniques, experienced a period of cancer regression but after several months eventually died. It is obviously critical that we determine at a psychobiologic level what is occurring which determines success or failure with the technique. As with other self-regulation procedures, the differences may be less inherent to what is cognized or visualized and more in terms of what is actually somatically internalized. Ultimately, it may be that successful application lies with the imagery being associated with a pervasive state of relaxation and nonstressfulness. This is important because some patients are prone to use highly aggressive and anxiety-eliciting imagery in their efforts to combat cancer (e.g., bees stinging the cancer cells). The evidence would suggest that the images used be consistent with a state of bodily relaxation. Green and Schellenberger used the analogy of teacher and classroom to convey the desired relationship between imagery and relaxation; the classroom must be quiet to hear the teacher. Other suggestions for effective visualization include: providing patients with a sound rationale for the power of imagery and visualization to affect physiology and ensuring that the visualization is felt inside as a body experience.

> Critics of imagery and visualization techniques argue that the use of these techniques is premature because there are insufficient research data to warrant their use, and that the placebo effect, not imagery, accounts for positive results. It is further suggested that using imagery and suggesting that the patient can play a role in the disease process give the patient false hope. The false-hope criticism is never valid. Hope is neither true nor false; hope is hope, and few people today would argue that patients should not have hope. (Green & Schellenberger, 1991, p. 287)

The research of McClelland (1989) may eventually shed light on the psychological processes by which visualization is able to alter physiologic function. McClelland made a distinction between implicit as opposed to explicit motives. Implicit motives are inferred by analysis of associative thought streams generated by projective tests while explicit motives are measured directly by self-report measures. Implicit motives, according to McClelland, are based on emotional learning and might be more closely linked than explicit motives to the physiological systems that control healthy functioning of the body.

Two implicit motives which have been studied in relation to visualization and the immune system are need for power and affiliation. The power motive is defined as "the desire to have impact on others, by influencing, persuading, helping, arguing with, or attacking them," while the affiliation motive is defined as "the desire to establish, maintain, or restore warm relationships with other people, not as a means to an end, but as an end in its own right" (Jemmott, 1987). McClelland's argument is that a strong need for power reduces a person's immunologic competence only if the person's need for power is inhibited or blocked. In one study, individuals were shown a film which was designed to arouse the power motive. The analyses showed that the subjects with high inhibited power motivation exhibited evidence of decreased immunocompetence as measured by decreased salivary IgA concentrations one hour after the film.

In a second study, McClelland attempted to elicit the need-for- affiliation motive by having undergraduates observe a documentary film about Mother Teresa which demonstrated her selfless love for the poor, for abandoned babies, and for the terminally ill. Subjects' salivary IgA levels increased significantly after watching the film but returned immediately to baseline following the film. However, if subjects were encouraged to maintain the "glow" by reliving in their imagination experiences in their lives of love, they were able to maintain the higher salivary IgA level for a longer period of time. A further analysis revealed that although half the college students were inspired by the Mother Teresa film, the other half reported a conscious reaction of depression or dislike. Both groups showed similar salivary IgA changes to the film. Further analysis of the projective test protocols of the subjects revealed the presence of a special type of affiliation motivation which is called "Affiliative Trust." Apparently, this form of affiliation reflects a positive feeling toward cooperative relationships in contrast to a negative cynical feeling toward cooperative relationships. Students who wrote stories about positive rather than cynical affiliative relationships after seeing the film were the ones whose IgA increased. McClelland also referred to some data which indicated that Affiliative Trust, when measured as a trait, is associated with a higher helper to suppressor T cell ratio. Individuals with positive expectations toward others who are generally optimistic and not pessimistic tend to be healthier. The implicit motivational research of McClelland and colleagues represents an interesting approach to the study of personality factors in health. Whether it is possible, using projective assessment, to tap subtle dimensions of psychobiologic functioning that have eluded traditional self-report measures remains to be seen.

NOVATION THERAPY

Grossarth-Maticek and Eysenck (1991a) developed a therapeutic strategy for cancer-prone individuals which they call novation (meaning "renewal") behavior therapy. The approach reflects their belief that cancer patients manifest the Type C personality primarily in terms of: (1) emotional repression and expression of anger and anxiety, and (2) feelings of hopelessness-helplessness and depression in response to interpersonal stress. They have applied their personality model to heart disease as well, but present discussion is restricted to the treatment of cancer patients:

> The method has been called 'Creative Novation Behaviour Therapy,' and is characterized particularly by an insistence on personality differences between healthy and disease-prone individuals, and a stress on changing personality and behavior in ways delineated by these differences. 'Novation' indicates that new types of behavior are to be developed, and 'creative' suggests that the patient is to be encouraged to develop these novel behaviors through self-observation and experience of the consequences of his/her actions. Another name for the method of treatment sometimes used is 'Autonomy Training,' because the major aim of the treatment is to stimulate an individual to look toward the long-term positive results of different types of behavior and self-evaluation. Autonomy training teaches that behavior which leads to short-

term positive but long-term negative results should be avoided, very much as behavior which leads to both long-term and short-term negative results should be avoided. (p. 2)

The fundamental personality dimension of cancer-prone individuals in need of development is emotional autonomy. According to Grossarth-Maticek and Eysenck (1991a), these individuals exhibit an exaggerated attachment and orientation to other people and objects. That is, their reactions are highly dependent on the behavior of a particular person(s), making autonomous self-regulation impossible. The high dependence on emotionally important others leads cancer-prone individuals to a position where they themselves cannot gratify needs except through these needs-satisfying persons. They are completely unable to make themselves independent of the object or persons in question.

Through autonomy training, individuals are taught to recognize their dependent object relationships and provided with practical skills for reducing tension and stress in situations which previously created feelings of hopelessness, helplessness, and anxiety. The therapeutic process is quite structured and draws on a number of existing cognitive and behavioral strategies and techniques. During the initial session, it is explained that the patient himself must play an active role in determining the behaviors which will bring about the increased autonomy in his long-term actions. The therapeutic objectives are definitely large-scale and not likely easily attainable. Patients are required to describe their present self-concept, the behavioral patterns which maintain this concept, and then engage in new behavioral patterns which, if successfully implemented, will lead to long-term positive results. A cancer patient, for example, described her most important psychic difficulties and desires as:

> "(a) I cannot stop thinking, and the thoughts go round and round on the one theme, that as a woman I am rejected and worthless; (b) I have longed, during my whole life, to be close to my parents, my boyfriend, and my woman friend, but have never achieved this, and for this reason I become depressed and still more convinced that I am worthless as a woman. I can visualize now, in my illness, how the metastases spread, but not how I can become partly healthy, either physically or mentally."

> .... "I can tell you both what I do not want and what I do want. I am quite clear that I do not want to enter a therapy, in which something is being done to me, in which the therapist only wants to confirm his own views, and is not really capable of taking an interest in me. I would like to be free of endless torturing thoughts of being worthless as a woman and that other people just tolerate me. I would like to be

self-sufficient and in this way to strengthen my psychic strength so
that I can overcome the illness better. (p. 11)

Just how many cancer patients possess this negative self-image and would
also describe their goals of therapy in this fashion is unknown.

Specific behavioral techniques include visualization of independence,
cognitive restructuring, social skills training in aggressive distancing, emotional expressiveness, distress management, and training to achieve a be-
havior-directing hierarchic value structure. This very complex program of
behavior/personality change requires approximately 30 hours of therapy.
The objectives lend themselves well to a group format as the members are
able to draw on each other's support and communications. Grossarth-
Maticek and Eysenck (1991a) believe that the innovative or "novational"
aspect of their therapy lies in their global therapeutic strategy and objective rather than in the tactics employed. Rather than focus on specific
symptoms and their management, their goal is to change the behavior and
personality of cancer-prone people to that characteristic of people not
so prone.

In a second paper (Grosssarth-Maticek & Eysenck, 1991b), they presented some prelimary data which indicated that cancer-prone individuals
(i.e., Type C individuals free of cancer at time of study) who volunteered for
a therapy program based on these principles showed fewer deaths 13 years
later from cancer than a control group of Type C individuals which did not
receive this intervention program. In addition, they described some data
based on 24 pairs of cancer sufferers, matched for type and progress of
cancer, who were randomly assigned to novational therapy or control
group conditions. The survival averaged 5.07 years for the treated group
and 3.09 years for the control group. These differences could have resulted
from a number of nontherapy variables, but the authors believe not. They
cited an independent study (Spiegel et al., 1989) which found that a
group of women with breast cancer who received group therapy combined with self-hypnosis lived twice as long as a similar group who were
given only traditional medical treatment (36.6 months compared to 18.9
months).

It remains for the future to determine if the treatment strategy outlined
under novational therapy is more or less effective than strategies which do
not explicitly seek personality change. Grossarth-Maticek and Eysenck
(1991a) acknowledged the need for replication and at the same time concluded their paper with reference to provocative anecdotal data. These data
came from an unpublished study of seven patients who had experienced
spontaneous cancer regression. The patients had been disease-free for a
period of six years to 25 years and in all cases had shown a marked change
in their personality and behavior, away from Type C and toward autonomy.

BALANCED PERSPECTIVE

Although conclusions cannot be made at this point as to whether psychological factors may alter the course of cancer, we do know that every cancer patient needs to come to terms with the disease in his or her preferred way. Health professionals, friends and/or family of individuals with cancer need to be highly sensitive to what can and cannot be changed, not just in terms of a person's biology but also in terms of a person's psychology. Facing the prospect of death is a highly individualized existential experience and often leads to a search for meaning. Cancer patients wonder what they might have done to bring the cancer on and how much time they have left. It is also a time that they look back on their lives and "take stock" of both personal and interpersonal activities. A good percentage of patients find the resources to convert the disease into an experience of personal growth.

If psychological variables influence the course of cancer, we need to better understand what it is that cancer patients are supposed to do toward helping themselves. Advising cancer patients to change their personality, maintain "positive attitudes," or introduce more humor into their lives is intellectually and morally not acceptable, especially when death is inevitable and the patient feels guilt, confusion, and anger for not maintaining the proper frame of mind. The common denominator to most self-help techniques appears to be a subtle release of chronic tension levels within the person. Cousins' use of hand warming, for example, has the feature of providing patients with hope as well as directing their attention toward body relaxation. Similarly, claims for the use of humor might also be expected to release the person, in cathartic fashion, from subtle tension levels. There are some data indicating that humor is associated with enhanced immune system function. Martin and Dobbin (1988) reported that subjects with a strong sense of humor showed less immunosuppression in response to daily stress than subjects with less of a sense of humor.

Far too many cancer victims are being blamed and are blaming themselves for what may be their biologic destiny. These patients often believe that depression and anxiety about their disease should be suppressed, that they should maintain a "positive" attitude at all times. As a rule, cancer patients try to avoid potentially overwhelming feelings and consider themselves to be doing well if they don't cry or worry. "Doing defenses (keeping occupied) are commonly employed. Many believe that a positive attitude will help them to heal, and that 'negative' thoughts and feelings (often those most appropriate to their psychological if not biological reality, like fear, anger, and sadness) can cause their cancer to recur. Therefore, they terrify themselves when they experience their true feelings and strive to suppress and control them" (Hoffman, 1988). In some instances, appropriate psychological/psychiatric counseling may be necessary:

E.D., an intelligent, educated 46-year-old married real estate entrepreneur, was initially seen at the time her breast cancer was diagnosed. She had her own therapist, a behaviorist, who had been treating her for a phobia, and she declined further support. Years later, when she was confronted with progressive metastic disease, she requested further psychiatric consultation. . . . At the same time, the patient's husband insisted that a positive attitude would cure her, and that any 'negative' emotions, like fear, might contribute to recurrence. This belief was strongly reinforced by the patient's new support group. . . . to whom the patient and her husband turned for faith and healing. After church healers had repeatedly prayed for the patient and laid on hands, the patient was unable to suppress her 'negative' feelings like despair and terror, and tentatively asked the Breast Center psychiatrist for help. She then embarked on outpatient psychotherapy, augmented by family therapy. This eventuated in home hospice care with psychopharmacotherapeutic intervention to manage her pain, depression, and anxiety, until she died. (Hoffman, 1988, p. 185)

Individuals working in psychosocial oncology are faced with the difficult task of accommodating cancer patients who demand treatment based on popularized notions of wellness. According to Cella (1990), cancer victims have gone well beyond the data in their expectations, making it difficult for clinicians to know exactly what approach to adopt. Competing with "evangelists" who preach inspirational messages of love and hope is not ethical given the lack of supporting evidence. At the same time, Cella wondered whether a diluted and mundane approach of a standard stress-management program might, like too low a dosage of chemotherapy, be ineffective:

At issue here is the question of whether "holistic" oncology can be practiced in moderation or whether moderation of the message somehow removes its healing power. If hope "heals" by fostering faith in cure—in other words, if faith-healing is a teachable commodity—must that faith be unbridled? Must a person hope for and believe in total cure, or can that person hope with equal vigor for some approximation? . . . To *expect* cure of metastic disease as the end product of any therapeutic effort, whether that effort is biological or psychological, is excessively ambitious. To hope for cure is natural and human. If cure is not attained, as it usually is not, then physical decline and death do not signify failure. . . . This is the challenge to the health promoter: to encourage optimism, hope, laughter, and whatever else might improve a seriously ill person's quality of life without burdening that person with guilt or, worse yet, with a hollow drivenness toward the unlikely. (pp. 20–21)

Cella (1990) proposed a doctrine of cancer wellness that can be used to guide psychosocial interventions with cancer patients. The doctrine is based on a number of beliefs, one of which is the notion that people who take responsibility for their health and general well-being are better at dealing with cancer than those who do not. This in no way means that they are responsible for their disease. Even if personal coping styles contributed in some way to the disease onset, this is no more the case than with any other disease. Reflections on self-blame need be discouraged, unless such reflections might be utilized for coping with present stress in a more adaptive fashion. A second belief involves hope, not just hope for recovery but hope for other aspects of life as well. Fostering hope without promise of cure is very important:

> Our role is to help patients find the appropriate level and kind of hope. For example, if a patient comes to us with unrealistic expectations, such as hope for complete remission of metastic disease, we do not try to dispel his or her belief in this possibility, nor do we overtly reward that belief by elaborating on unproved ways to bring about remission. If a patient is in despair, we do not encourage that despair, nor do we respond with only a sad, empathetic nod. We struggle with the patient to understand the despair and its function; then we attempt to help the patient discover alternatives to that despair. If hope for cure or remission is no longer tenable, improved palliation, physician-patient communication, family relationships, and personal satisfaction may be the goals. (p. 24)

There is no single approach to wellness, and finding the ideal approach for each individual is a collaborative process, involving first of all the patient and, second, members of the health care team. "The important belief to promote is that people have the inner ability to make a meaningful difference, that the direction of change must come from within the person who has made a commitment to change" (Cella, 1990). We cannot forget, in dealing with cancer, that we all eventually die. It may appear callous to say this to a person who is dying of cancer but if presented in a sensitive fashion such an understanding can "replace panic with perspective" (Cella, 1990). Most people are not dying in the moment and it can be of immense clinical value to have them change their perspective—to have them realize that at this moment they are alive and can contribute to their ongoing well-being. Cancer patients, of course, don't "need cancer to change" but they can be encouraged to make the best of it. Many cancer patients do acquire a deeper understanding of themselves and are able to maintain a sense of personal dignity and quality of life during the course of the illness.

5
Psychopharmacology: Mood Disorders and Addictions

DRUGS AND THE PSYCHOBIOLOGIC PERSPECTIVE

This chapter examines the pharmacological treatment of clinical anxiety and depression. Both emotional conditions are considered as mood disorders and, more often than not, both conditions are found to occur concomitantly in the same patients. Chemotherapy is the most popular method for controlling mood disorders and it is often assumed that these conditions can be managed through drugs alone. Professional journals regularly promise powerful medications for stopping intrusive thoughts, relieving psychological pain, lifting depression, improving self-esteem, and providing hope. These changes can seldom be achieved by drugs alone and therapeutic effects which accompany chemotherapy need to be understood within the individual's larger psychobiologic context. The old dictum, "drugs do not create new behavior, they only influence existing behavior" remains true today in spite of the explosion of knowledge and developments in this field.

Drug treatment approaches for anxiety and depression have a seductive appeal for both physicians and patients. Medication allows the physician, when faced with the request for treatment, to deal with the condition immediately. Also patients are relieved that their symptoms are due to some "chemical imbalance" to be corrected by the drug and not to their personality or some other factor within their responsibility. Drugs, with their images of scientific control, dampen the idea that people's moods are also governed by thoughts and feelings. There is growing evidence that patients' responsiveness to medication is in large part the result of psychobiological reactions within patients themselves.

This chapter also examines the psychobiology of addictions. There is a common framework for understanding all addictive behaviors, with particular emphasis on the addictive experience and its determinants. Finally, the chapter describes a treatment framework based on the concept of relapse prevention.

MODES OF PSYCHOACTIVE DRUG ACTION

Models of drug action are heavily based on physiochemical events that occur at synaptic sites throughout the nervous system. The synapse is the gap that separates the axonal membrane of one neuron from the dendritic membrane of an adjacent neuron. Synaptic junctions also occur between neuronal endings and the muscles being innervated. The axon terminal makes close approximation with the dendrite through a narrow space called the synaptic cleft. The synaptic cleft separates the presynaptic membrane (the axon and the axon terminal) from the postsynpatic membrane of the dendrite. Mitochondria (the metabolic factories of the cell) and numerous small synaptic vesicles are located in the presynaptic terminal. Basically there are five steps or somewhat independent processes that take place during the synaptic transmission process (Figure 5.1). Steps 1 and 2 are presynaptic events involving the synthesis, storage, and release of neurotransmitter. Steps 3 and 4 involve the extracellular action of the transmitter; that is, diffusion, and receptor activation, and metabolic destruction of transmitter. Step 5 involves the reuptake of the chemical transmitter and results in the cessation of information transfer.

The synthesis of the neurotransmitter occurs within the synaptic vesicles. Synaptic vesicles are produced from proteins in the cytoplasm of the cell body, which eventually make their way through the axon to the terminal buttons. Synaptic vesicles protect neurotransmitters from degradation by enzymes in the surrounding cytoplasm. When a nerve action potential reaches the end of an axon, there is believed to be an opening of calcium channels at the terminal button. The opening of the channels allows calcium ions ($Ca++$) to enter the button and to trigger the release of neurotransmitter. Neurotransmitter release starts with a vesicle moving toward the presynaptic membrane and fusing with it (Pinel, 1990). With contact, the membrane opens and the neurotransmitter is released from the vesicle into the synaptic cleft. The transmitter molecules then move across the cleft and combine with receptor molecules on the external surface of the postsynaptic membrane to produce a postsynaptic potential.

The binding of the neurotransmitter molecule with the postsynaptic receptor is believed to result in changes in chemically gated ion channels in the receptive membrane. In some neurons, ion channels that permit the greater inward flow of sodium ($Na+$) ions than the outward flow of potassium ($K+$) ions result in an excitatory postsynaptic potential (EPSP) and depolarization. In other neurons, EPSPs are produced by the closing of $K+$ channels that are normally open while the neuron is at rest. Inhibitory postsynaptic potentials (IPSPs) are produced by the opening of channels which allow the efflux of $K+$ ions. There is also an indirect mechanism

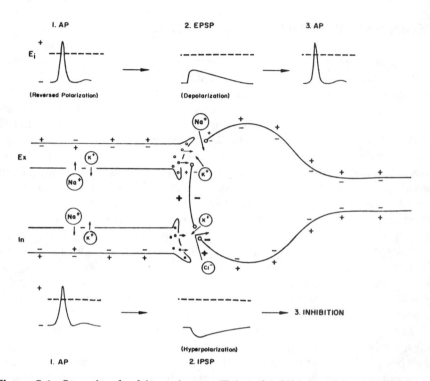

Figure 5.1. Steps involved in excitatory (Ex) and inhibitory (In) neurohumoral transmission.

1. The nerve action potential (AP), consisting in self-propagated reversal of negativity (the internal potential, E^i, goes from a negative value, through zero potential, indicated by the broken line, to a positive value) of the axonal membrane, arrives at the presynaptic terminal and causes release of the excitatory (o) or inhibitory (•) transmitter.

2. Combination of the excitatory transmitter with the postsynaptic receptors produces a localized depolarization, the excitatory postsynaptic potential (EPSP), through an increase in permeability to cations, most notably Na^+. The inhibitory transmitter causes a selective increase in permeability to K^+ or Cl^-, resulting in a localized hyperpolarization, the inhibitory postsynaptic potential (IPSP).

3. The EPSP initiates a conducted AP in the postsynaptic neuron; this can, however, be prevented by the hyperpolarization induced by a concurrent IPSP.

The transmitter is dissipated by enzymatic destruction, by reuptake into the presynaptic terminal, or by diffusion. R. J. Lefkowitz, B. B. Hoffman, & P. Taylor. (1990). Neurohumoral transmission: The autonomic and somatic motor nervous systems (pp. 84–121). In A. G. Gilman, T. W. Rall, A. S. Nies & P. Taylor (Eds.), *Goodman and Gilman's The pharmacological basis of therapeutics.* New York: Pergamon Press. Reprinted by permission.

which leads to changes in postsynpatic membrane potentials. In this case the bind of the transmitter molecule to the receptor leads to additional changes in the cytoplasm. Second messengers are produced which have further effects on the ion channels. One such messenger is cyclic adenosine monophosphate (cAMP) which is produced from an enzyme which is released when a neurotransmitter binds to a receptor.

The termination of the effect of the transmitter is, in some cases, controlled through enzymes which deactivate the transmitter by breaking it down into its constituent parts. For example, the effect of cyclic AMP on the ion channels of the postsynaptic potentials is only brief because it is quickly destroyed by the enzyme phosphodiesterase. The more common method of deactivation involves reuptake of the neurotransmitter molecules from the synaptic cleft by the presynpatic neuron. allowing the neurotransmitter molecules to be recycled for use again.

There are three major classes of neurotransmitters; acetylcholine, monoamines, and amino acids. Acetylcholine (Ach) was first identified as a transmitter chemical in the peripheral nervous system. It is also present in large amounts in brain tissue. Following synthesis, acetylcholine is thought to be stored inside the nerve terminal within synaptic vesicles until it is released into the synaptic cleft upon arrival of an action potential. The acetylcholine then diffuses across the cleft and attaches itself to receptors on the dendrite of the next neuron. Once acetylcholine has exerted its effect on the postsynaptic membrane, its action is terminated by the enzyme acetylcholine esterase (AChE).

There are four monoamine neurotransmitters—norepinephrine, epinephrine, dopamine, and serotonin. The term catecholamines describes the first three as they are all synthesized from tyrosine (i.e., tyrosine → L-DOPA → dopamine → norepinephrine → epinephrine). Catecholamines are inactivated by the enzymes monoamine oxidase (MAO) and catechol o-methyltransferase (COMT). It is believed that the postsynatpic effects of catecholamines are terminated primarily by an active process—their reuptake across the presynaptic nerve membrane back into the presynaptic nerve ending. Dopamine cell bodies are located primarily in the substantia nigra, a midbrain nucleus with axons that connect to a group of structures called the basal ganglia. The dopamine neurons play an important role in movement and loss of dopamine is associated with Parkinson's disease. Most norepinephrine cell bodies are situated in the brainstem, which contains structures heavily involved in emotional behavior. Serotonin, also called 5-hydroxytryptamine or 5-HT, is widely distributed within the brain and is involved with body temperature, sensory perception, and sleep.

The amino acid neurotransmitters are present in the majority of fast-acting synapses within the central nervous system. Four widely studied amino acids are glutamate, aspartate, glycine, and gamma-aminobutyric acid (GABA). The brain contains high concentrations of aspartic acid, GABA, and glutamic acid, and the spinal cord contains high concentrations of glycine. Aspartic acid and glutamic acid appear to be universally excitatory; that is, their application to virtually any brain cell results in increased activity of that cell. GABA and glycine appear to be universally inhibitory.

Neuropeptides also serve as neurotransmitters. Peptides are short chains of amino acids and were first investigated as hormones (i.e., released into the bloodstream by endocrine glands). One by one, however, the peptides have been identified within neurons. Neuropeptides have far-reaching effects because they are released into the extracellular fluid, ventricles, and bloodstream. For this reason, neuropeptides are often called neuromodulators:

> Unlike conventional neurotransmitters, whose function is to carry local excitatory or inhibitory messages across synapses, neuromodulators increase or decrease the sensitivity of large populations of neurons to the local effects of neurotransmitters. Neuromodulators are thought to act through receptors whose activation produces gradual, long-lasting metabolic changes in their neurons via secondary messenger systems. . . . , rather than immediate brief changes in ion flow. . . . Neuromodulators are thought to influence behavior by regulating emotional and motivational tone. (Pinel, 1990, p. 153)

There are at least five ways in which a drug could potentiate the synaptic action of the transmitters. First, it might increase the rate of synthesis of the transmitter substance. Second, the compound might potentiate synaptic transmission by blocking the enzymes responsible for the metabolism of the transmitter. Third, a drug might augment the action of transmitters by inducing its release from the presynaptic nerve terminals, thus increasing the amount of transmitter available to stimulate the postsynaptic receptors. Fourth a drug might prolong the action of transmitter at its postsynaptic receptor by blocking its active uptake from the synaptic cleft back into the presynaptic nerve terminal. The principle of reuptake into the nerve terminal and then into the storage vesicles is crucially important, because there are drugs that may block either the active uptake process into the nerve terminal (thus potentiating the synaptic action of the transmitter) or the uptake of the transmitter from the intracellular fluid in the nerve terminal back into the synaptic vesicles. Such a block of active reuptake of dopamine appears to be the primary mechanism of action of cocaine. Finally, drugs may stimulate the postsynaptic receptor, mimicking the effect of the transmitter.

ANXIOLYTICS AND THE BENZODIAZEPINE RECEPTOR

Antianxiety or anxiolytic drugs are classified as sedative–hypnotic compounds. The benzodiazepines are among the most commonly prescribed anxiolytic drugs. These drugs have been used as a panacea for the treatment of anxiety in spite of concern that they have similarities in addictive potential to the opiates and barbiturates. Some investigators continue to see these drugs as dangerous and cite cases of serious addiction while others feel that the benzodiazepines are relatively safe.

Chlordiazepoxide was the first benzodiazepine synthesized and the first to be used clinically. There are many benzodiazepines available, most of which differ in potency, absorption, onset and duration of action, elimination half-life, and active metabolites. There is no real agreement as to what these differences mean in terms of observed clinical effects. The half-lives for some of the major benzodiazepines are: chlordiazepoxide, 5–10 hours; diazepam, 30–60 hours; oxazepam (serax), 5–10 hours. Elimination half-life is considered an important factor in benzodiazepine choice. A short half-life, for example, is often seen of value with elderly patients as benzodiazepines with this characteristic (e.g., serax) would be less likely to accumulate and produce prolonged sedations and side effects. Short half-life benzodiazepines are also claimed to facilitate sleep of insomniacs without morning "cloudiness." Unfortunately, the same short half-life benzodiazepines, when discontinued, result in a rapid drop in the serum level, leading to a higher incidence of withdrawal reactions or rebound insomnia.

The usual indications for the use of benzodiazepines are as anxiolytics, muscle relaxants, hypnotics, and as anticonvulsants. Although certain benzodiazepines are singled out as specific for each of these uses, they are all similarly effective in the short-term management of anxiety. A modification in dose can turn an anxiolytic into a hypnotic or anticonvulsant. Benzodiazepines have been found to be most commonly prescribed for women, the elderly, and those with high levels of emotional distress and somatic problems.

The concept of the benzodiazepine receptor combined with the inhibitory transmitter GABA, is at the heart of understanding the action of benzodiazepine drugs. GABA is an inhibitory neurotransmitter said to be present in 30% of brain synapses. There are two different types of GABA receptors, called GABAa and GABAb. The GABAa receptor, when occupied by GABA, leads to an increased flow of negative chloride ions through chloride channels into the cell, thereby hyperpolarizing the cell and inhibiting its function. There is evidence that benzodiazepines increase the inhibitory effect of GABA by increasing the affinity of GABAa receptors for

GABA and thus prolonging the opening of the chloride channel. Brain benzodiazepine receptors are found in diverse regions throughout the forebrain and brainstem, with the most dense regions including the olfactory bulbs, hippocampus, amygdala, cerebellum, and lamina IV of the cortex.

Drug trials consistently show that benzodiazepines are better than placebo in treating anxiety disorders but not that much better. Reviews indicate that over 55% of studies find a "statistical advantage" for benzodiazepines over placebo. Unfortunately, a psychobiologic dependence often develops in patients taking a benzodiazepine in therapeutic doses for a period of several months. Rickels et al. (1986) observed a high rate of relapse (63%) in the year following treatment with either 6, 14, or 22 weeks of diazepam. Most patients sought further medical help for their condition and most received medication. Michelson and Marchione (1991) reviewed a study which involved 500 panic disorder patients who were assigned to treatment with the high-potency benzodiazepine alprazolam (Xanax) or placebo:

> Sixty percent of clients on alprazolam versus 30% of the placebo clients were panic-free after eight weeks of treatment at dosages as high as 10 mg per day. Many of these clients could not be withdrawn off the drug because of psychological dependence. Of those who discontinued the medication, 30% suffered rebound panic attacks worse than the panic attacks for which they had originally sought treatment. Finally, 90% of these clients experienced relapse following medication withdrawal. (p. 108)

There are very few unwanted effects associated with benzodiazepine use. Drowsiness occurs in some individuals but this can be controlled by reducing dosage. Tolerance to the anxiolytic effects or escalation of dose are observed infrequently. When anxiety disorder patients are tapered gradually off benzodiazepines, the large majority have no severe withdrawal symptoms. However, withdrawal from benzodiazepines in the absence of additional therapy is likely to be associated with a return to predrug levels of anxiety (Wardle, 1990). Return of the original symptoms upon gradual tapering documents a need for continued treatment rather than addiction. Most behavioral clinics combine benzodiazepine treatment with some form of cognitive behavioral therapy, the assumption being that concurrent benzodiazepine use may optimize conditions for new learning. Benzodiazepines represent a powerful tool for assisting patients in managing their anxiety and distress during the initial stages of behavioral treatment. However, patients on long-term benzodiazepine use generally do poorer in behavioral treatment programs than those who are not taking benzodiazepines (Wardle, 1990). Benzodiazepine withdrawal syndrome, when it does occur, can often be distinguished from a return of the pretreatment anxiety symptoms on the basis of specific withdrawal symptoms, such as increased sensitivity to light, noise, or other sensations; abnormal perception of motion; and muscle twitching.

TRICYCLIC MEDICATIONS

Tricyclic antidepressants (TCAs) have gained an important role in the treatment of both anxiety and depression disorders. The term "tricyclic" reflects the basic three-ring chemical structure of these compounds; it also serves as a type of shorthand to separate TCAs from a distinctly different group of drugs with antianxiety and antidepressant properties known as monoamine oxidase inhibitors (MAOIs). The MAO inhibitors are a small group of drugs that have long been considered alternative drugs for the treatment of major depressive illness; they all have in common the ability to block the enzyme monoamine oxidase. As mentioned earlier, monoamine oxidase is an enzyme located within the nerve terminals of norepinephrine, dopamine, and serotonin neurons. Blockade of this enzyme (which normally modulates the amount of transmitter present) allows transmitters to accumulate in the nerve terminals. As a result, larger amounts of transmitter are released when neuronal stimulation occurs. MAOIs are generally viewed as less effective than the TCAs in the management of severe depression. Subsequently, they were relegated to the role of drugs of second choice in the treatment of depression.

TCAs have a mode of action different from the MAOIs as they inhibit or block the neuronal uptake of norepinephrine and serotonin into the presynatpic nerve terminals from which they were originally released. Some TCAs are potent norepinephrine reuptake inhibitors with weak effects on serotonin, whereas others have preferential impact on reuptake of serotonin. The trycyclics do not have a stimulating or mood-elevating effect in normal individuals.

Clomipramine hydrochloride (Anafronil) is a potent serotonin reuptake blocker that is used to decrease the symptoms of obsessive-compulsive disorder (OCD). An obsessional symptom is described as a "recurrent or persistent idea, thought, image, feeling, or movement which is accompanied by a sense of subjective compulsion and a desire to resist it, the event being recognized by the individual as foreign to his personality" (Steketee & Foa, 1985). Obsessions usually refer to the thoughts, images, or action that generate anxiety. They are often recognized by the sufferer as being senseless, at least initially. The individual also recognizes that the obsessions are products of his own mind but at the same time cannot control their presence. Compulsions are behaviors that refer to the attempts to alleviate the anxiety aroused by the obsessions. The behaviors are repetitive, purposeful, and intentional. They are usually performed in a stereotyped fashion and are designed to prevent some dreaded event or situation. Patients know, for example, that ritualistic washing is absurd and senseless but feel some dreaded consequence beyond anxiety will occur unless they wash. Most common are the patients who have contamination obsessions (Insel, 1990). These patients worry about having an infection or disease that requires washing or showering. Consequently, they show a great deal of avoidance behavior and will not use public rest rooms or certain rooms in their house, or will refuse to go shopping for fear of contaminating their surrounds. Persons with obsessional doubt are the next most frequent OCD group (they are often called "checkers" as opposed to "washers"); these individuals have to go back and check that a bump in the road was in fact not a body or they have to make certain 30 or 40 times that a door is locked.

OCD is relatively infrequent as a presenting clinical condition but the low frequency of presentation may reflect the fact that sufferers are afraid of telling their families or physicians about their "bizarre" or "crazy" symptoms. Flament, Rapoport and colleagues (Flament et al., 1988) interviewed 5,600 high school students using a checklist of questions about the presence or absence of obsessions, rituals, and compulsive traits. As part of the initial screen, they also asked questions about how strong the urge was to complete the compulsions and about the severity of worry or distress associated with each obsession. Of these 5,600 students 114 (2%) scored above a predetermined cutoff that was suggestive of significant obsessive compulsive symptoms. These 114 were subsequently interviewed by psychiatrists and 15 of the 114 met criteria for clinical diagnosis of OCD. Average age of onset is usually 19 years (late adolescence or early twenties). The disorder appears to have a familial basis as between 21% and 25% of nuclear family members of obsessive compulsive probands also suffer from OCD (Rasmussen & Eisen, 1990).

Clomipramine is a selective blocker of serotonin reuptake and is known to be more effective than placebo in the treatment of OCD. Some studies have reported clomipramine to be better than the norepinephrine reuptake blocker desipramine in reducing symptoms of OCD, leading to speculation that an abnormality of brain serotonin function may be at the basis of OCD (Rapoport, 1989). The anxiety levels in patients with OCD are very high and some clinicians believe that clomipramine, when it works, does so by inducing "down-regulation" of serotonergic responsiveness. The predominant neurobiological hypothesis regarding the pathophysiology of OCD is that abnormal regulation of brain serotinergic function is related to at least some aspects of the disorder.

OCD is an extremely difficult disorder to control with medication alone and few patients are asymptomatic at end of a clinical drug trial. The majority of studies simply report "improved" or "better," and even here the numbers responding are often in the 50% to 60% category. Although studies generally follow a double-blind crossover design, their duration seldom exceeds eight weeks and the symptoms often return. In addition, patients who strongly hold the belief that their compulsive rituals are necessary to forestall future catastrophes (i.e., those with "overvalued ideas") have poorer outcome with drug treatments. For example, the patient who really believes that someone will die if she does not wash her entire house every day is unlikely to give up the rituals with chemotherapy alone.

Mary is a 28-year-old married female, with two children. She felt contaminated by "poisons," which in actuality were most often dust flecks, skin flakes, mineral deposits on drinking fountains, "spots" on food produce, etc. Her primary fear was that these contaminants would somehow get from her body onto others and result in possible poisoning. The fear was so severe that on some occasions she would imagine seeing liquid from antifreeze or solvent containers in supermarket aisles "spill" onto the floor and in some way reach her clothes. Also, normal dust flecks would become potentially poisonous, making it necessary for her to engage in considerable checking to make certain that none of the "poison" remained behind. Mary was not afraid of contaminating family, friends, and therapists because, in her words, she knew that she would see these people again. Her fear was for the countless strangers that passed by and she dreaded not knowing what might have happened to them. Mary's primary compulsion to relieve anxiety was hand and body washing. She would have numerous showers throughout the day in an effort to cleanse her body. The disorder eventually cost her a career in special education as she was unable to function in the presence of children without having fear of contaminating their environment. Mary also used reassurance as a compulsion to reduce the anxiety. Following contact with a contaminant, she would repeatedly ask her husband, therapist, or someone in authority, such as hospital poison control experts, whether a few grains of "poison," transmitted from clothing, produce, etc., might kill someone. Her anxiety would immediately diminish upon receiving the reassurance but would return within a few moments and require further reassurance. A trial of clomipramine was partially successful as the patient experienced a significant reduction in her obsessive thinking and general anxiety. However, her condition eventually deteriorated and resulted in an admission to a psychiatric inpatient program. During her stay in the program she was momentarily denied access to washing and showers but she eventually substituted coke and other available liquids for water.

Behavioral treatment is a recommended alternative to chemotherapy and consists of two related techniques, *exposure* and *response prevention* (Steketee & Foa, 1985). The exposure treatment consists of repeatedly exposing patients for prolonged periods (45 minutes to 2 hours) to situations/circumstances that provoke anxiety and discomfort. Patients with washing rituals are required to touch their particular "contaminated" objects. In time, it is assumed that the associated anxiety will gradually diminish and extinguish. With Mary, exposure consisted of 15 daily sessions in shopping malls. The most frightening situation involved having her touch fruit produce, especially strawberries, as she was convinced that the contact would in some way contaminate the remaining produce. Her preferred solution to the dilemma would be to buy all the produce on the stand.

Response prevention consisted of refusal to provide her with reassurance that no harm would befall other shoppers and also restricted water use. The recommended procedure for washing is to allow "supervised showers" of 10 minutes' duration, once every five days. This aspect of treatment could not be enforced as the patient's family had given up on trying to help. Some reduction in the intensity and frequency of obsessive behavior was achieved with the exposure but the patient was far from cured. Both drugs and behavior therapy can be limited with very severe occurrences of OCD. With less severe occurrences of OCD, there is some agreement that exposure and response prevention lead to meaningful improvement in 60% to 85% of patients. There is also some evidence that clomipramine alone yields only limited and transient benefits during the first few weeks of treatment (Marks et al., 1988).

TCAs not only have limited treatment effectiveness for anxiety and depression disorders but their continued use may result in the development of side effects, which at times can prove quite dangerous. TCAs have a number of side effects, one of the most surprising being a paradoxical reaction characterized by arousal, restlessness, worsening insomnia, and increased anxiety; patients with such reactions appear literally "wired" on TCAs. A more frequent class of side effects is related to TCA's anticholinergic effects (i.e., blocking of acetylcholine receptors). Such side effects include dry mouth, blurred vision, urinary hesitancy, and constipation. TCAs can also produce cardiac side effects as well as sensations of hangover, fatigue, heavy feelings in the limbs, or having "cotton" in the head.

PLACEBO AND DOUBLE-BLIND DESIGN

It is widely assumed that a patient's clinical response to a drug is based on the additive effect of "specific" and "nonspecific" factors. The specific factors refer to the physiochemical effects of the drug while the "nonspecific" factors refer to a number of effects which collectively are termed the placebo effect. *Placebo* is Latin for "I shall please" and is defined as "any component of therapy that is deliberately or knowingly used for its nonspecific, psychologic, or physiologic effect, or that is used unknowingly for its presumed or believed specific effect on a patient, symptom, or illness, but which, unknown to patient and therapist, is without specific activity for the condition being treated" (Shapiro & Shapiro, 1984). When a patient goes to a therapist for treatment there is the normal expectation that the patient will receive help, and almost regardless of the type of treatment the patient receives, including the infamous "sugar pill," most patients will experience some improvement. Given the nonspecific component of treatment, it becomes necessary to demonstrate that a proposed therapeutic drug provides more benefit than would be expected from just placebo treatment.

The notion that specific (drug) and nonspecific (psychological) treatment factors can be studied independently reflects an effort to keep mind and body issues separate:

> The so-called physiological effects of a drug are treated as if they were of an entirely different class from the "psychological" ones. "Placebo effects" are regarded as a nuisance to be screened out. Obviously, "psychological effects" are fully as physiological as those attributed to a drug's biochemical action. Placebo responses occur in tissue and are physiologically "real." However, the current set among biologically-oriented researchers is to act as if one category of drug action is real and the so-called psychological aspect is imaginary. One can understand the attitude of biological researchers whose goal is to create an agent that selectively eliminates a "psychiatric symptom" by initiating changes in some biochemical system. Their focus is on events in that system and other potential influences are extraneous. However, human response categories cannot be separated into such neat categories, and in fact, we know little about the potential amount of spread of the physiological events, representing the psychological experience of taking a drug, to the specific biochemical system that drug is supposed to influence "directly." (Fisher & Greenberg, 1989, pp. 316-317)

Although the nature of the placebo may vary, depending on the nature of the active treatment, in drug trials the placebo takes the form of a pill or capsule identical in appearance to the "active" medication. In this way, neither the patient nor the therapist knows which medication the patient is receiving, and the clinical trial is referred to as double-blind. This procedure is employed to prevent the bias that might result from either the patient or the therapist knowing the true nature of the treatment. Patients are randomly assigned to the various conditions in order to prevent the bias of assigning the "best" patients to the drug treatment condition. Drug studies also use an initial placebo washout procedure not just to wash out the effects of prior medication but also to weed out those patients who are likely to deviate from study procedures either by taking nonstudy medication or by missing scheduled appointments.

The double-blind condition may not be as "blind" to the participants as is commonly assumed. According to Greenberg and Fisher (1989), physicians and nurses can often discriminate which patients are receiving active drug and which are receiving placebo. This is an especially serious problem because studies have shown that if bias can operate, it will. The less controlled the evaluation of a therapeutic procedure the more the experimenter and subject can bias the outcome. Clinical improvement rates are generally much higher in open drug trials than in blind drug trials. In addition, across studies which have employed double-blind designs, the magnitude of therapeutic effect has been observed to correlate positively with the magnitude of placebo effect. Thus, if the drug effect was large, the placebo effect was large. This suggests that despite the use of the double-blind there was a "spread of intensity of therapeutic expectation" for the active drug to the placebo. One study cited by Fisher and Greenberg (1989), asked physicians and patients being treated for depression to guess at the end of six weeks of treatment (involving either imipramine, phenalzine, or placebo) whether an active or inactive substance had been administered. Both patients and physicians were able to correctly guess the appropriate conditions at high levels of accuracy (79% and 87%). When the patients were grouped into those who had or had not responded to the treatments, it was found that responders were more accurate than nonresponders in identifying whether they had received active drug or placebo. At least in this study, the double-blind condition clearly failed to conceal treatment conditions from both the physicians and patients.

One vital source of information with therapeutic potential within the double-blind design are the cues supplied by the body sensations activated by the drug. Patients can learn to discriminate between drug and placebo largely from subtle cues provided by body sensations and symptoms. We saw earlier that the TCAs in particular can produce a variety of body sensations, including tremor, dry mouth, sweating, and constipation. Inert placebos might initiate some body sensations but nothing of the magnitude of the active substance. Subjects in a drug trial are generally warned to expect certain side effects and if they do not experience them, they may conclude that they have been given a placebo, or that the drug is ineffective for them. Conversely, those who do experience side effects may feel that the drug is working and will not think that they have received inert or ineffective medication.

Probably in the great majority of studies of the effectiveness of antidepressants involving a comparison with an inactive placebo there have been significant differences in the body experiences of the drug and placebo groups. Such differences could signal to the patients involved whether they were receiving an active or inactive agent and they could, further, supply discriminating cues to all personnel (e.g., nurses) responsible for the patients' day-to-day treatment. In the case of the personnel, one would expect that they would adopt different attitudes toward those they identified as being "on" versus "off" active treatment and consequently communicate contrasting expectations. . . . Those patients receiving an inactive placebo have fewer signals (from self and others) indicating they are being actively treated and should be improving. By the same token, patients taking an active drug like imipramine receive multiple signals that may well amplify potential placebo effects linked to the therapeutic context. (Greenberg & Fisher, 1989, p. 23)

To further support their thesis, Greenberg and Fisher described a review by Thomson (1982) of a large number of double-blind placebo-controlled studies of trycyclic antidepressants. Thomson discovered that of those which used an inert placebo, 59% found a superior therapeutic effect for the trycyclic. Of those which used an active placebo, atropine, only 14% of the studies reviewed showed a superior effect for TCA. It is possible that atropine, because of its anticholinergic effects, served as an antidepressant. It is also possible, however, that active placebos such as atropine produce indirect therapeutic benefits through changes in nonspecific body awareness. An active placebo may more convincingly arouse body sensations that affirm a potent agent has been taken into one's body. Interestingly, the efficacy of a placebo may in some contexts be correlated with the number of side effects it produces. In the same fashion, the clinical effects of active drugs may be partially linked simply to the changes in body experience they induce. Greenberg and Fisher (1989) described a study which found that ratings by normal subjects of their "well-being" after ingesting lithium chloride did not correlate with plasma lithium concentrations, but rather with amount of nausea experienced. The peripheral effects of lithium (viz., nausea) and not blood concentration levels were best predictive of subjective drug effects. These data imply that there may not be a tight relationship between dosage level, concentration of drug in the blood, and improvements in mood.

Greenberg's and Fisher's (1989) observations concerning awareness of body responses accompanying placebos may apply to active drugs as well. If body experiences are an ongoing component of the drug-taking procedure then we need to better understand their role in determining therapeutic response. Fisher and Greenberg (1989) pointed out that the amount of self-awareness mediates important response systems and "it is logical to expect that agents intensifying body sensations will also increase self-body awareness. An active drug may not only be more easily recognized as a "real" treatment but may also stimulate special "self-feelings" that can influence various levels of behavior. The fact that blindly ingesting a placebo is a perceptibly different experience than taking an active agent means that there is only a superficial experimental similarity between the two conditions. In fact, perceptible change in body awareness may be at the basis of improvement following psychotherapy. Positive body experiences in combination with perceived therapeutic expectation of those administering the treatment may lead to therapeutic change. Conversely, highly charged negative attitudes and feelings may cancel out the direct biochemically derived therapeutic effects of a number of drugs.

Fisher and Greenberg's (1989) thesis concerning body awareness and drug-placebo effects may ultimately shed light on the psychobiologic processes that maintain the intense and debilitating feelings of depression. Why, for example, when the condition is severe, do those afflicted feel as if they are in pain or dead inside? Why do such feelings seem to dissipate with time?

Light Therapy

An example of a treatment which leads to rapid symptom relief in some forms of depression and which may owe its therapeutic effects to altered body awareness is light therapy. The technique has an ancient history and is currently experiencing a revival in the treatment of depression, seasonal doldrums, and sleep problems. There is a possibility that any therapeutic effects which occur with light may result from indirect enhancement of the patient's somatic awareness:

> In 1910, Dr. J.H. Kellogg, superintendent of the Battle Creek, Michigan Sanitarium, published Light Therapeutics: A Practical Manual of Phototherapy for the Student and the Practitioner. Light treatment was provided at the Battle Creek Sanitarium to 4,000–5,000 invalids yearly for conditions such as malarial cachexia, diabetes, gangrene, obesity, chronic gastritis, cirrhosis, hysteria, and writer's cramp. For melancholia, Kellogg recommended arc lights and buttermilk. (Kripke et al., 1989, p. 342)

Bright light is currently being used to treat seasonally-based somatic symptoms which collectively are called winter depression or seasonal affective disorder (SAD). The depression has its onset in fall or winter and recovery occurs by spring or summer. Most investigators believe that the condition is unique in symptoms when compared with the more typical depressive disorder seen in clinics. For example, neurovegetative symptoms of decreased appetite, poor sleep, and weight loss characterize depression in general, while individuals experiencing SAD exhibit a "reverse" neurovegetative profile characterized by increased appetite, weight gain, and sleep time (hypersomnia). Seasonal doldrums are quite common in regions with major climatic changes. Terman (1989) completed a random telephone survey of over 200 citizens of New York City and asked them to rate the degree of seasonal change in sleep length, social activity, mood, weight, appetite, and energy according to specific months of the year. They were also asked to rate the degree to which seasonal changes presented a personal problem in their lives. Approximately 50% of the respondents reported lowered energy, 42% reported increased sleep, 31% reported less social activity, and 31% reported feeling worst throughout the winter. Twenty-five percent reported that the changes were sufficient to cause a personal problem.

Terman (1989) presented a graphic comparison of the survey respondents with similar data obtained from a psychiatric sample of SAD patients. The data are shown in Figure 5.2. The upper panel presents the month-by-month responses separately for the items "feel best" and "feel worst." The patients showed a pattern of feeling best and worst which followed the onset of spring and fall respectively. The normals showed a more complex and less pronounced pattern. The graphs in the lower panel were derived by subtracting the "feel best" responses from the "feel worst" responses; thus if the frequencies for the two categories were equal during any month, the relative frequency score would be 0.0. Note that the SAD patients were quite uniform in their responses from month to month, as evidenced by the large amplitude changes for the group as a whole. The normal population showed a lower amplitude oscillation with a noticeable summer slump. Normals feel best in May and June followed by a slump in July and August. In addition their swing to depressed mood occurs later in the fall, relative to SAD patients.

Until very recently, ultraviolet light was considered important for therapeutic effects, and treatment consisted of exposing the skin, while shielding the eyes, to ultraviolet "light baths." At present, phototherapy consists of very little ultraviolet light and is directed at the eyes rather than the skin. A number of controlled studies have now demonstrated that bright light is associated with improvement in SAD (Rosenthal et al., 1989). These studies have often involved crossover designs where two treatments (bright light versus room light) are administered for one week each, separated by a week of withdrawal from light treatment. Response to treatment can often be detected by the fourth treatment day and relapse following withdrawal of light can also be detected by the fourth day of withdrawal. It is impossible to control for placebo effects, especially since the magnitude of the placebo effect may be expected to vary directly with the intensity of the light administered.

Light intensity is presumed to be critical and is administered at an intensity (e.g., 2500–10,000 lux) far in excess of ordinary room light (500 lux). Some patients, however, have been observed to improve at exposures of 300 lux. It is difficult to know if other parameters make a difference. Length of treatment session has been studied, with claims made that ses-

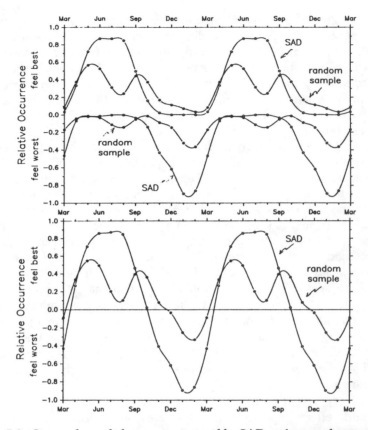

Figure 5.2. Seasonal mood changes as reported by SAD patients and respondents to a random-sample population survey. Top panel shows relative frequencies of response to separate questions in which the months of feeling worst and feeling best are identified. Bottom panel meshes these separate questions into a continuous score in which the proportion feeling worst is subtracted from the proportion feeling best (Terman, 1989). Reprinted by permission of The Guilford Press.

sions of two hours' duration are generally better than sessions of 30 minutes. The light spectrum might also be expected to make a difference, assuming that in nature it is the summer sunlight that is responsible for reversing the symptoms of SAD. Most researchers have used full-spectrum fluorescent light in their studies. Full spectrum fluorescent lights have more blue light and near-ultraviolet light, and less yellow and green light, than regular fluorescent lights. There is no evidence that light spectrum itself is the curative factor as full spectrum lighting is not necessary for a therapeutic effect to occur (Rosenthal et al., 1989).

The mechanisms and processes responsible for the antidepressant effects of light are unknown. Initially, there was enthusiasm for eye-mediated changes in melatonin, which is a hormone of the pineal gland. It was assumed that SAD might be a photoperiodic phenomenon similar in some ways to hibernation (Kripke et al., 1989). In hamsters, melatonin also shows seasonal rhythmicity, with higher levels in winter and lower levels in summer. Another photoperiod theory that has been advanced to explain the therapeutic effects of light is based on circadian rhythms. It is assumed that the light restores, in some unknown manner, normalcy to the patient's circadian rhythm patterns.

What might be the contributions of psychobiology to the therapeutic effects of light? Most people associate warm light with body-soothing sensations as well as calm and inner tranquility, as evidenced by the great numbers who seek escape from winter climates by traveling to regions nearer the equator. Also, bright light may lead to improvement in depressives who are experiencing primarily negative body symptoms rather than negative cognitive symptoms. That is, rather than dwelling on thoughts of feeling shunned, doomed, stupid, inferior, inadequate, etc., the SAD patient may be focusing on the somatic aspects of the disorder, that is, lethargy, spiritlessness, "paralysis of will." Light therapy, in some indirect fashion, might activate positive body sensations associated with feeling bubbly, zestful, radiant, spirited, and energetic.

SOMATIC-COGNITIVE INTERFACE IN DEPRESSION

For most, if not all, occurrences of depression, there is a very large psychological or cognitive component to the condition. This is true even though the vast majority of cases of clinical depression are managed solely with antidepressant medication. To patients, the ongoing painful nature of their condition—the deep lack of interest in family, friends, and work—and accompanying somatic symptoms is not only bewildering but also leads them to feel that their condition must be due to some brain dysfunction that is beyond their control or influence.

The key diagnostic symptoms of severe clinical depression, as outlined by the American Psychiatric Association (1987) are dysphoria and an inability to experience pleasure. The dysphoric mood is characterized by symptoms such as feeling sad, hopeless, low, down in the dumps, and irritable. In general, less severe forms of depression are dominated by cognitive symptoms while more severe occurrences of the condition are characterized by a perceived dominance of somatic symptoms, that is, fatigue, weight loss, insomnia.

Psychological models of depression focus on identifying characteristics of the depressive's beliefs, attitudes, and general thinking style which make them susceptible to episodes of depression symptoms. The symptoms, in effect, are the result of faulty patterns of thinking. These models place a greater emphasis on the conditions leading to depression rather than the conditions maintaining depression. Beck (1967) described the operation of a negative cognitive triad: negative views of the self, the world, and the future, as representative of thought content in depression. Further, Beck argued that the information processing of depressed individuals can be characterized as systematically biased in a negative direction. The model is typically presented as a diathesis-stress model, in which latent dysfunctional attitudes are triggered by distressing life events. That is, the dysfunctional thinking style remains inactive until certain negative event perceptions occur.

Some therapists recommend an A-B-C framework in which the beliefs at point B are seen to mediate the consequences (symptoms) at point C in response to a given situation or circumstance at point A. Most depressed individuals attribute their distress to some major, trait-like failing in themselves; that is, they appear to have an active depressotypic self-schema. In other patients, the patient's view of self may not be so negative but his or her view of the world is very bleak. In either case, the patient's expectations of securing the kinds of things from life that would be satisfying and fulfilling are negative.

The hopelessness theory of depression (Abramson, Metalsky & Alloy, 1989) posits that some occurrences of depression originate from (a) the individual's negative expectations regarding highly valued outcomes, combined with (b) expectations of helplessness about changing the likelihood of occurrence of these outcomes. Vulnerability to depression derives from this negative attributional style of explaining the causes of life events. The model of depression is depicted in Figure 5.3. Depression begins with the individual's perceived occurrence of negative life events or nonoccurrence of positive life events. Why and when do negative events such as failing an exam or breaking up a relationship lead to depression in some individuals and not others? According to the authors, there are three types of inferences that depression-prone people make that determine whether they develop a sense of hopelessness and accompanying symptoms of depression. First, they attribute the negative events to stable and global causes ("I failed because I am stupid") rather than unstable and specific causes ("I failed because I did not study the right material"). Second, they infer consequences of the negative event that lie outside the perceived causes. "For example, a student may attribute low scores on the Graduate Record Examination (GRE) to distracting noises in the testing room (an unstable, specific attribution), but infer that a consequence of the poor performance on the GRE is that he or she will never be admitted to a graduate program in mathematics . . ." (p. 361). Finally, there are, in addition to inferred

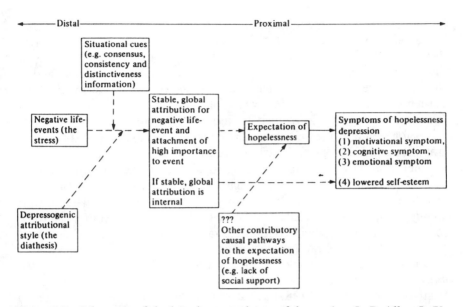

Figure 5.3. Schematic of the hopelessness theory of depression. L. B. Alloy, L. Y. Abramson, G. I. Metalsky, & S. Hartlage (1989). The hopelessness theory of depression: Attributional aspects. (British Journal of Clinical Psychology, 27, 5–21.) Reprinted by permission of the British Psychological Society and author.

consequences of negative events, also inferred characteristics of the self related to negative self-worth, undesirability, etc. The symptoms of depression, including motor retardation, sadness, lack of energy, and suicide represent the outcome of this central cognitive state of hopelessness. The authors also acknowledged that once a person becomes hopeless, it is possible that "some biological or psychological processes are triggered that need to run their course and do not dissipate as quickly as hopelessness."

A variant of the learned helplessness model has been used to explain why women are apparently more prone to depression than men. Studies of clinical depression report nearly twice as many women as men being diagnosed with depression. Community surveys also generally report a higher incidence of depression in women than men. Interestingly, studies based on college students have found no differences, leading to the suggestion that only women with "exceptionally good mental health" go to college while "men who go to college may be more representative of the mental health of men in general" (Nolen-Hoeksema, 1987). According to Nolen-Hoeksema (1987), women receive more "helplessness training" than men. Not only are they trained to be dependent on others, they are also denied the markers of success (promotion, salary) made available to men. Equally critical are differences in how men and women respond to their mood, when the feelings of depression are beginning. It is hypothesized that men, when depressed, tend to engage in activities designed to distract themselves from their mood ("I avoid thinking of reasons why I'm depressed," "I do something physical."). Women, when depressed, tend to be less active and to ruminate more about the possible causes of their mood and the implications of their depressive episodes ("I try to determine why I am depressed," "I cry to relieve the tension."). Women are more likely than men to blame themselves for feeling depressed. The more ruminative response style of women amplifies and prolongs their depressive symptoms.

Albert Ellis (1987), the founder of rational emotive therapy, hypothesized that depression-prone individuals engage in an absolute or necessitous form of thinking that he labeled "musturbation." To quote Ellis, "when people *merely* wish, prefer, or desire to achieve goals . . . and when they fail to do so and they think they will continue to fail, they will tend to feel distinctly . . . sad and regretful but *not* depressed. When, however, they consciously or unconsciously . . . convince themselves that they *should, ought, and must . . . achieve the success and approval they desire, they then* make themselves depressed" (1987, p. 123). In similar reasoning, Beck (1967) invoked the "tyranny of the shoulds" as contributing to depression. Brown and Beck (1989), however, were unable to detect differences in the frequency of scores on the "Shoulds Scale" between depressives, anxiety patients, and a psychiatric control group (patients with a diagnosis other than affective or anxiety disorder, e.g., personality disorders, sexual disorders). Items comprising the Shoulds Scale are presented in Table 5.1. The three groups exhibited similar average scores to the scale, suggesting to Beck that necessitous thinking is not specific to depression. It may also not be specific to psychiatric conditions.

Perfectionism represents a personality trait that is governed by a necessitous thinking style and excessive perfectionism and has been identi-

TABLE 5.1. Contents of the Shoulds Scale

If I try hard enough I should be able to excel at anything I attempt.
A person should try to be the best at everything he undertakes.
To be a good, moral, worthwhile person, I must help everyone who needs it.
I should always have complete control over my feelings.
I should be happy all the time.
I should be able to please everybody.
A person should do well at everything he undertakes.
I should set higher standards for myself than other people.
I ought to be able to solve my problems quickly and without a great deal of effort.
A person should be able to control what happens to him.

(Brown & Beck, 1989, p. 319)

ied as a source of depression and suicide in some college students (Halgin & Leahy, 1989). Perfectionists go beyond high achievement in their quest for excellence; their goals are set so high as to be unattainable, leaving them in a state of persistent dissatisfaction with themselves. Some authors have suggested that the perfectionism of some individuals evolves from interactions with perfectionist parents, "whose own self-esteem is contingent on the success of their children." In these cases, parents reinforce their child's desire for excellence in academic or social worlds while they react anxiously to failure, viewing it as a poor reflection on themselves. These children, in a desperate pursuit of parental love and acceptance, strive to be flawless. Perfectionist children, after performing in an outstanding manner, can conclude that they are okay and that they deserve to feel good. On the other hand, when they are less than perfect, they feel terrible. There are societal contributors to perfectionism as well—there is emphasis on perfectionism and achievement within education and there are also unrealistic models of "success" in the larger society.

Although the cognitive model of depression has intuitive appeal, researchers have had difficulty documenting a depressogenic attributional thinking style outside of the presence of depression. When depressed, individuals do report considerable negative thinking in their attitudes toward themselves, the present, and the future. These patterns of depressive thinking also increase the likelihood that depression will persist. Patterns of thinking during depression characterized by generalized hopelessness ("my future is bleak," "it's just not worth it") and global negative self-evaluation ("what's the matter with me?" "I'm worthless") were predictive of poor recovery (Dent & Teasdale, 1988). However, when in remission or symptom-free, depressives sometimes differ from normals in attributional styles and sometimes do not. Therefore, we cannot be certain that cognitive states like hopelessness are not simply symptoms rather than causes of depression. Dent & Teasdale postulated that the state of the information-processing system is affected by emotional state. With depression present, negative interpretations and memories become more active while positive interpretations and memories become less active. It is not clear what causes the initial shift toward depressive ideation.

In spite of the difficulty researchers have had documenting the existence of a pervasive depressogenic thinking style in depression-prone individuals, cognitive therapy remains a popular alternative to chemotherapy in the control of depression. Rather than work on the somatic symptoms, cognitive therapy is directed toward the negative and dysfunctional thinking style of the depressed patient (Beck, 1967). Two concepts necessary for understanding the rationale to cognitive therapy are *automatic thoughts* and *underlying assumptions*. Automatic thoughts are viewed as reflexive cognitions occurring in various situations. The thoughts are typically linked to affect and make sense in terms of a person's present affective state. The thoughts are not unconscious but rather operate from a "back-channel" of the stream of consciousness. Underlying assumptions are even less apparent to patients than automatic thoughts in the stream of consciousness and refer to more abstract views, attitudes, and principles that govern a person's behavior.

One of the first goals of cognitive therapy is to teach patients to identify and monitor automatic dysfunctional thoughts. Patients are seldom aware of having these thoughts unless they are taught to recognize them. The following example illustrates the power of automatic thoughts in controlling mood change and depression onset. The patient in question was experiencing what he thought was endogenous depression, a term which was initially used to describe depression due to biological events and which was also independent of precipitating life events.

> John, a mildly depressed 38-year-old married journalist, noticed that, the day before, he awoke "a bit less depressed" than usual, but soon his depression came back again, worse than ever. John thought that this was proof of the endogenous nature of his depression, because a previous psychiatrist had explained to him that sadness is at its worst, for "endogenous patients," early in the morning. During this assessment, John, trying to identify accurately the events that followed his "seemingly good" awakening the day before, was very sad and not much interested in the procedure. He thought that no "real illness" could be cured by talk. The therapist then asked whether his wife had gotten up before him or after him. Taking on a still gloomier look, John answered that she had gotten up after him. He said angrily that his wife completely disregarded his suffering, and that often, taking advantage of the fact that he arose earlier than usual ever since he got "sick," she would ask him to prepare breakfast! It was not hard to make John see that, as soon as he heard his wife saying "Now that you're up, dear, will you get breakfast ready?," his mood changed. He had become angry, just as he did now; he had started to think that his wife did not understand him and did not love him and *after that* he had become sad. (Guidano & Liotti, 1983, p. 176)

The automatic thoughts in this case are characterized by rejection, anger, and a feeling of being unloved.

The initial goal of cognitive therapy is to teach patients to recognize the presence of automatic thoughts. With practice and homework, patients can become quite effective at recognizing these thoughts as well as the connection between these thoughts and negative emotional reactions. Patients are also taught to examine the evidence supporting a particular negative thought ("She does not love me") as well as to explore alternative interpretations of particular events that make them feel depressed. They are also instructed in the use of more reasonable thoughts and, later in treatment, provided with guidance in identifying and modifying the underlying assumptions or beliefs that contribute to their depressogenic thinking style.

The "deeper" aspect of a patient's depressogenic cognitive makeup (i.e., underlying assumptions) can often be broached on a developmental basis with patients. In some instances the underlying assumption is a pervasive fear of loneliness which itself is avoided through hard struggle:

> If you try hard, if you are strong, if you have enough willpower, if you are nice and never get angry (a good person does not get angry), if you are long-suffering and sacrifice yourself for others, if you work hard, and if you love people then perhaps you will succeed in avoiding loneliness and misery. A generic feeling,"there's something wrong with me," and a remedy, "I have to fight my fate," become the foundations for building personal identity. (Guidano & Liotti, 1983, p. 191)

A further quote from patient John illustrates the early sense of loss and loneliness and also a connection between the innocent request from his wife, the elicitation of automatic thoughts, and the connection to underlying assumptions:

> My father was often away from home; he was a salesman and he had to travel a lot to other cities. No, I didn't resent his absence; you have to work to live, and life is so hard. . . . He was too tired to play with me when he was at home. . . . My mother was rigid; all she wanted was for me to be the best in class. . . . She used to say that life is full of difficulties, and you have to be very well prepared for them. . . . I can't forgive the way she behaved when my father grew old and had to retire; she refused to admit that he was really worn down, she wanted him to go on working, she forced him to work in the house, preparing meals and cleaning the floors . . . it was awful. (Guidano & Liotti, 1983, p. 188)

Cognitive therapy is widely considered to be equal if not more effective than drug therapy in the control of depression (Greenberg & Fisher, 1989). Overviews have shown that when placed side by side in the same studies, cognitive therapy has proved as successful as drug therapy in the alleviation of depression (Hollon, Shelton & Loosen, 1991). In a multicenter study, Elkin et al. (1989) compared the effectiveness of imipramine hydrochloride, a TCA, with cognitive and interpersonal therapy in the treatment of depression. A total of 250 patients with major depressive disorder were randomly assigned to one of four 16-week treatment conditions: cognitive therapy, interpersonal therapy, imipramine plus clinical management, and placebo plus clinical management. Cognitive therapy was based on providing patients with cognitive strategies and techniques designed to help correct negative distorted views about themselves, the world, and the future, and the underlying maladaptive beliefs that give rise to these cognitions. The interpersonal therapy concentrated on helping the patients better understand their own interpersonal problems and conflicts and developing more adaptive ways of relating to others. The clinical management component provided guidelines, not only for the management of medication and side effects and review of the patient's clinical status, but also for providing the patient with encouragement and support if necessary. The clinical management component approximated a "minimal supportive therapy" condition.

At the end of 16 weeks, all treatments, including the placebo plus clinical management condition, had led to improvement. The researchers found that the depressed patients responded equally to the drug treatment and the psychotherapy treatment. The order of treatments was quite consistent—with imipramine-clinical management doing best, placebo-clinical management doing worst, and the psychotherapies generally in between. Overall, the treatment group differences were not that large at the end of treatment. However, when the patients were regrouped on the basis of the severity of their depression some clear-cut differences emerged. When the patients were divided on the basis of pretreatment severity scores, imipramine appeared to be the most effective mode of treatment, with the two psychotherapies in between. The interpersonal therapy group actually did better than the cognitive therapy group.

An innovative aspect of this study was the inclusion of the clinical management component with both imipramine and placebo. The clinical management addition consisted of having the patients seen once a week for 20 to 30 minutes by a well-trained and experienced psychiatrist, who not only administered the medication and reviewed symptoms, side effects, and general functioning, but also offered support and encouragement. In the typical drug study, patients are given their coded capsules and sent home with no encouragement. The addition of this component likely enhanced the effectiveness of both imipramine and placebo and further explained the failure of the psychotherapies to show superiority over active drug treatment. It is significant that minimal supportive therapy and expectations regarding the medication, along with the generally supportive research and treatment environment, was sufficient for many patients to achieve a significant reduction in depressive symptoms.

A potential advantage to cognitive therapy is the expectation that successful application of the procedure would lead to removal of the conditions which render the individual susceptible to depression, thereby reducing the chances of relapse. Relapse is the major limitation of using medication alone to treat depression. According to Greenberg and Fisher (1989), the percentage of patients who improve in the long term following the use of antidepressant medications is quite low. They believe that antidepressant medications are far less potent in alleviating depressions than is generally assumed. Belsher and Costello (1988) reviewed the relapse literature and showed that approximately 50% of patients relapse within two years of recovery. Other researchers have noted that approximately two-thirds of depressed patients become symptomatic again during the first year after ceasing to take medication.

There are some data suggesting that cognitive therapy is more effective in preventing depression relapse. Blackburn, Eunson, and Bishop (1986) presented two-year follow-up results for patients with unipolar depression who had initially been assigned randomly for treatment with either cognitive psychotherapy or pharmacotherapy, or a combination of both therapies. Across the two-year period, the relapse rates were 23% for those treated with cognitive therapy, 21% for those treated with cognitive therapy and drug therapy, and 78% for those treated with drug therapy alone. After reviewing a number of additional studies which have examined this question, Hollon et al. (1991) concluded that cognitive therapy does seem to protect the patient against relapse of depression. They pointed out, however, that the studies supporting this conclusion have not followed patients beyond two years and what may have been demonstrated is a short-term advantage of cognitive therapy over prematurely-terminated chemotherapy. Studies which have continued patients on medication beyond the standard four to eight weeks have demonstrated much lower rates of remission. Kupfer and Frank (1987) presented some initial data suggesting that relapse rates can be held to less than 10%, four months after recovery, if a combined treatment consisting of psychotherapy, an educational workshop, and medication is administered. When advocating drug therapy and cognitive therapy combination treatments, it is necessary to remain sensitive to the difficulty patients often have in attributing treatment gains to their own efforts and not the drug. Effective medication fading procedures need to be incorporated into combined drug and psychological treatments to help minimize faulty attributional judgments and maximize patients' sense of personal mastery (Greenberg & Fisher, 1989). Patients accustomed to using drugs are often unwilling to consider functioning without their use, leading to a lifetime dependence on the drug.

DRUG ADDICTION AND CRAVING

Prolonged psychoactive drug use often leads to new problems that were not foreseen in the initial use of the drug. Whether initial use was medical or recreational, addictive behaviors associated with drug use may develop. These behaviors are set apart from other behaviors by the individual's overwhelming involvement and fear of having to live without continued drug self-administration (Donovan, 1988). From a psychobiologic perspective drug use resembles a form of upward rather than downward determinism, as individuals appear to have no self-control over their actions. In cases of addiction, strong overpowering cravings seem to dominate the individual's existence to the point that all other sources of reward are abandoned in favor of gratifying the addictive behavior. Current models of addiction recognize that such cravings are more than biologically determined and depend to a significant extent on a multiple of factors, including the person's psychological makeup (mood states, personality, expectations about the drug effects), the environment, and values and morals reflected in the larger society.

One of the more significant developments in current addictions writings is the recognition of commonalities across addictive behaviors. Whether the problem is one of excessive eating, drug use, gambling, or other behaviors, there are important similarities in the phenomenological states and controlling conditions of the addictions involved. Donovan outlined a number of communalities across addictive behaviors that are important for our discussion:

1. the addictive experience represents a powerful and immediate technique for changing one's mood and sensations;
2. changes in arousal associated with stress, pain, or negative moods (depression, boredom) tend to increase the likelihood of the addictive behavior;
3. both classical and instrumental conditioning contribute to the addictive process;
4. the addictive experience, although providing the individual with a degree of control over his/her immediate subjective experience (i.e., increased positive mood, decreased negative mood), is associated with addictive behaviors that are excessive and beyond control. These aspects of addiction taken together are known as the "paradox of control."
5. relapse following treatment is very common with all addictive behaviors and is under the control of individual, situational, and physiological factors;
6. addiction is not inherently related to a given drug; thus substitution of one drug (e.g., alcohol) for another drug (e.g., cocaine) may lead to a relapse in the use of the first drug and/or addiction to the second drug. It is the person who becomes addicted, and the addictive experience may be associated with a number of drugs;
7. in spite of high relapse rates, a number of individuals do overcome their addictions without professional assistance. There are known

stages through which these individuals progress on their way to recovery.

Dual System Model of Addiction

Why is it that drugs are so powerful in their dependence capabilities? Why is it so difficult for addicts to discontinue chemical use? Early efforts to answer these questions focused primarily on the negative aspects associated with physical dependence on a drug, that is, addicts use drugs in order to avoid the negative withdrawal symptoms of not taking the drugs. Ignored in this explanation is the fact that many addicts use drugs simply for the powerful pleasure-producing qualities. Anecdotal support for this view is provided by addicts themselves:

> Everything is about getting high and any means to get there becomes rational. . . . if it means stealing something from somebody close to you, lying to your family, borrowing money from people you can't pay back, writing checks that you can't cover, it doesn't matter as long as you can get high. . . . if you are sitting around a table with others freebasing and one falls on the floor and dies you don't call for help because that's more cocaine for the rest of you.

It is evident that the pleasure-producing as well as the negative-reducing capabilities of drugs must have a physiological substrate. Current thinking holds that the effects of a number of addictive drugs, including amphetamine, cocaine, opiates, barbiturates, alcohol, nicotine, and caffeine are mediated by common brain mechanisms (Wise, 1988). The conditioning concepts of positive reinforcement and negative reinforcement were utilized by Wise to explain different underlying mechanisms associated with the ability of some drugs to produce positive effects and the ability of other drugs to reduce negative effects. As defined by Wise, "positive reinforcement is any stimulus that brings pleasure or euphoria to a subject who is already in a normal mood state." Negative reinforcement, on the other hand, refers to a stimulus that terminates or ends distress and returns a subject to a normal mood state. Opiates and other addictive drugs are known to have effects on both positive and negative reinforcement, with each type of reinforcement being controlled by different brain mechanisms.

Positive reinforcement is believed to be mediated by dopamine systems in the medial forebrain bundle and the midbrain region of the substantia nigra. The median forebrain bundle is a large bundle of fibers that courses through the lateral hypothalamus and innervates a number of structures. It is recognized as being involved in mediating the reinforcing effects of brain stimulation at some sites. The ventral tegmentum and associated substantia nigra are midbrain nuclei that are part of the brain dopamine system (Figure 5.4).

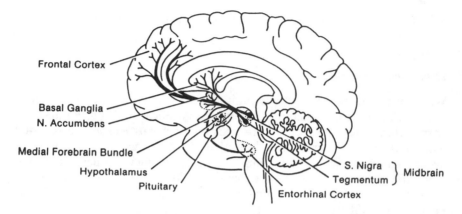

Figure 5.4. Dopamine systems in the brain. William A. McKim, *Drugs and behavior: An introduction to behavioral pharmacology,* **2e, c1991, p. 257. Reprinted by permission of Prentice Hall, Englewood Cliffs, New Jersey.**

The nucleus acumbens is considered to be the center of the dopamine circuit, and if these neurons are removed in animals, drugs such as amphetamine become less rewarding. The brain dopamine system is not associated with dependence or withdrawal symptoms following a direct opiate injection. Injections of opiates in areas believed to be involved in negative reinforcement, specifically the periventricular gray matter, are associated with dependence and withdrawal symptoms. The periventricular gray matter is the portion of brain tissue surrounding the ventricles containing the cerebrospinal fluid. Evidence in support of a link between opiates, negative reinforcement, and the periaqueductal gray comes from work studying social distress. Opiates reduce social isolation distress cries in animals and opiate antagonists produce such cries even in animals that are not socially isolated. Thus the periaqueductal gray is a likely candidate for the site at which opiates can have negative reinforcing actions relating to "psychological pain" as well as physiological pain and withdrawal distress.

The implications of this model for understanding cravings are as follows: First, the mechanisms for the drug's ability to produce positive reinforcement are distinct from the drug's ability to produce negative reinforcement. The positive reinforcing effects of ventral tegmental opiate injections alone are capable of maintaining drug use and self-administration habits that define psychological dependence in the absence of any withdrawal distress or obvious source of pain or discomfort. The positive reinforcing nature of some addictive drugs is often underestimated. Studies have shown, for example, that the craving for self-administration of synthetic cocaine is strong enough that animals will under certain conditions starve to death rather than give up the opportunity for more administration. Second, there is a basis for postulating the existence of common mechanisms underlying both positive and negative reinforcing effects across a number of addictive drugs. As mentioned previously, it is known that a number of addictive substances have similar reinforcing effects and the dual system model points to a common biological mechanism for these effects:

> Opiates and cocaine activate the same neural circuitry, and either drug will be a stimulant to reestablish drug taking in ex-addicts who are currently drug free. That is, a detoxified heroin addict is at significant risk from cocaine as well as from heroin; a detoxified cocaine user is at risk from "recreational use" of heroin as well as from recreational use of cocaine. This is widely assumed by clinicians, and many rehabilitation programs require total drug abstention as a condition of treatment. The possibility that nicotine, alcohol, and even caffeine may activate the same neural circuitry suggests other drug stimuli that may put an ex-addict at risk. (Wise, 1988, p. 125)

The intrinsic positive and negative reinforcing powers of addictive drugs make it easier to understand the power these systems acquire over the individual's thoughts, feelings, and behaviors. According to Ludwig (1988), in such instances the brain becomes an "organ of rationalization rather than of rationality." Because the individual has to live with an addicted biology, his mind tries to legitimize his intentions and behaviors so that he need not feel guilty. Ludwig gave examples of the thinking styles of addicts within the context of several themes or "scripts" which represent rationalizations to justify intense cravings:

> With the *escape script,* individuals wish to avoid the discomfort aroused by unpleasant situations, conflicts, or memories. Failure, rejection, disappointment, hurt, humiliation, embarrassment, discontent, or sadness all tend to demand relief. Rather than openly confront a critical employer or unappreciative spouse, endure boredom and frustration, or lie awake at night worrying, individuals only want to eliminate their misery. . . . It is not necessarily intoxication they want. They only want numbness, the absence of problems, and peace.
>
> Yvonne portrayed this type of thinking well, shortly after the breakup with her boyfriend. She had known the rift was coming, but still it was a shock. For the first couple of days after it happened, she numbly went about her business, forcing herself to cope, but then difficulty with sleeping started and one morning she awoke just wanting to scream. On that particular morning, she finished in the bathroom, put a kettle of water on the stove, and then wandered into the pantry, aimlessly searching about. But for what?
>
> 'God, I'm pissed,' she muttered silently to herself. 'After all I did for the bastard. You can't trust any man. They're all shits. How could I be so dumb . . . so naive . . . so idiotic? It's just not worth it, staying sober. For what? . . .'

She stood on the stool and, apparently without awareness, reached toward the back of the shelf for the bottle of gin that had been stashed away there some time ago,

'I need a martini . . . something,' a voice inside of her declared. 'Something powerful . . . strong and fast. I need to stop thinking about this . . . and go blotto. It's driving me crazy. . . . So what if I take a drink, maybe two. Nobody really cares anyway.' (p. 21)

Other scripts used by addicts involve needing a drink/drug to relax, to socialize, or to find romance. One script focuses on the sensual and pleasurable aspects of the alcohol itself, the "smooth, silky flow of liquid down one's throat." A young construction worker described by Ludwig gave up drinking with his buddies after work because of the difficulties it caused with his wife and previous job. He took considerable ribbing from his buddies so on one occasion decided to join them solely for the social interaction. He had a few sodas and no strong craving for alcohol. However, his wife expressed displeasure at this activity. On a future occasion, however, he was not to be so lucky:

And then one very hot, muggy day after work, when he was feeling thirsty and irritable, he took one sip of the coke and found himself sickened by it. 'Ugh, it's sweet,' he muttered to himself, and watched the other fellows happily guzzling their beer. But for some reason, this time the desire to join the others in a beer was compelling. 'Not that I crave it,' he told himself, 'but just for the taste and to be social. Beside, it wasn't beer that got me in trouble last time, it was the booze. I always could handle beer.' (p. 28)

We see in these individuals how thoughts and feelings surrounding drug use can be influenced if not determined by bodily changes and also how difficult it must be to maintain abstinence in the presence of these changes. Although the addict's thoughts and feelings are not solely the result of underlying biologic processes, we can see the power of the positive reward system and can understand why many addicts believe in the positive outcomes of drug use, ranging from enhanced positive moods, and increased social interaction and intimacy, as well as increased cognitive function and creativity (Donovan, 1988).

The treatment implication of the dual system model of addictions is obvious: programs must be designed to deal not only with the withdrawal symptoms of addictions but also the positive reinforcing capabilities of drugs. The problem of drug craving is a "dual" biological problem and depends as much on the biology of positive reinforcement as on the biology of withdrawal symptoms and one that is likely to depend on the biology of memories of past reinforcements as on the biology of drug-produced physiochemical changes.

If drugs of abuse activate positive reinforcement mechanisms directly and centrally, they may do so with much greater intensity than can ever be summoned by environmental stimuli like food, water, or the reinforcing beauty of nature, art, or music. Whereas the signals from natural reinforcers depend on sensory transducers and the propagation of nerve impulses across axons and synaptic junctions, drugs can activate reinforcement mechanisms centrally, saturating receptor mechanisms that may never be saturated as a consequence of natural reinforcement. Modern technology—involving the refinement and synthesis of drugs and their administration in high purity and concentration, directly into the blood supply—may allow us increasing capability to develop reinforcers with greater potency than the biologically significant stimuli of food, fluids, and sex partners. To the degree that drug reinforcers compete successfully with more natural reinforcers, they constitute a serious risk to health and to social institutions as we know them. They have the potential to seduce us from what is good for us. . . . (Wise, 1988, p. 127)

Alcoholism, Personality, and Brain Mechanisms

A model of alcoholism that parallels to some extent positive and negative reward systems has been developed by Cloninger (1987). He proposed that different brain systems are at the basis of certain personality attributes which themselves may, under appropriate circumstances, contribute to alcoholism. There are two personality or temperament types which lead to two general subgroups of alcoholics, labeled as Type 1 and Type 2 (Table 5.2). Type 1 alcoholics are late-onset alcoholics and engage in very little spontaneous drinking or aggressive behavior when drinking. They are dependent individuals, experience considerable fear and guilt, and would use alcohol as a means of reducing harm avoidance (negative reinforcement). Type 2 alcoholics develop alcoholism early and have a tendency to engage in persistent alcohol-seeking and aggressive behavior, analogous to a form of self-stimulation (positive reinforcement). Most alcoholics have some features of both types. He hypothesized that women tend to develop loss of control (Type 1) alcoholism with later onset and associated guilt and depression. Men, on the other hand, are more prone to exhibit the characteristics of Type 2 alcoholism—fighting when drinking, arrests for reckless driving, and inability to abstain before age of 25. The Type 1 alcoholic-prone individual would have a personality characterized by personality/temperament features of hypervigilance, apprehension, and anticipatory worrying. In contrast, Type 2 alcoholic-prone individuals would be inattentive, distractible, impulsive, and easily bored.

Cloninger believes that there is a genetic basis to his proposed personality-alcoholism link. He reported that alcoholism is three to five times

TABLE 5.2. Defining Features of Type 1 and Type 2 Alcoholics (adapted from Cloninger, 1987).

Characteristic features	Types of alcoholism	
	Type 1	Type 2
Alcohol related problems		
Usual age of onset	After 25	Before 25
Spontaneous alcohol seeking	Infrequent	Frequent
Fighting and arrests when drink-ing	Infrequent	Frequent
Psychological dependence (loss of control)	Frequent	Infrequent
Guilt and fear about alcohol de-pendence	Frequent	Infrequent

as frequent in the parents, siblings, and children of alcoholics as in the general population. This conclusion was based on a large-scale adoption study in Sweden, which examined over 1,700 individuals who were born to single women and adopted by nonrelatives at an early age. In Sweden extensive centralized medical, criminal, and personal records are kept on the entire population. All instances of insobriety resulting in legal, family, medical, or personal difficulties are recorded by a Temperance Board. By using the extensive information available, he was able to classify the biologic parent, given that alcoholism was present, as Type 1 or Type 2. He found that both genetic predisposition and life circumstance were necessary if the adopted-away sons were to express susceptibility to loss-of-control (Type 1) alcoholism. Thus, genetic predisposition or a provocative postnatal environment, but not both, did not increase the risk of alcoholism in the adoptees. If both occurred in the same person, the risk of severe alcohol abuse was more than doubled. In contrast, in adopted-away sons of fathers with spontaneous alcohol-seeking characteristics (Type 2), the risk of alcoholism increased regardless of environmental background. In these families the risk of alcohol abuse in the adopted-away sons of type 2 alcoholic fathers was nine times that in the sons of all other fathers.

The daughters of Type 1 alcoholics were at increased risk, largely because the mothers of these individuals were often alcohol abusers. The daughters of Type 2 alcoholics were not at increased risk for alcoholism and for this reason Type 2 alcoholism was called "male-limited." In summary, this study showed that men and women do not exhibit the same patterns of abuse; at least one form of alcohol abuse is inheritable and found exclusively in men; daughters of alcoholic mothers are particularly susceptible regardless of the presence of abuse in fathers; environmental factors are significantly associated with the most common type of alcohol abuse. These data may or may not be representative of other populations.

Personality attributes associated with Type 2 alcoholism are hypothesized to be related to self-stimulation and the dopaminergic system. Individuals with a predisposition to alcohol-seeking behavior may have a greater dopaminergic response to alcohol. Type 1 alcoholics, on the other hand, are hypothesized to have an inheritable tendency to respond intensely to aversive stimuli, thereby facilitating learning to inhibit behavior in order to avoid punishment, anxiety, and frustrated omission of expected rewards.

Although certain inherited behavioral dispositions may be necessary components of vulnerability, it is unlikely that these behaviors in infancy are sufficient by themselves to cause substance abuse in adulthood. Many intervening factors undoubtedly play important roles in influencing the ultimate likelihood of an adverse outcome, for example, parental rearing style, peer influence. learned habit patterns of coping, and cultural and social sanctions. Where alcohol is prohibited, such as in certain Moslem nations, there is little alcoholism. It appears that the inheritability risk factor for alcoholism is best viewed, along the lines proposed by Cloninger, as a behavior-genetic vulnerability factor. Traits such as heightened activity level, high emotionality, reduced attention span-persistence, low sociability, and low "soothability" have been identified by a number of writers (Tarter & Edwards, 1986). Thus, the child with poor emotional and behavioral regulation is particularly inclined to develop a personality disorder; this personality disposition is associated with an increased risk for alcoholism. Children who by temperament are highly active, for example, are more likely to have mothers who are submissive. Also, sons of alcoholic fathers more frequently experience physical and sexual abuse and suffer the various adverse consequences of living in a family with chronic discord. In such families the use of punishment legitimizes and reinforces aggressive (Type 2) behavior in the child.

CLASSICAL CONDITIONING, DRUG TOLERANCE, AND WITHDRAWAL

All addictions programs recognize the power environmental cues have in contributing to the craving experience and potential drug use. It is instructive, in this regard, to examine some basic animal research which demonstrated the very significant influence of environmental factors in the development, maintenance, and treatment of addictive behaviors. The two most important characteristics of addictive behaviors and long-term drug use are tolerance and dependence. Drug tolerance may be defined as a state of progressively decreasing responsiveness to a drug. A person who develops tolerance requires a larger dose of the drug in order to achieve the effect originally obtained by a smaller dose. For example, the analgesic effects of heroin, the motor discoordination caused by alcohol, and the appetite-suppressing quality of amphetamines all diminish with repeated drug usage, such that more of a drug must be taken each time to achieve the same level of effect.

Drug dependence is a different phenomenon. Drug dependence has been defined as a "syndrome in which the use of a drug is given a much higher priority than other behaviors that once had higher value. The existence of drug dependence varies along a continuum and the term "addiction" is usually reserved for severe instances of dependence (Jaffe, 1990). Physical dependence refers to an altered physiological state which is produced by the repeated administration of the drug to prevent the occurrence of the withdrawal or abstinence syndrome that is characteristic of the drug. It is assumed that prolonged drug use leads to a form of "latent counteradaptation" in the nervous system which becomes manifest in the form of rebound or overshoot phenomena when the drugs are stopped or an antagonist is administered. For example, the long-term use of morphine may lead to a compensatory increase in cyclic AMP which would lead to the rebound excitability of neurons in the locus ceruleus during opioid withdrawal (Jaffe, 1990).

The counteradaptational processes that eventually produce observable withdrawal symptoms begin with the first dose. Thus, it is possible that the use of short-acting drugs to induce euphoria or reduce tensions can result in relative dysphoria or an exacerbation of these same tensions as the drug effects wane. The rise in unpleasant feelings may then lead to continued use of the drug. The relationships between drug tolerance, dependence, and addiction are extremely complex and likely to include variables beyond the drug-produced physiological changes. Jaffe (1990) described the withdrawal or abstinence syndrome associated with morphine as follows:

> About 12 to 14 hours after the last dose, the addict may fall into a tossing, restless sleep that may last several hours but from which he awakens more restless and more miserable than before. As the syndrome progresses, additional signs and symptoms appear, consisting of dilated pupils, anorexia, gooseflesh, restlessness, irritability, and tremor. With morphine and heroin, nonpurposive symptoms reach their peak at 48 to 72 hours. As the syndrome approaches peak intensity, the patient exhibits increasing irritability, insomnia, marked anorexia, violent yawning, severe sneezing, lacrimation, and coryza. Weakness and depression are pronounced. Nausea and vomiting are common, as are intestinal spasm and diarrhea. Heart rate and blood pressure are elevated. Marked chilliness, alternating with flushing and excessive sweating, is characteristic. Pilomotor activity resulting in waves of gooseflesh is

prominent, and the skin resembles that of a plucked turkey. This feature is the basis of the expression "cold turkey" to signify abrupt withdrawal without treatment. Abdominal cramps and pains in the bones and muscles of the back and extremities are also characteristic, as are the muscle spasms and kicking movements that may be the basis for the expression "kicking the habit." The respiratory response to CO_2, which is decreased during opioid administration, is exaggerated during withdrawal. (p. 534)

The term "psychologic dependence" is often used to separate the environmental and behavioral influences of dependence from the physiological processes which determine dependence. There is some evidence, however, that the psychological and physiological determinants of dependence are closely connected. These connections were demonstrated by Siegel (1979) using the classical conditioning paradigm. Within his model, the drug administration procedure, the drug itself, and the accompanying drug-produced changes are analyzed within a conditioning framework. The drug constitutes the unconditioned stimulus (UCS) and the drug-produced physiologic changes the unconditioned response (UCR). The conditioned stimulus (CS) consists of stimuli regularly associated with drug administration, such as the setting, sight of the needle, thoughts of drug use, etc.

The key to understanding a conditioning explanation of drug tolerance and drug withdrawal is the concept of the conditioned compensatory response. Repeated drug use is associated with two opposing responses, the drug response and an opposite competing response. When a drug is first used, as shown in Figure 5.5, the drug's effect is solely the result of drug-produced changes (UCRs). With repeated administration, the compensatory response, which is also the conditioned response (CR), begins to develop. In this instance, the CR is opposite in direction to the UCR. With repeated administrations, the drug-compensatory response gains in strength and eventually rivals the drug-produced UCR, with the net effect being a very small drug effect or even a drug effect in opposite direction to the UCR. The development of the conditioned compensatory response constitutes drug tolerance.

Drug dependence within this model constitutes the occurrence of a full-blown compensatory response in the absence of a drug-produced response. The usual drug cues associated with the compensatory response are not counteracted by actual drug administration. Siegel acknowledged that for this model to work, responses indicative of withdrawal need be opposite in direction of the responses produced by the drug. This is apparently the case for the opiates. Many of the symptoms of opiate administration (hypotension, hyperthermia, contraction of pupils, relaxation, analgesia)

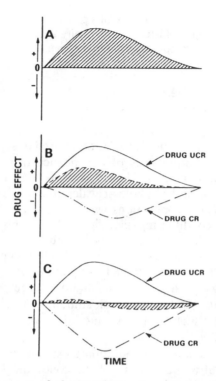

Figure 5.5. Development of the conditioned compensatory response (Siegel, 1979). Reprinted by permission of Academic Press.

are opposite the effects noted when the drug is withdrawn (hypertension, hypothermia, dilatation of pupils, anxiety/insomnia, pain).

Withdrawal symptoms associated with drug craving are to a large extent under the control of environmental cues that have been associated with drug use. It is widely recognized that the sight of drug paraphernalia, friends using drugs, money, and even thoughts and talk of drug use are capable of eliciting powerful withdrawal cravings. A treatment implication of this model is that drug abstinence, in the presence of cues other than those associated with the drug, would not be an effective therapeutic procedure for the treatment of drug-dependence. For example, placing an individual in a "detoxification" center should not necessarily alter the connection between previous drug cues and the drug-compensatory CRs. Most treatment programs now recognize the withdrawal-producing potential of environmental cues associated with addictive drug use and efforts are made to extinguish the withdrawal responses in the presence of these cues.

RELAPSE PREVENTION MODEL

All treatment programs concerned with addictive behaviors are plagued by high relapse rates. Relapse rates for the addictions are cited as being in the range of 50% to 90%; such rates are based on clinical populations and it may be that persons who attempt change on their own are more successful. Recognition that return to substance abuse is the rule rather than the exception has led to some significant alterations in treatment approaches. Instead of examining preexisting personality/motivational variables that might predict resumption of addictive behavior, the focus is on events contributing to postcessation drug cravings and use. What happens after treatment has ended is seen as having a greater impact in determining outcome than what happens during the treatment phase. Posttreatment factors such as the patient's emotional/coping style, employment/living environment, and social support are seen as critical determinants of the patient's ability to maintain and strengthen postcessation changes. So important are these parameters to successful outcome that their omission would be seen as a sign of a treatment program doomed to failure.

The most influential approach is the relapse prevention model of Marlatt and colleagues (Marlatt & Gordon, 1985; Brownell et al., 1986). Marlatt makes a distinction between "lapse," which is an initial return to drug use, and "relapse," which is a full return to drug use. "When a slip or mistake is defined as a lapse, it implies that corrective action can be taken, not that control is lost completely." Traditional thinking on the dangers of relapse is similar to the analogy of a person standing at the edge of a cliff where "the slightest disruption can precipitate a fall from which there is no return." The relapse prevention model assumes that lapses do occur and that the addict needs to recognize and regulate high-risk situations that contribute to their occurrence. Research on the determinants of relapse suggests that stressful life events during the postcessation interval increase the likelihood of resumption of drug use. Relapse prevention consists of providing patients with the appropriate *intrapersonal* and *interpersonal* skills to minimize the impact of lapses and thereby prevent full-blown relapses.

Inpatient/outpatient relapse prevention programs utilize a variety of behavioral strategies for dealing with high-risk situations. For many individuals, high risks include negative emotions associated with stress, depression and anxiety, situations associated with drug use, and thoughts and feelings associated with craving and withdrawal. The variables deemed important by Marlatt are typically presented within a skill learning therapy framework and include the following topics (Monti et al., 1989):

1. Managing thoughts about alcohol
2. Awareness of anger and anger management

3. Relaxation and imagery techniques
4. Cue exposure
5. Enhancing social support networks
6. Planning for emergencies

Learning to recognize and alter alcohol-related thoughts is a most difficult challenge, especially in the initial days of drying out. Being dry refers to stopping drinking and eliminating alcohol from one's system but does not mean being committed to this forever. Being sober refers to the substitution of a more positive frame of mind and lifestyle for that associated with drinking. Only a small percentage of alcoholics experiences delirium tremens or D.T.s (hallucinations, confusion, seizures). The vast majority of alcoholics experience less serious withdrawal symptoms, including irritability, morning sweats, or just feeling lousy. This period represents a dangerous time as susceptibility to relapse is very high.

Surviving detoxification is only the beginning of the struggle. Individuals can remain irritable, restless, and depressed for up to four to six months and can have difficulty sleeping and thinking for up to a year. It is not surprising that their thoughts are so vulnerable to alcohol and other drug use during this period. Alcoholics often attempt to fight their cravings head-on, with what is called counterpoint thinking. That is they try to use mental energy to block the unwanted thoughts related to drug use. Unfortunately, this strategy often fuels and strengthens the very unwanted thoughts:

One alcoholic I interviewed prayed fervently, day and night, for strength to resist the urge. Another would meditate, argue with himself, eat honey, take a hot bath, jog, start making phone calls to friends, try to read, or smoke incessantly when he was by himself in an effort to keep the tempting thought from taking possession of his mind. While deliberate distraction may successfully keep the urge at bay, it unfortunately reinforces the notion that there is something to be frightened about. This, in turn, paradoxically gives even greater power to the unwanted thought. (Ludwig, 1988, p. 98)

There are more successful strategies for altering craving-related thoughts without directly blocking their presence. One strategy is "playing the script out" by first imagining how nice it would be to have a drink followed by imagining how rotten it will feel afterwards. Other strategies include shifting thoughts to activities other than drinking:

Some clients and clinicians find imagery exercises to be a potent force in controlling thoughts and urges to drink. A client who feels that he/she is about to be overwhelmed or engulfed by urges to drink can be helped by imagining scenes that portray urges to drink as storms that will end with calmness, mountains that can be climbed, or waves that can be ridden. Every client can find a personal image to help him/her maintain control until the urge peaks and then dissipates. Other useful images include being a warrior or explorer who can "slice through" urges (e.g., the enemy, the thick tropical underbrush) and carve out a path to safety. Images can be made more vivid by using relaxation techniques and by referring to all the senses (e.g., seeing the thick green jungle, hearing the sword swishing through the leaves, smelling the tropical plants, etc.). (Monti et al., 1989, p.82)

Alcoholics also tend to focus on the immediate positive aspects of drinking and to ignore the longer-term negative consequences of drinking. This may be all the more likely in high-risk situations. Thoughts about the positive effects of drinking enable alcoholics to rationalize their decision to drink, since the short-term "pros" of drinking usually appear to outweigh the long-term "cons" of drinking. Alcoholics are taught to catch themselves thinking about the positive consequences of drinking ("One little drink will help me relax at this party") and substitute a more balanced viewpoint for decision-making ("Stop! Remember the last time I got drunk, I punched someone out . . .").

Awareness and sharing of inner feelings is also a common objective of drug abuse programs (Vos, 1989). Quite often drug addicts have developed a negative self-image and difficulty in expressing inner emotional conflicts. They have a strong tendency to underestimate themselves and an overwhelming feeling of not being recognized as individuals with unique feelings and thoughts. Self-destructive tendencies may need to be recognized and altered before significant behavioral changes can occur. Some alcoholics, for example, experienced considerable rejection and aggression in childhood and learned to protect themselves against such events by believing that they are themselves to blame. In this way, they are able to believe that the parents actually loved them and things were not as bad as they seemed. Freeing themselves from such a past is associated with considerable pain, rage, and fear. However, by experiencing these emotions in a therapeutic environment, the patient learns to integrate the past into his/her present personality and begin developing a positive self-identity. Clinically, drug addicts must develop a strong sense that they can cope with life's demands without having to drink—what has been called a sense of self-efficacy. Alcoholics, in the early stages of treatment, often have high confidence that they will never drink again, only to have this confidence shattered upon returning to their natural environment.

Recognizing the role of situational or environmental cues is also important in recovery from drug use. Regardless of the addict's original reasons for drug use, the drug use eventually takes on a life of its own. We demonstrated the power of environmental cues with Siegel's (1979) conditioned compensatory response model. Addicts themselves are well aware of situational determinants of drug cravings:

> It's just like I guess an alcoholic who has to walk down the street and pass a bar without getting a craving for a drink. Drugs are everywhere, especially areas where I live and the areas I have to travel through. You have people standing on the corner selling drugs openly; if you drive by, they stop your car and offer you various things. You're approached sometimes with free drugs. They try to scare you into a situation where something is going to trigger you and get you started again. There are a lot of triggers . . . a sum of money . . . if you get your hands on $50.00 at one time, that's a hit. . . . other things like the paraphernalia involved . . . the smell of matches that you use when freebasing, or if someone lights a cigarette around you, you might start thinking about getting high.

Ludwig (1988) noted that there is a high degree of individuality associated with drug cues. Alcoholics who were asked to pinpoint conditions under which cravings appeared described inner tension, including nervousness, shakiness, and irritability, as the most common trigger for drinking. Specific cues were not mentioned by the majority of subjects, although some alcoholics identified social events, hot weather activities, and even taking a bath as problematic. The heavier the reported drinking, the greater the number of situations in which it was reported to occur.

A technique specifically designed to break the connection between environmental cues and cravings is called *cue exposure therapy*. The technique is designed to help addicts who have gone through detoxification to resist drug use outside the hospital. The therapy is based on extinction theory—that, by presenting drug cues which are not followed by drugs, the cues will lose their craving value. A dramatic variant of this approach was popular in the 1950s and was based on aversive conditioning rather than extinction. Succinylcholine was administered by intravenous drip to alcoholics immediately after letting them handle, sniff, and taste their preferred alcoholic beverage. This induced a sudden respiratory paralysis along with a smothering feeling and a sensation of dying. Although this conditioning created a number of distressing symptoms in the presence of alcohol, it did not in the long run stop the individual from drinking. The technique does not control for the many cues in the alcoholic's natural environment that contribute to alcohol consumption. Antabuse (disulfiram) is another of the aversive techniques whereby alcoholics are required to ingest the substance daily. Antabuse prevents the metabolism of alcohol and leads to a rapid buildup of acetaldehyde. In the absence of alcohol, Antabuse produces few effects in the body. However, following alcohol ingestion, the individual experiences a number of severe symptoms, including throbbing headache, nausea, and vomiting. The problem with this form of treatment is that it does not remove the urge to drink and sooner or later the alcoholic will discontinue its use.

With cue exposure therapy, the goal is to initially help addicts recognize the connection between environmental cues and cravings and then devise strategies to weaken the connections (Monti et al., 1989). One of the main problems in treating addicts is having them recognize a need for this type of therapy. After detoxification, many people feel great and are naive about the scope of their problem in that they feel that once they have cleared themselves of the drug they have cleared themselves of the problem. The value of this concept is that it brings to the addict's attention the role of environmental stimuli in maintaining drug use. During cue exposure treatment sessions, stimuli which are frequently associated with drug use are presented in the absence of drugs. It is unknown whether the extinction of cravings which takes place during clinical sessions generalizes to the addict's natural environment. The clinical procedure also involves having addicts avoid cues that are high in risk or providing them with alternative activities for high-risk times of day. Its success as a technique likely depends on how well the addict is able to cope with the other multiple determinants of drug use.

Interpersonal factors are also considered a major determinant of relapse. Absence of appropriate social skills may restrict an individual's alternatives in a social situation and also decrease the likelihood of obtaining social and emotional support from others that may be necessary to maintain abstinence. Social anxiety, for example, may prevent the individual from feeling comfortable socially without alcohol or some other drug present in his/her system. Many therapists believe that addicts need instruction in problem-solving and social skills more than traditional psychotherapy. Addicts themselves often reject psychotherapy and are more comfortable with programs which strengthen their skills in areas of money management, education, parent/child relationships, parenting skills, recreational activities, emotional control, and communication (Stark, 1989).

Given the multitude of factors that determine drug addiction, it is understandable why relapse prevention is itself a high-risk endeavor.

Imagine a person in a high state of distress because of a recent marital argument and pressure at work. The individual attends a party where the expectations are to relax and enjoy. Several of his/her friends are already drinking and having a good time (modeling influences). Coping will be determined by the individual's general and specific coping skills and self-efficacy expectations. Self-efficacy percepts will be influenced by the individual's current stress level and history of coping in similar situations. The individual's expectations about the short- and long-term effects on behavior will also be important. That is, the individual may emphasize the immediate positive outcome expectations of the effects of alcohol (e.g., relaxation and euphoria) while ignoring the longer-term negative consequences (e.g., hangover, depression, accidents). If drinking is initiated, various actual reinforcing effects of alcohol may come into play. In sum, a combination of social learning, situational, cognitive, and biological/psychophysiological factors will interact with one another. (Monti et al., 1989, p.10)

Although the challenges facing recovering addicts are enormous, there are a number of successful programs to which they can turn for assistance.

6
Pain

COMPLEXITY OF PAIN

Survey data would suggest that just about everyone is at risk of developing a pain problem during the course of a lifetime. Surveys have reported between 55%–60% of adult Americans describe themselves as experiencing back pain one or more days during the year (Fordyce, 1988). Migraine headache, chronic daily headache, and abdominal pain are also known to occur with a very high incidence and to cause enormous financial, emotional, and interpersonal costs to those afflicted. The magnitude of the population at risk for chronic pain disorders is itself reason for improving our understanding of the processes involved. To the sufferer, pain is a signal that something is physically wrong in the body location associated with the pain. Quite often this is the case and pain can be seen as a sensory signal indicative of specific tissue damage. This view, however, is generally regarded as too simplistic in understanding the majority of pain problems seen in clinics. Many occurrences of pain persist beyond the expected period of healing (e.g., back pain) or recur for no apparent reason (e.g., migraine headache). Even in cases with tissue damage present, it has proved impossible to link, in a one-to-one or isomorphic fashion, the amount of tissue damage present and the degree of pain experienced.

The best known example against assuming one-to-one relationships between tissue damage and pain comes from Beecher (1959). He noted that wounded soldiers when taken to a hospital often requested very little morphine for wounds which were clearly associated with considerable tissue damage. Many of the soldiers either denied having pain from their wounds or had so little pain that they did not want any medication to relieve it. Why, he wondered, would such extensive injuries cause less pain in soldiers than in civilian patients with similar wounds undergoing surgery? Beecher reasoned that the total situation and its meaning must have modified the soldiers' psychological reaction to the tissue damage, such that, at least for the moment, tissue damage was not interpreted as pain. According to Wall (1989a), it is not unusual to find a mismatch between the degree of bodily injury and the pain level experienced. Civilian patients admitted to an emergency room with the substantial injuries of everyday life report no acute pain in some 40% of the injuries, more pain than one might expect in 40%, leaving only 20% in the expected range. This huge variation is not random, nor is it to be attributed to "shock" or "distraction." The working premise in pain research and therapy is that there is no simple relationship between injury and pain.

Clinical pain is generally divided into superficial, deep, or neuropathic pain (Ness & Gebhart, 1990). Superficial pain arises from the stimulation of cutaneous structures, is often well localized, and evokes specific protective responses. Deep pain is the most frequently seen pain in clinic and is more difficult to localize. The pain originates from internal structures such as the heart, abdomen, and reproductive organs. Moreover, the pain may radiate and be perceived as originating from a larger area. For example, pain originating from an inflamed joint may make an entire limb ache. Internally, the link between tissue damage and pain is often very elusive. Neuropathic pain occurs following disease or injury involving peripheral sensory and/or motor nerves. Neuropathic conditions can be especially difficult to treat. The pain is often described by the sufferers as "burning," "electric shock," "tingling," "pricking," "itching," and "cold" (Boureau, Doubrère, & Luu, 1990).

There are many examples of individuals who, after recovering from physical injury, continue to suffer extreme pain in the absence of any apparent damage. Damage of peripheral nerves is sometimes accompanied by pain that persists long after the tissues have healed and the nerve fibers have regenerated. Such pain may occur spontaneously or may be triggered by innocuous stimuli such as touch or a change in air temperature. The intensity of pain may increase over the years and may even spread to other areas of the body. These observations suggest that the nervous system may undergo changes following injury, both peripherally and centrally, such that previously nonpainful stimuli become capable of eliciting pain, at least under some circumstances.

Wall (1989a) stated that when an axon nerve is cut across there is an immediate violent and repetitive discharge in all types of axons. The discharge dies down within seconds and the cut end becomes relatively insensitive for some time as the ends seal over:

> Within a day of an axon having being cut, the end seals over and sprouts begin to grow out. During the first week each axon sends out multiple sprouts, up to 50 from a single axon. These search out and probe surrounding tissue. Many curl back and run along intact axons toward the central nervous system. If an axon sprout succeeds in entering a Schwann cell tube [cells that compose myelin sheaths of peripheral axons], it continues to grow toward the periphery and the unsuccessful sprouts from that axon disappear. If axon sprouts fail to

locate a distal Schwann cell, they probe for short distances into surrounding tissue. During the second week some of the multiple sprouts disappear but others remain to form a neuroma [new nerve cells]. (p. 8)

According to Wall, such sprouts exhibit greater spontaneous nerve activity than normal axons as well as greater sensitivity to mechanical stimuli and chemical stimuli associated with the sympathetic nervous system (e.g., norepinephrine). He provided clinical observations of patients who had developed pain and abnormal sensitivity in the area supplied by a single nerve that had been injured. All the patients underwent nerve resection and within 72 months all experienced the pain in the same area as before the operation. This unfortunate result suggests that peripheral nerve damage may result in changes central to the lesion which are not necessarily reversed by surgery directed at the area of the original injury.

There are numerous experimental and clinical examples of the pain response either under- or over-exceeding what is expected in terms of presenting stimulus/injury. Most theorists now believe that the impact of "pain" stimuli on the nervous system cannot be understood without taking into account the ongoing state of the nervous system. "No stimulus, and consequent afferent barrage arrives in a blank open central nervous system. There are always other events occurring in the periphery which are signaled to the CNS as the normal steady background barrage. The stimulus-produced afferent barrage arrives in a CNS which is set in a particular state of excitability, depending on many past and present factors" (Wall, 1989a).

The goal in this chapter is to provide, through theory and clinical examples, a psychobiologic perspective for dealing with pain disorders. In spite of increasing awareness of the psychobiologic complexity of pain, there remains a tendency to separate "physical" pain from "psychological" pain, and also to view the former as "real" or legitimate pain and the latter as "imaginary" pain. The origins of most pain problems are not fully understood, making it important to be very careful in dealing with a patient's ongoing pain and suffering. The appearance of chronic pain after lesions in the nervous system is not necessarily related to the pathogenesis, etiology, or any specific lesion site. For example, infarctions in the thalamus may sometimes be associated with pain and sometimes not. Also damage at almost any level of the nervous system where there is interference with processing of somatosensory information (peripheral nerves, dorsal roots, spinal cord, brain stem, thalamus, and cortex) may all lead to the same chronic pain syndrome. Pain due to life-threatening disease is not easily distinguished from pain due to psychophysiologic origins and in rare occurrences can in fact have both origins. The dilemma facing individuals afflicted with pain that persists is that they cannot understand why the medical profession is unable to help and what it is they are to do to improve their condition.

To help appreciate the complex nature of pain and its multiple components, it is useful to keep in mind the definition proposed by the International Association for the Study of Pain (Merskey, 1979):

> Pain is an unpleasant sensory and emotional experience associated with actual or potential tissue damage, or described in terms of such damage (p. 249).

The definition encompasses both the sensory and emotional components of the experience and also attempts to dissolve, at the subjective level, the distinction between organic and nonorganic pain. Pain is always subjective and highly individualistic in origin and experience.

PHYSIOLOGICAL MECHANISMS

Two very old doctrines from sensory physiology have been used to explain the physiological origins of pain. One doctrine is based on *intensity* and the second doctrine is based on *specificity* (Malliani, Pagani, & Lombardi, 1989). The intensity doctrine assumes that pain is caused by an excessive stimulation of receptive structures. Within this doctrine, pain may occur with any kind of stimulation as long as the stimulation is excessive. Thus, anything very hot, very cold, or pressing very hard on the skin, or a very bright light to the eyes, causes pain. If pain is due to excessive stimulation of other kinds of sensation, then there is no stimulus-specific modality of pain. According to this approach, the many differences in the discharge characteristics of sensory receptors and nerve fibers are the source of the various kinds of sensation that are experienced. Sensory receptors are a class of specialized nerve endings at which physical, chemical, or electromagnetic incoming signals are changed into nerve-action potentials. The intensity approach assumes that the discharge patterns of a rapidly adapting receptor and of a slowly adapting one are different. The spatial and temporal discharge patterns of the peripheral nerve fibers and fibers connecting to them within the central nervous system may represent a code that, being finally decoded, produces different kinds of sensation. The intensity approach is illustrated by the fact that mild tactile stimulation of the cornea causes a feeling of touch whereas a stronger tactile stimulus causes pain. The difference in sensation is assumed to be due to increased discharge and spatial summation of the same nerve endings and fibers and not due to the stimulation of sensation-specific nerve endings and fibers.

Alternatively, pain has been conceived of as a specific sensation, that is, the result of excitation of a unique physiologic apparatus with characteristics which make it responsive only to a "nociceptive" stimulus. This view has its origin in the doctrine of specific energies advanced by Johannes Muller in 1840 (Malliani et al., 1989). Muller advanced the idea that different types of nerve fibers respond to different stimuli because of their special receptive structures; as a consequence the activity in each particular nerve fiber always gives rise to the same sensation, whether the stimulus acts internally or externally. In 1895 von Frey proposed that the quality of a skin sensation depends, initially, on the type of sensory receptor that is stimulated. He demonstrated that punctate stimulations of certain spots of the skin could elicit a distinct unpleasant sensation, while similar punctures applied to nearby spots evoked only a tactile sensation. Although such a functional spotted map is not reliable, these classical observations remain relevant to current specificity explanations of pain.

Specialized receptors in the skin and associated peripheral fibers do exist for the mediation of pain. Physiologic research (Campbell, 1989) has managed to isolate highly specialized types of sensory fibers which alone or in concert with other specialized fibers provide information to the central nervous system about the environment and about the state of the organism itself. In the case of the sensory capacity of the skin, it is known that stimuli may evoke a sense of cooling, warmth, or touch. Warm fibers are predominately unmyelinated fibers and have been shown to signal exclusively the quality and intensity of warmth sensation. There are also thinly myelinated fibers that encode cooling and different classes of mechanoreceptive afferent fibers, keenly sensitive to deformations of the skin.

The remaining class of cutaneous receptors is distinguished by a relatively high threshold to the adequate stimulus, be it heat, mechanical, or cooling stimuli. Because they respond preferentially to noxious (injurious or potentially injurious) stimuli, they are termed *nociceptors*. Two groups of nerve fibers have been implicated: the unmyelinated C fibers and the myelinated A-delta fibers. C fibers and associated receptors, termed C-fiber nociceptors, are the most common type of cutaneous nociceptors. These nociceptors are generally responsive to both heat and mechanical stimuli and are called C-fiber mechano-heat nociceptors (CMHs). The thermal threshold of CMHs in primates is typically greater than 38 degrees C, but less than 50 degrees C. Two types of A-fiber nociceptors (AMHs) responsive to heat and mechanical stimuli have also been identified, the primary difference being in terms of quickness of response: type I AMHs are believed to signal pain from long-duration stimuli while type II AMHs are believed to signal first pain sensation. A comparison of the C-fiber and type I A-fiber responses to a prolonged painful stimulus is illustrated in Figure 6.1.

Peripheral nerve fibers enter the spinal cord through the dorsal horn. Sensory neurons within the dorsal horn are packed within the dorsal horn

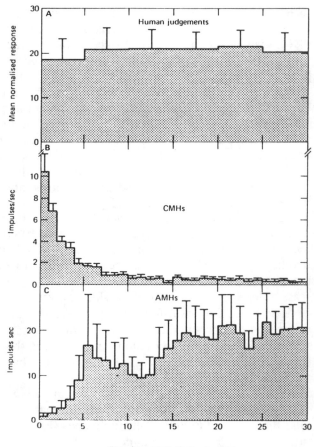

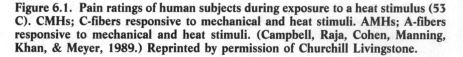

Time from onset of stimulus (sec)

Figure 6.1. Pain ratings of human subjects during exposure to a heat stimulus (53 C). CMHs; C-fibers responsive to mechanical and heat stimuli. AMHs; A-fibers responsive to mechanical and heat stimuli. (Campbell, Raja, Cohen, Manning, Khan, & Meyer, 1989.) Reprinted by permission of Churchill Livingstone.

into several layers or laminae (Wall, 1989b). C fiber afferents terminate primarily in laminae 1 and 2, which together make up the area called the substantia gelatinosa. A-delta afferents terminate primarily in laminae 1, 2, and 5. Although there are nociceptive-specific neurons in these laminae, Wall (1989b) cautioned against understanding the activity of these cells without taking into account "the circumstances under which it is observed." To illustrate, he noted that A-delta and C fibers most commonly innervate neurons with a wide dynamic range within the dorsal horn. These neurons respond to brush, touch, pressure, pinch, heat, and chemicals. However, their range can be substantially altered if descending impulses are blocked. In some instances their excitability may be reduced, in other instances it may be increased. The significant point is that these neurons can change their excitatory/inhibitory response and receptive field characteristics following changes in descending neural control systems.

Nociceptive information from peripheral receptors and fibers ascends in the central nervous system over two pain signaling systems, the lateral system and the medial system (Melzack, 1990). As shown in Figure 6.2, the lateral system tracts project to the sensory cortex while the medial system projects through the central core of the brain stem, terminating in various areas within the limbic system. The lateral system is designed to mediate acute phasic pain characterized by a sudden onset and relatively quick dampening. The medial system, according to Melzack, may be involved more with the emotional rather than sensory aspects of pain. It is not well suited for identifying the specific site of body injury but it does seem to be suited for maintaining "diffuse, unpleasant feelings for some time after an injury has occurred."

Specific structures within the cerebral cortex known to be involved in pain include the anterior cingulate gyrus (part of the limbic system located just above the corpus callosum), primary somatosensory cortex (SI), and secondary somatosensory cortex (SII). SI is located in the precentral gyrus of the frontal lobe and SII lies anterior to SI. The involvement of these regions in pain sensation was demontrated by Talbot et al. (1991) using magnetic resonance imaging (MRI) and positron emission tomography (PET). A heat stimulus (48 to 49 degrees C) and a warm stimulus (41 to 42 degrees C) were applied to subject's forearm during the actual PET scan. The technique allowed for the study of changes in cerebral blood flow to specific regions within the cortex across the stimulus presentations. All subjects rated the heat stimulus as painful and the warm stimulus as below pain threshold. The most prominent region of blood flow activity during the heat stimulus was the anterior cingulate gyrus followed by SII and SI. All significant changes were restricted to the region of the cortex contralateral to the stimulated arm. These data are consistent with both the intensity and specificity doctrines as changes in cerebral blood flow, although specific to brain regions, occurred to both the warm and heat stimuli; the increases were simply greater for pain than warmth.

The view that pain is under the control of a number of highly specialized and interactive peripheral and central systems had its beginnings in 1965 with the proposal of the gate-control theory (Melzack, 1973; Melzack & Wall, 1983). The theory was introduced to account for (a) the high degree of physiological specialization of receptors, nerves, and spinal tracts in the central nervous system; (b) the direct influence of psychological processes on pain perception and response; and (c) the persistence of clinical pain

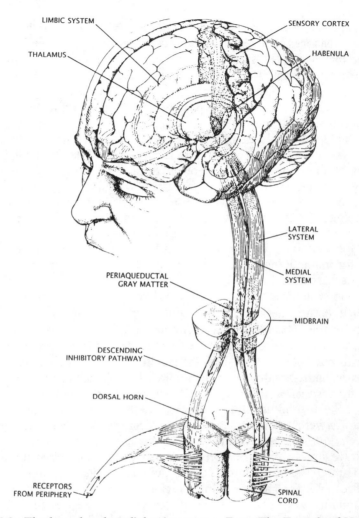

Figure 6.2. The lateral and medial pain systems. From The Tragedy of Needless Pain, by Ronald Melzack. Copyright © (1990) by Scientific American, Inc. All rights reserved.

after healing. The model proposes that the nervous system possesses a number of mechanisms which "control" the transfer of impulses from afferent fibers to cells which in turn trigger the various effector systems and which evoke sensation. A schematic of the model is presented in Figure 6.3.

Nerve-impulse patterns entering the dorsal horn of the spinal cord are not transmitted, in an uninterrupted fashion, directly to the brain. Rather, the impulses first pass through the cells of substantia gelatinosa, which is the region of short, densely packed nerve fibers, diffusely interconnected, run-

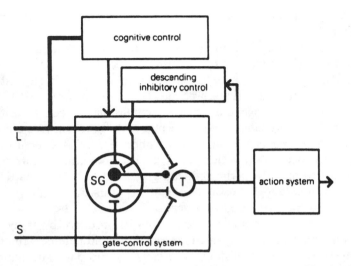

Figure 6.3. The gate-control theory of pain; (L) Large diameter fibers; (S) small diameter fibers; (SG) spinal-gating mechanism; (T) spinal cord transmission cells. Reprinted by permission of R. Melzack.

ning the length of the spinal cord. The role of these cells within the model is to serve as a gate by "selecting and computing" combinations of the signals which impinge on them. Some combinations sum and aid each other. Other combinations evoke inhibitions so that one input excludes the effect of the other. As shown in Figure 6.3, large (A-beta) and small (A-delta, C) diameter fibers enter the dorsal horn with their continued influence mediated in part by effects on the substantia gelatinosa (SG) interneurons. The SG has both excitatory (white circle) and inhibitory (black circle) functions and may operate both presynaptically and postsynaptically. Melzack and Wall (1983) emphasized that the substantia gelatinosa may or may not prove to be "the primary vehicle for gating" and in fact there is evidence that modulation occurs at other levels within the dorsal horn and the nervous system.

There are also descending pathways from the brain to the dorsal horn which have mainly inhibitory effects on the firing of dorsal cells. The hypothesis that descending systems contribute to pain modulation was supported by the discovery of the phenomenon of *stimulation-produced analgesia* (SPA). SPA is a highly specific suppression of pain produced by electrical stimulation of discrete brain sites. These sites include regions in the medulla, midbrain, and lower limbic structures (Liebeskind & Paul, 1977). During SPA, animals remain alert and active and normal behaviors such as eating are not interfered with. Responses to noxious stimuli, however, are absent. The analgesic effect can be isolated in that the stimulated animal ignores a pinch to one limb and responds normally with a pinch to another limb.

An equally significant discovery in the study of descending nociceptive-modulation mechanisms was the identification of the endogenous opioids. Endogenous opioids are peptide neurotransmitters which are distributed throughout the central nervous system (Fields & Basbaum, 1989). At least three families of endogenous opioid peptides have been identified: B-endorphin, Met-enkephalin, and dynorphin. All three peptides are present in the pituitary and are found in a number of central structures which contribute to nociception. A number of different opioid receptors have also been identified and the periaqueductal gray (Figure 6.2), in particular, is known to contain a high density of opiate receptors. All families of opioids are present in the periaqueductal gray.

Stimulation-produced analgesia can often be produced by applying electrical stimulation in regions which are rich in opioid peptides. In addition, the analgesic effects of such stimulation can be reduced with the administration of naloxone, a drug which blocks the actions of morphine, indicating that opioids must be involved in the analgesic effects otherwise observed. The mechanism of action of the opioids is unknown, one hypothesis being that they inhibit inhibitory neurons and thereby disinhibit output neurons in analgesia-producing regions (Fields & Basbaum, 1989). It is not clear if the different opioid systems and associated receptors control different modalities of pain sensation (mechanical, heat) or different types of responses (sensory, affective) to painful stimuli. It is also not clear if these systems play a role in chronic pain disorders. Levels of endorphins have been reported to drop rather than increase during pain episodes and also in no case has naloxone been observed to modify either pain threshold or the "spontaneous" appreciation of pain in human chronic pain patients (Millan, 1986).

PSYCHOLOGY OF PAIN TOLERANCE

Professionals in the medical, paramedical, and dental fields are well aware of the wide variation in pain experiences exhibited by individuals to similar physical stimuli. Procedures that should hurt sometimes do not, and quite benign and presumably nonpainful interventions may produce an intense reaction in some patients. One explanation is that there exist individual biologic differences in pain sensitivity. This view implies that there are some categories of persons who are constitutionally more or less sensitive to the effects of tissue damage.

Researchers who study individual differences in pain sensitivity distinguish between measuring the threshold of pain and tolerance for pain.

Threshold is the point on a continuum where a patient first perceives or defines the sensation as painful. Tolerance is the point at which the individual is not prepared to accept higher levels of stimulation or continue to endure present levels. It has been suggested that pain threshold is more related to sensory variables while pain tolerance is more loaded towards psychological variables. For example, there is no evidence that cultural/racial differences exist for pain threshold but there is evidence that cultural/racial differences based on language and pain behavior exist for pain tolerance (Zatzick & Dimsdale, 1990).

The notion that pain threshold and pain tolerance are under the control of different variables is supported by the work of Chen and colleagues (Chen et al., 1989). They demonstrated a dichotomy reflecting individual differences in pain responsivity to the cold-pressor chronic pain. In their research, subjects were required to immerse both hands in an ice-water bath for a maximum of five minutes or until they could no longer tolerate the cold water. Subjective pain was measured with both a visual analog scale (VAS) and the Melzack Pain Questionnaire (MPQ; Melzack, 1987). The VAS consists of a 100 mm line anchored with "not at all" to "pain as bad as one can imagine." The MPQ allows for the assessment of sensory ("throbbing," "aching"), and affective ("tiring-exhausting," "fearful") and calculating scores for sensory, affective, and evaluative dimensions of pain. Examples of both scales are presented in Figure 6.4.

Using this procedure, Chen et al. (1989) identified both a pain-tolerant (PT) and a pain-sensitive (PS) group. The pain-tolerant group (PT) in each of their studies tolerated the required five minutes of cold-pressor test while pain-sensitive (PS) subjects only tolerated a grand mean of 60 seconds. It is not clear why subjects vary so much in their sensitivity to cold-pressor pain. The researchers found some evidence using MPQ that the two groups are similar on the sensory dimension but differ on the affective and evaluative dimensions, which suggests that "central hypothesis of affective and cognitive integration during pain perception may clearly discriminate PS from PT subjects."

CHILDBIRTH LABOR PAIN

The complexity of pain is clearly evident from studies of women who have described the pain associated with childbirth labor. Although the majority of women experience labor as extremely painful, there remains considerable variation in women's reports of labor pain. Melzack and colleagues (Melzack et al., 1981) had women in labor respond to the adjectives from the MPQ. The reported pain levels were significantly greater for those with first pregnancies than for those who had given birth before. Both groups rated

SHORT-FORM McGILL PAIN QUESTIONNAIRE

RONALD MELZACK

PATIENT'S NAME: _____   DATE: _____

	NONE	MILD	MODERATE	SEVERE
THROBBING	0) ____	1) ____	2) ____	3) ____
SHOOTING	0) ____	1) ____	2) ____	3) ____
STABBING	0) ____	1) ____	2) ____	3) ____
SHARP	0) ____	1) ____	2) ____	3) ____
CRAMPING	0) ____	1) ____	2) ____	3) ____
GNAWING	0) ____	1) ____	2) ____	3) ____
HOT-BURNING	0) ____	1) ____	2) ____	3) ____
ACHING	0) ____	1) ____	2) ____	3) ____
HEAVY	0) ____	1) ____	2) ____	3) ____
TENDER	0) ____	1) ____	2) ____	3) ____
SPLITTING	0) ____	1) ____	2) ____	3) ____
TIRING-EXHAUSTING	0) ____	1) ____	2) ____	3) ____
SICKENING	0) ____	1) ____	2) ____	3) ____
FEARFUL	0) ____	1) ____	2) ____	3) ____
PUNISHING-CRUEL	0) ____	1) ____	2) ____	3) ____

NO
PAIN |———| WORST
                                                     POSSIBLE
                                                     PAIN

Figure 6.4. Short form of the McGill Pain Questionnaire. Reprinted by permission of R. Melzack.

the pain at intensity levels higher than levels reported for clinical pain conditions (e.g., cancer and back pain). Although the average intensity of the pain scores was very high, there remained considerable variability in pain scores. That is, while some women described the pain as very severe, others found it to be only moderate or mild in intensity. Prepared childbirth training had minimal effect as women who received training reported lower pain scores but a high percentage of these women still requested epidural analgesia. Other researchers have found no difference in perceived pain during labor of women who were given childbirth training and women who were not given training.

Labor pain has usually been assessed only during the active phase of labor, when it is most intense. However, pain is also experienced by many women during the early or latent phase of labor and there is some evidence that pain level experienced during this phase is predictive of later events. Wuitchik, Bakal, and Lipshitz (1989) measured pain and cognitive distress during latent, active, and transition phases of labor. Latent labor was defined as the time the woman first perceived contractions as occurring regularly 12–15 minutes apart, with no loss of contractions, to the time dilatation first exceeded 3 cm. Active labor was defined as the time between 3 cm and full dilatation. Transition was defined as the period from full dilatation until delivery.

Subjective pain was assessed with the Present Pain Intensity Scale (PPI) of the MPQ. The PPI consists of six adjectives ranging from "no" pain to "excruciating" pain. Another aspect of this study involved the assessment of cognitive distress experienced by the women across the phases of labor. They were asked to report the thoughts and feelings that were occurring during and between contractions.

To examine the relationship between pain during latent labor and labor progress, the PPI scores for the latent labor phase were classified into pain groups: discomforting (ratings: 0–2), distressing (rating: 3), and horrible/excruciating (ratings: 4–5). Mean lengths of the latent and active phases for the three groups are presented in Figure 6.5. Women in the horrible/excruciating group had much longer labors than women in the distressing and discomforting pain groups. Women in the horrible/excruciating group had a 26.3% incidence of cesarean delivery, compared with a 0% incidence in the discomforting group. The authors recognized the chicken-egg dilemma with these data as physical factors might have been responsible for the differences in pain levels and longer labors. However, separate analyses

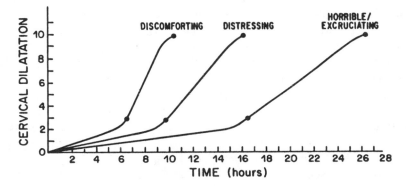

Figure 6.5. Relationship between pain in latent labor and cervical dilatation. Reprinted with permission from The American College of Obstetricians and Gynecologists. (Obstetrics and Gynecology, 1989, 73, 35–42.)

conducted on physical risk factors revealed no differences between the groups. Moreover, groups did not differ in terms of the length of time they had been in labor when the pain ratings were obtained.

The data from this study indicated that early experience of severe pain and distress-related thought may predispose the woman to a long and painful labor. High pain during latent labor may precipitate increases in catecholamines and cortisol that can attenuate uterine activity. The observation that pain and distress during early labor may set the stage for later events has implications for childbirth training and for the significant other who is present during labor. The data point to the importance of providing women with early support and intervention. By intervening early, it becomes possible to allow the distressed woman to regain and maintain a sense of control over the evolving labor process. For the future, it might be possible to design a form of "panic management" training for the woman (and spouse) who maximizes her ability to regulate the critical psychobiologic processes very early in latent labor, before events move beyond her influence.

NEURALGIA AND PHANTOM LIMB PAIN

There are a number of clinical pain conditions which persist beyond the period of healing. Postherpetic neuralgia is an example of such a condition and owes its origin to herpes zoster which is a common self-limited disease characterized by pain and skin rash. It is caused by reactivation of varicella zoster virus. The clinical onset of zoster begins with the onset of pain in the area of affliction. The characteristic blisterlike rash usually appears a few days after the onset of pain and may take weeks to heal. In most patients the course is self-limited, both rash and pain disappearing completely. In others there is irreversible skin damage and sensory loss. In a significant number of acute zoster patients there is persistent pain, in others the initial pain subsides and a second pain, often of distinctly different character, begins. Whether persistent or recurrent, pain that is present beyond the period of active skin lesions is called postherpetic neuralgia (PHN). PHN can be defined as pain arising in or persisting in areas affected by herpes zoster at least three months after healing of the skin lesions (Rowbotham & Fields, 1989). Patients with PHN collectively describe three distinct components to their discomfort: a constant, usually deep pain, a brief recurrent shooting or shocking tic-like pain, and a sharp radiating sensation evoked by light touching of the skin (called "allodynia" and defined as pain produced by nonnoxious stimuli). The mechanism(s) of the persistent or recurrent pain and allodynia of PHN is unknown. One theory is that the pain of zoster is due to relatively selective damage to afferents with larger diameter myelinated axons and consequent loss of their predominately inhibitory action on higher order nociceptive transmission neurons in the spinal cord dorsal horn. Other possible explanations include cutaneous impulse generation from partially damaged primary afferent nociceptors or intact but sensitized primary afferent nociceptors. PHN is a frequent complication of herpes zoster in the elderly. Local anesthetic drugs administered by skin infiltration (e.g., lidocaine) into the area of maximum pain produce pain relief that, when successful, is much more complete than that achieved by tricyclic therapy. Moreover, the duration of relief in some cases extends beyond the time taken for the medication to wear off. Although lidocaine has a short (1-2 h) half-life, some patients experience relief following each skin infiltration that lasts from one to four weeks (Rowbotham & Fields, 1989).

Phantom limb pain is another example of persistent pain following healing. Phantom limb is a natural and expected consequence of amputation. Most amputees report feeling a phantom limb almost immediately after amputation of an arm or leg. The phantom limb is quite real in experience to the extent that the person who feels it may try to actually use the limb in question. Patients with Parkinson's disease have reported, following amputation, a tremor sensation that resembled the sensation which occurred prior to the amputation. The phantom also usually moves, when the person walks, in perfect coordination with the other limbs. Phantoms of other body parts feel just as real as limbs do. An arm may be experienced as either hanging limply along the side of the body, moving freely while walking, or as being in a fixed position (Jensen & Rasmussen, 1989).

At first, the phantom limb feels normal in size and shape, but as time passes, the phantom limb begins to change shape. "Telescoping" refers to a shrinkage of the phantom, where the digits of the hand or the foot gradually approach the stump to which they finally become attached. The time it takes for telescoping to develop and be completed varies, but the process is generally completed within the first year. The frequency and intensity of phantom limb sensations also diminish as time goes by. In some patients, the phantom experience lasts for a few weeks whereas for others it may persist for a few years. Usually only islands of the missing limb are felt. For example, in the hand the thumb and index are the most prominent parts felt, while in the leg the great toe, the instep, and the heel are the most vividly felt parts.

Phantom limb can become the site of severe and excruciating pain. In the literature severe phantom pain is generally reported to occur in .5%–5% of amputees. Phantom pain is mainly localized distally in the phantom limb. Persistent severe pain is seen only in a small percentage of these individuals. Many internal and external stimuli are capable of modifying the phantom limb sensation, including distress, touch, weather change, cold, heat, and stimulation elsewhere.

The origins of phantom limb pain are unknown. The physiologic changes that take place at the site of nerve injury (formation of sprouts and neuromas, spontaneous activity, increased sensitivity) have been implicated but not proven to initiate and maintain phantom limb pain. The hypersensitivity of the residual nerves and developing sprouts to stimulation may represent one explanation for the exacerbation of phantom pain by environmental changes (temperature, wind, barometric pressure) and situational stress. Changes in dorsal horn neurons which have lost their neuronal afferent input may play a role in triggering phantom limb phenomena. Increased excitability as well as expansion of receptive fields have been documented to occur in the dorsal horn following peripheral nerve injury (Wall, 1989a).

Also implicated in phantom pain are central or cortical changes that occur following peripheral injury. Brain structures involved in the control of a limb that has been amputated continue to respond to the stimulation of adjacent skin areas. At a more general level, Melzack (1989) postulated the existence of a central biasing mechanism within the brainstem reticular formation that exerts an inhibitory influence at all levels within the sensory system. If through the loss of a limb a large number of sensory fibers are destroyed, the inhibitory influence of this mechanism will decrease, making it more likely that a pain response will occur to almost any stimulus. There may also be distinct nociceptive pathways and mechanisms that transmit sensations resulting from peripheral nerve damage as opposed to normal pain sensations. Yarnitsky, Barron, and Bental (1988) presented a case of a 72-year-old amputee with a five-year history of phantom pain who, upon experiencing a stroke in the region of the posterior internal capsule (involves thalamic-cortical pathways), saw the complete disappearance of phantom pain. Although motor function and normal sensation were present, the phantom pain had not returned at the end of a seven-month follow-up. Unfortunately, surgical intervention of these structures and pathways seldom produces more than transient relief.

SENSORY PAIN CONTROL TECHNIQUES

All cultures have learned to treat pain with counterstimulation which itself is often pain producing (Melzack, 1989). One of the oldest methods is "cupping," in which a glass cup is heated up and then inverted over the painful area and held against it. The cooling air inside the cup contracts, leaving a partial vacuum and resulting in the skin being sucked up into the cup. The procedure produces bruising of the skin with concomitant pain and tenderness. Cauterization is yet another ancient method. Generally the end of an iron rod was heated until it was red-hot, and was then placed on the painful area such as the back or leg in patients with low back pain. The procedure, of course, produced pain and subsequent blistering of the area that was touched by the cautery. The same effect was achieved by two other procedures: rubbing blistering fluids into the skin, or applying a cone of moxa (made from the leaves of the mugwort plant) to a site on the body, setting the tip of the cone aflame, and allowing it to burn slowly until it approached or reached the skin ("moxibustion").

Transcutaneous Electrical Nerve Stimulation (TENS)

Electrical stimulation of the skin, called transcutaneous electrical nerve stimulation, or TENS, is based on the notion that peripheral activation of A beta fibers might lead to sensory modulation of pain via inhibitory action generated in the dorsal horn of the spinal cord. The arrangement of inhibitions mediated by A beta fibers is largely segmental, requiring that the TENS administration be in the region of the body where the pain is located. The electrical pulses produced by the stimulator are designed to be of just sufficient intensity and frequency to excite the afferent fibers in a nerve adjacent to the painful region and at the same time not damage the skin. The technique is also capable of producing poststimulation analgesia; patients with causalgia, a neuropathic condition characterized by intense burning pain, have exhibited poststimulation effects lasting from five minutes to 10 hours. A major difficulty with the technique is that the efficacy of the treatment tends to fall with time. The rate of attrition is often very high after one year of use. The technique has no known side effects and the only contraindication would be presence of a pacemaker.

TENS is often combined with other forms of therapy such as heat and massage. It is difficult to know what the effects of TENS are per se in such treatment sessions, as patients often enjoy the massage and interpersonal aspects of therapy as much if not more than the TENS. Also, having to come to the clinic for therapy forces the patient to take time out from a hectic schedule and relax. Aside from the therapeutic benefits of the therapy itself, this gives the patients time to think and prepare for whatever else their day may bring. TENS therapists generally recognize that these aspects of treatment are probably as important in terms of the patients' getting better as the physical benefits of the therapy.

Acupuncture Analgesia

Acupuncture therapy originated in ancient China some 2,000 years ago. Originally, acupuncture was based on the theory that all vital organs of the body are connected through tubular systems or meridians that radiate underneath the skin. Life energy or "ch'i," was believed to flow through the meridians, and its excess or deficit produced pain and disease. The insertion of needles into points along the meridians served to correct imbalances in the life energy. Acupuncture charts are extremely complex and consist, traditionally, of 361 points which lie on 14 meridians, most of which are named after internal organs, such as the large intestine, the heart, or the bladder. The points chosen for treatment are held to be influenced by the time of day, the weather and a multitude of other variables. There is no evidence to support the meridian theory and even the Chinese do not consider the meridian theory as a reasonable explanation for the effectiveness of acupuncture.

Modern acupuncture sites often bear no resemblance to the classical needle point locations; instead, locations are often selected which are trigger points, tender areas, or in the region adjacent to the pain. Also, electrical stimulation is commonly used. Modern or "Western" acupuncture also bears no resemblance to traditional acupuncture therapy:

> The traditional acupuncturist will take a medical history including details of sleep, appetite, etc. He/she will be interested in the patient's psychological state and will consider the impact of the patient's lifestyle on their complaint. The acupuncturist will also assess subtler signs such as the quality of the pulse, the coloration of the tongue, the complexion, and the patient's smell. . . . To follow this procedure fully leads to a diagnosis couched in traditional terms along with a treatment plan that is individual to each patient.
>
> . . . .the important fact to note is that the traditional acupuncturist might, for example, treat 10 tension headache subjects in 10 different ways. This is not because he or she has failed to notice the similarity in symptomatology but because a great deal of other information, both physical and psychological, contributes to the final diagnosis. In the same way, a psychotherapist might feel that there were a variety of different causes for depression each of which needed to be treated differently. . . .To a traditional acupuncturist much of the acupuncture that is practised in the West is akin to unqualified persons handing out antibiotics at random to sick people. (Vincent & Richardson, 1986, p. 3)

The two most commonly treated pain conditions where acupuncture has been researched are headache and low back pain. Patients often report considerable initial relief following acupuncture. A review of the literature (Richardson & Vincent, 1986) concluded that following acupuncture, "clinically significant short-term pain relief is usually achieved by from 50% to 70% of patients suffering chronic pain." Unfortunately, the majority of these patients do not maintain their improvements at six- to twelve-month followup. Comparisons of acupuncture at classical sites with needle insertion at random or irrelevant locations have produced a mixture of findings, with some studies favoring the classical sites and other studies reporting no difference. One explanation for the failure of acupuncture to produce long-term changes is based on Melzack's (1989) central biasing notion which was discussed under phantom limb pain. It is not understood what happens physiologically when a needle is inserted into a classical site, a tender region, or some other location. Melzack hypothesized that the analgesic properties of acupuncture may be central rather than peripheral or extrasegmental rather than segmental. Intense inputs from needle stimulation activate small-diameter fibers which project to the cells in the periaqueductal gray. These in turn activate a serotonergic system that ultimately modulates transmission through the dorsal horn. The entire system, then, comprises a complex feedback loop in which small-fiber inputs comprise the feedforward segment while the descending inhibitory system is the feedback segment. Within such a model, peripheral stimulation would lead to only transitory changes in the biasing systems and discontinuation of stimulation would be followed by a return of the pain.

MIGRAINE AND DAILY TENSION HEADACHE

Migraine headache and tension headache, taken together, are the most frequent pain conditions seen in medical clinics. The migraine headache is usually distinguished from the tension headache on the basis of pain location, quality of pain, and presence/absence of associated symptoms. The migraine attack is marked by a one-sided or unilateral pain. The pain may have a sharp and/or pulsating quality. Some migraineurs experience a warning or aura phase prior to the onset of the pain. The most dramatic prodromal symptoms involve the visual system, with the person being frightened by the sudden appearance of blind spots (scotomata), zigzag patterns, or flashing colored lights (Figure 6.6). Such symptoms may disappear with the onset of the head pain, but the patient may report the appearance of new symptoms, especially those associated with the autonomic nervous system (nausea, vomiting, hypersensitivity). Early studies found high concordance rates for migraine in families but more recent data show far lower rates, largely because of improvements in the manner in which the data were collected. Migraine headache susceptibility is likely present in all of us to some extent.

Neurologists generally separate migraine from tension headache on the basis of pain quality, pain location, and presence/absence of associated symptoms. Tension headache is experienced as a pain of pressing/tightening quality, bilateral in location and not accompanied by nausea. The frequency of the attacks determines whether the diagnosis is episodic (present less than 15 days per month) or chronic (present more than 15 days per month). In reality, it is often impossible to distinguish migraine from tension headache because of the high degree of symptom overlap of the two con-

Figure 6.6. Example of scintillating scotoma. From S. L. Hupp, L. B. Kline & J. J. Corbett, Visual disturbances of migraine, *Survey of Ophthalmology*, 1989, 33, 221–236. Reprinted by permission.

ditions (Bakal, Demjen, & Kaganov, 1984). Symptom similarities between chronic migraine and tension headache sufferers are usually far greater than symptom differences. Both groups of headache sufferers, as diagnosed by neurologists, experience tension headache symptoms (bilateral pain, dull and aching pain), vascular symptoms (unilateral pain, throbbing pain), and autonomic symptoms (nausea, vomiting) roughly to the same extent. Individual differences in symptoms do exist but these tend to be unique to the individual presenting with headache and do not lend themselves to simple classification.

The underlying physiology associated with the migraine and tension headache is largely unknown. The classic thesis for migraine is that vascular changes outside the skull are responsible for the events that lead to pain. A two-phase change in the extracranial vasculature was believed to take place, with arteriolar narrowing or vasoconstriction in the extracranial arteries and smaller vessels occurring during the first or prodromal phase followed by vasodilatation during the painful phase. The notion that migraine head pain is associated with extracranial vasodilatation was first demonstrated in a classic study by Graham and Wolff (1938). They administered ergotamine tartrate, a vasoconstrictive substance, to subjects during the headache phase of a migraine attack and simultaneously recorded extracranial pulse activity from the superficial temporal artery. Some subjects showed decreases in pulse amplitudes that were interpreted as due to the vasoconstrictive effect of the ergotamine. Some subjects also showed a decline in the subjective intensity of the headache, with the decline mirroring the changes in the pulse wave amplitudes. Wolff failed to report just how many subjects showed this pattern and the study has never been adequately replicated. In spite of this, the model served as a physiological basis for headache for over 50 years. Furthermore, ergotamine tartrate remains for many the drug of choice for the treatment of an acute migraine attack.

A frightening variation of the vascular migraine is the cluster headache. It was so named because the attacks have a clustering character; the person may be headache-free for a number of weeks or months and then suddenly begins to experience very severe attacks of unilateral nonthrobbing pain in the eye region. The attacks occur with a frequency of one to three times a day, each lasting for approximately 45 minutes. This pattern may occur for several weeks or months only to cease and be followed by a long remission period. This is a relatively rare condition and occurs in less than 1% of the headache population.

Current theories of migraine are deemphasizing the presumed vasodilatation of the extracranial vasculature and concentrating instead on biochemical events occurring within the brain itself (Welch, 1987). The 5-hydroxytryptamine (5-HT) receptor system, for example, continues to receive attention as the principal system that mediates the effects of antimigraine drugs (Peroutka, 1990). 5-HT is a potent intracranial vasoconstrictor and is hypothesized to rise during the prodromal phase of the attack and decrease during the painful phase of the attack. The number one drug used to treat the majority of mild to moderate attacks is Aspirin. It is not known if Aspirin exerts its effects through analgesia, antiinflammation, or some other mechanism. Severe cases of migraine are treated with ergot preparations (Cafergot, Ergotamine). Although often effective, ergotamine drugs also cause a number of side effects, one of the most unpleasant being nausea, which also often occurs as part of the migraine episode. One theory of migraine is that unknown events lead to the opening of arteriovenous connective shunts in the head. Blood is diverted from the capillary beds and ischemia and hypoxia result. Based on this hypothesis, antimigraine drugs would work by closing these shunts and restoring normal blood flow. 5-HT agonists may work by blocking release at terminals of normal transmitters such as 5-HT, norepinephrine, and acetylcholine. There are a number of prophylactic agents for migraine, including propranolol (Inderal), amitriptyline (Elavil), and methysergide (Sansert). These drugs are consumed on a q.d (every day) or t.i.d (three times a day) basis.

These drugs are all believed to be potent blockers of 5-HT receptors or the uptake of 5-HT receptors.

Identifying Headache "Triggers"

Most headache attacks in chronic sufferers occur in the absence of identifiable causes or triggers. Indeed, migraine has been defined as a "paroxysmal" disorder, a disorder that appears without obvious provocation. Migraine sufferers themselves often devote a good portion of their lives trying to identify the factors responsible for their condition but generally have difficulty being successful. Bright light, pollution, and carbon monoxide have often been suspected as being responsible for migraine attacks. Foodstuffs are also frequently cited, especially those containing monosodium glutamate, alcohol, and chocolate. There is very little evidence to support a relationship between particular foodstuffs and migraine onset. Countless migraine sufferers have tried antimigraine diets without experiencing significant relief.

There are some events which will reliably produce or worsen headaches in headache-prone individuals. Alcohol is one such stimulus, possibly because of its known vasodilatory properties. Most people who have a headache in response to some physical event (eating hot dogs, swimming, sex) do so because they are already headache sufferers and not because of the event per se. A common belief among many migraine sufferers is that their condition is precipitated by adverse weather conditions, particularly hot dry winds (e.g., the desert winds of Arizona, the Santa Ana of Southern California, the Chinook of Canada). In spite of the prevalence of this belief, there is no real good evidence of a strong relationship between weather change and headache onset. A study of migraine sufferers attending a clinic in London found no relationship between headache onset and changes in wind velocity, temperature, barometric pressure, and humidity (Wilkinson & Woodrow, 1979).

Simply identifying one or two "stressors" in a headache sufferer's life is not the same as identifying the "trigger" for the condition. Usually, the identified events are illustrative of the individual's way of reacting in a variety of similar situations. These situations may involve themes such as nonemotionality, worry, anger, perfectionism, and/or lack of assertiveness. There are isolated instances when situational change through job change, marital therapy, and/or divorce produce dramatic symptom relief but this is generally not the case. Most of these individuals have had headache since early adolescence and carry their headache predisposition with them into the present. Also, situational change, such as a vacation in the sun, even if accompanied by a short-term reduction in pain, does not necessarily lead to awareness of why the pain disappeared. Patients returning from a sun vacation who experience relief during the trip (many do not) usually remark with surprise how good it felt not to have pain and how their relief must have had something to do with differences in atmospheric pressure or pollutants. Within days, they are usually back to prevacation headache levels.

Chronic headache is especially difficult to understand in terms of external causes, especially when the condition becomes daily. The two most common complaints of chronic headache sufferers are : (a) the attacks have become more frequent and longer over the years, and (b) the attacks appear to occur for no apparent reason. Chronic headache sufferers generally describe their condition as having an intermittent beginning, and with repeated attacks evolving to a state where the pain is always present to some degree. The pattern of pain for such an individual is described as follows:

6:00 A.M.: Woke up feeling sick, sore neck, some nausea. Took some Tylenol. Pain slightly over one eye.

10:00 A.M.: Sitting in class, feeling sick, eyes hurt, side of head beginning to throb. Difficult to concentrate.

2:00 P.M.: Feeling worse, went to exercise class, some dizziness, went home, took some Forinal, lay down.

8:00 P.M.: Pain a bit better, studying for a test, feeling exhausted, went to bed.

This verbal record is for one day of headache activity but is often descriptive of the person's life for the past several months, if not years. Each day begins much the same, with the beginnings of pain or actual headache already present. It is not surprising that such individuals have difficulty identifying specific triggers for their condition. The condition is also difficult to alter with self-regulation techniques.

Some physicians believe that the excessive use of medication is what is maintaining the problem and that the first step in patient treatment is to remove the medication. The condition has been called analgesic rebound headache (Michultka et al., 1989) on the assumption that the sufferer has developed tolerance to the medication and runs the risk of experiencing exacerbation of headache intensity and frequency for several weeks after medication is discontinued. There is little evidence that medication discontinuation alone will lead to resolution of the headache condition.

Headache susceptibility, in chronic cases, appears to have become a learned or acquired property of the individual. The ultimate cause of the condition resides within the headache sufferer himself, "in the form of a continuous and multifaceted condition involving cognitive, behavioral, physiological, and biochemical events" (Bakal et al., 1984). If headache susceptibility resides within the individual, then understanding and preventing headache requires changes to one's internal milieu or psychobiologic predisposition to headache.

The precipitation of headache, in the chronic case, is seldom due to a specific trigger. Rather, the disorder appears to acquire a degree of autonomy from situational events which are known to trigger headache in occasional headache sufferers. Critical for understanding headache onset/ maintenance in the clinical patient are the symptoms which precede the actual onset of the headache attack. By learning to recognize the first signs of the condition, headache sufferers can begin to appreciate the factors within themselves that contribute to the disorder.

Preheadache Warnings

Headache sufferers are generally aware of headache activity long before the attack reaches a severe level. There is usually no perceived coping value to this activity, other than indicating that they must prepare for the pain, sickness, disappointment, and suffering which inevitably follow. Why dwell on a condition that is going to get worse, they say, better to get on with the day. However, how the sufferer deals with the first signs of the developing headache determines to a large extent the course of the attack and the long-term outcome of the condition.

The first sensory signs of impending headache usually go unnoticed. If attention is directed internally, however, the sufferer will notice sensations of tension, pressure, and/or heaviness in the head region. Table 6.1 contains a number of symptoms which are frequently reported by headache sufferers on the day of their attack. The symptoms listed in the first column are primarily sensory in nature while the symptoms listed in the second column are primarily affective in nature.

Is it possible to use the premonitory symptoms to reverse the developing attack? The answer is yes, as long as the sufferer is able to adopt the

TABLE 6.1 Premonitory Headache Symptoms Experienced on Day of Attack (adapted from Amery, Waelkens, & Vandenbergh, 1986).

pallor	depressive feelings
altered facial expression	inactive
photophobia	lacking contact
phonophobia	tearful
nausea	irritable
dizziness	difficulty concentrating
aching muscles	
adynamia	
paresthesias	

appropriate psychobiological coping strategy. The strategy is congruent with being mentally and physically at ease and resembles in pure form the state achieved during restful sleep. In 1863 John Hilton published a classic text titled *Rest and Pain* with the theme that rest to an injured tissue is essential to its recovery (Walls & Philipp, 1953). With everyday headache, sleep is generally the most effective natural means for alleviating the pain. Indeed, the evolutionary significance of headache may be its protective function to signify tissue fatigue and the need of the body and mind for restorative rest. Chronic headache sufferers seldom feel rested or "restored" following a night's sleep. They begin each day feeling much as they did prior to entering sleep, if not worse. A similar nonrestorative sleep pattern has been described by Moldofsky (1986) to characterize a number of chronic pain disorders. The key symptoms are muscle ache, nervousness, irritability, "flu-like" sensations, and loss of appetite.

Reports from headache sufferers indicate that there may be a self-regulatory "window" associated with the onset of the premonitory symptoms. If recognized and managed at a very early stage with effective coping strategies, headache sufferers can learn to abort attacks and at the same time reduce overall headache susceptibility.

There are likely no specific psychological thoughts that contribute to this condition. However, themes surrounding anger, worry, anticipation, agitation, and so forth, especially if carried into sleep, probably contribute to the cascade of biochemical changes which lead to headache onset. Also significant in the chronic condition are the thoughts and feelings which occur as a result of the developing symptoms. Demjen, Bakal, and Dunn (1990) asked patients with chronic headaches to monitor their thoughts over a number of headache episodes, just at the outset of and during the worst pain. The thoughts were categorized as to whether they were headache-related ("I am angry with myself for getting another headache," "I am depressed because I have another headache") or situation-related ("I feel annoyed about petty things," "Everyone is getting on my nerves"). The results showed that patients with continuous or near-continuous headache had a preponderance of headache-related thoughts relative to situation-related thoughts, suggesting that "headache disorders of increased severity are accompanied by a cognitive shift whereby the patient's primary concern moves from situational and interpersonal distress to distress associated with the disorder itself."

It is clear that how an individual reacts to developing headache symptoms has a significant bearing on the actual course of the disorder. Not panicking, lying quietly, and trying to lessen the symptoms in the early stages may often abort the attack or at least reduce its severity. A number of migraine patients seen in clinic have reported success in using preheadache prodromal symptoms such as visual disturbance as a cue to psychologically "back off and relax" rather than as a sign of an unavoidable attack. When successful, the attack does not follow. This is a fragile skill and not easily implemented, especially if one has to face the demands of the day (attending class, work, etc.). It does illustrate, however, the importance of not generating headache distress.

Treatment Framework

Teaching headache sufferers to identify and self-regulate the factors which contribute to their condition is not an easy task but can be done. A good strategy is to begin intervention by first increasing the person's awareness of the sensory/physiologic components of the disorder. Training in passive or autogenic relaxation (Chapter 2) is a good place to begin. The patient is introduced first to relaxation of arms and legs and then is encouraged to practice identifying tension in and relaxing specific muscle groups in the head, face, neck, and shoulder region. Next, the patient is given training in how to accomplish this task without the aid of tapes. This awareness is guided with the use of electromyogram biofeedback. Biofeedback is generally used in most pain clinics to enhance a patient's sensory awareness of subtle muscle tension levels in muscle groups which are a problem (Duckro, 1990). This awareness can be developed to a level which often cannot be attained with relaxation tapes alone. Headache patients who listen to a tape and cognitively relax may not physically relax. Or they may relax some of the "easier" muscle groups (arms and legs) but have difficulty with specific muscle groups, especially in the region of the neck, eyes, and temple. Some patients, for example, have "furrowed" foreheads, "Bette Davis" eyes, or rigid jaw muscles, and find it difficult to alter activity from these muscles, especially while interacting with others or carrying out activities. Also, many headache sufferers have developed a style of blocking early sensations from consciousness for fear that the pain will become worse. Biofeedback can often be used as part of a larger therapeutic strategy for overcoming these difficulties:

> Typically, the feedback is used to demonstrate and reinforce physiological change in the direction of low arousal . . . Further, the awareness and control of physiological arousal represents only one aspect of the overall therapy employed. It is this overall plan of therapy which is the substance of the intervention. For example, it is typically not sufficient that physiological learning be evidenced only in the consultation room. Generalization of this learning to situations in everyday life seems to be a necessary aspect of treatment. This is clearly a behavioral task. (Duckro, 1990, p. 291)

A problem that continuous headache sufferers experience with relaxation techniques is the fear that the pain will become worse. On occasion, patients who relax with biofeedback experience sharp, stabbing pains, described as lightning shooting through their heads. Typically, these individuals have been using, in an unconscious fashion, muscle tension to ward off the pain. As they "let go," there is almost a rebound effect and they are hit with even more severe pain. A clinical example of this phenomenon is the *weekend migraine*. Some individuals are able to avoid a major headache attack throughout the week while at work. However, as soon as they slow down to relax, they are incapacitated with a severe headache. These patients will typically remark that during the week they were "too busy to have a headache," which again suggests the use of an active avoidance, coping style which finally breaks down at week's end. Some patients have ignored the pain and their body for so long that they are almost "numb" in the afflicted area. Emotionally, many of these people are overcontrolled and reluctant to express feelings, especially negative feelings, in an open fashion. Other patients are open "worriers"; they worry about being sick, about their spouse leaving, dying. Still others have "active" minds and have difficulty falling and staying sleep. Also not to be minimized are the potential presence of negative interpersonal factors.

Learning to recognize and alter preheadache and headache sensations in a clinic is only the beginning of migraine management. It is also the easiest of the changes necessary as the individual must now incorporate these skills into day-to-day functioning. This is not easy as they must adjust the way they have been functioning in a variety of contexts, ranging from how they handle feelings to what they are thinking before falling asleep. In short, they must become aware of subtle sensations associated with tightness, tension, and arousal in general that, left unmodulated, will result in a migraine episode. The problem is further compounded by the fact that there is no simple relationship between situational stress and migraine onset. The attack may appear, as in the case of the weekend migraine, for "no apparent reason" or just when the person was about to have a good time. With guidance, however, patients can usually begin to recognize situations and events that generate sensations of tightness and pressure. For example, a daily headache sufferer reported headache developing at the end of each day and could not understand why. She also noted that her mother would call four or five times a day and, with prompting, noticed that her shoulders became increasingly tense at the first ring of the telephone. Another patient noticed that her face became painful simply from watching television but, following self-monitoring, she noticed that the pain became worse after her husband entered the room and began making sarcastic comments about her choice of programs and inactivity!

The concept of headache personality has been examined extensively in the migraine literature. The consensus is that there are no personality traits which are unique to the condition. Migraineurs have been reported to be more depressed and anxious than headache-free individuals. One argument is that these symptoms are a consequence rather than a cause of the headache condition. In a study of children (Andrasik et al., 1988), it was found that the headache sufferers were more depressed and bothered by a greater number of somatic complaints than their headache-free counterparts. The older adolescents (between 13 and 17 years of age) also reported significantly greater anxiety, which the authors interpreted as resulting from frequent episodes of unexplainable, intense head pain.

Rather than debate whether personality variables are the cause or consequence of headache, it is better, from a therapy perspective, to help headache sufferers determine which traits might be exacerbating the condition and which traits might be used to lessen the condition. The following three case studies illustrate how personality variables interact with coping styles to bring on headache episodes:

> Patient no. 10, a married student nurse, displayed a strong positive relation between between 'expression of emotions/anger' and the occurrence of migraine attacks. . . .attacks typically occurred after being with her parents, whom she visited almost every weekend. Her parents expected her to help a great deal with the cleaning and maintenance of their house. Instead of refusing to cooperate on some of these tasks, she would avoid expressing her irritation and anger and try to meet all of her parents' demands. She would, however, blurt out her negative feelings as soon as she returned to her husband. But at that time a migraine attack would be well on its way.
>
> Patient no. 12, an elderly housewife, presented a strong relation between migraine attacks and 'comforting cognitions'. . . . It appeared that attacks occurred often when worrying about her drug-addicted son, who was wanted by the police. Although she tried, she was unable to comfort herself cognitively because of strong interference of anxiety and concern.
>
> Patient no. 16, a socially withdrawn biology student who shared accommodations with other students, showed a marked association between migraine attacks and 'social support'. . . . In her case seeking social support meant lamenting over noise or disturbances from others when in an attack. She otherwise would not share problems with others nor ask for help or advice concerning matters of everyday life. (Sorbi & Tellegen, 1988, pp. 355–356)

From these examples, it becomes understandable just how difficult it can be to alter a pattern of chronic headache activity. Patients who do improve following treatment often do so not through the daily practice of some behavioral technique but through the adoption of a subtle awareness of factors within themselves which contribute to the condition (Turk & Rudy, 1991).

LOW BACK PAIN AND PAIN BEHAVIOR

Low back pain, like headache, is a widespread pain condition and is a frequent source of activity limitation, even for otherwise healthy young adults. The majority of back pain episodes are acute, lasting a few days to a few weeks. For some 20%, however, the problem often lasts beyond a few weeks and leads to a chronic condition, often with accompanying disability. These individuals often show no sign of objective medical damage and begin to develop an outlook which reflects hostility, resentment, anxiety, and depression. In particular, they resent the medical system's inability to "fix" their condition and also the suggestion that they might be malingering in some fashion. At one time, they were characterized as "low back losers" on the basis of data produced by the Minnesota Multiphasic Personality Inventory (MMPI) which showed that chronic back pain patients, with and without signs of organicity, exhibited elevated scores on the Hypochondriasis (undue concern over health and bodily symptoms) and Hysteria (multiple physical symptoms for which there is no known physical basis) subscales, and a lesser elevation on the Depression subscale. This pattern of scores across the three scales is called the "conversion V" and is interpreted as a sign that these patients are using the back pain to deal with and solve emotional difficulties in a fashion that is socially acceptable. The general feeling today is that back pain patients, like other patients, are too individual to be grouped within a specific profile (Love & Peck, 1987). At the same time, many do exhibit a preoccupation with their condition, a belief that they are sick and suffering from some undiagnosed medical condition, They are often depressed as well but this may be as much a result rather than a cause of the persistent back pain.

For dynamic theorists, pain is a communication that goes well beyond the patient's physical injury; it concerns the pain from a life of giving without receiving and from the early childhood experiences that led to the preinjury behavior patterns typically reported by these patients. In a classic paper, Engel (1959) described the pain-prone patients as individuals who "are chronically depressive, pessimistic and gloomy people whose guilty, self-depreciating attitudes are readily apparent. . . . some seem to have suffered the most extraordinary number and variety of defeats, humiliations, and unpleasant experiences. . . . They drift into situations or submit to relationships in which they are hurt, beaten, defeated, humiliated, and. . . . seem not to learn from experience, . . . they conspicuously fail to exploit situations which should lead to successes. . . . Even though they complain of pain, for them pain is almost a comfort or an old friend. . . . It is an adjustment, a way of adaptation, acquired through psychic experience."

Engel believed that the origins of these attributes in pain-prone individuals had much to do with their upbringing. The parents were often physically or verbally abusive of each other as well as the child. One of the parents was often brutal in use of physical punishment and the other parent was submissive. Engel believed that such parents, although cold and distant, responded more when the child was in pain or ill. Thus, the child learned to invite injury to elicit an emotional response from the parent. As adults, they drift into pain-prone relationships in which they are hurt, beaten, defeated, and humiliated.

In some instances, pain patients can be described as hardworking, overactive, independent people who often give help to others to the point of self-sacrifice. They have been described as "pillars of society" or "solid citizens" (Blumer & Heilbronn, 1982), rather than "losers" who can't cope with adversity. Following the injury, however, the pillars begin to collapse and over time they become completely dependent and disabled by the pain.

> Although pain patients are now honorably removed from excessive work demands and able to receive otherwise unattainable care and attention, they must pay dearly in the coinage of chronic pain. Without pain, depression is the inevitable consequence and it is in this sense that the term "depressive equivalent" is used . . . the patients rarely acknowledge guilt about long absences from work and the other benefits they have gained via the illness, presumably because compensation is being paid for by the pain. Their pain may also be considered as the price they pay for the partially realized wish to be loved and the anger over not having received it [love] as children. (Catchlove, 1987, pp. 98–99)

The studies which have found support for the notion of early difficulties in family relationships and/or personality attributes of pain patients have often failed to use pain-free comparison groups. Abandonment, lack of affection, rejection, lack of physical affection, and physical abuse, although frequently reported in pain patients may also be present in comparison groups. When comparison groups are used, the attributes under study are usually not found to be unique to the pain patients. Gamsa (1990) compared pain patients and control subjects on a number of dimensions that have been previously implicated in the "pain-prone personality." These dimensions included the "Solid Citizen" measure, a measure of unmet childhood dependency needs, and a parental bonding questionnaire. The Solid Citizen measure was designed to mirror Blumer and Heilbronn's (1982) view of the pain sufferer as having an idealized self-image characterized by absence of problems in getting along with others, denial of personal problems, infrequent loss of control over temper, hardworking, and highly independent. Overall, the pain patients were similar to the control subjects in their responses to these questionnaires. Pain patients exhibited considerably higher depression scores and lower current life satisfaction scores than the nonpain controls but these differences are more likely to be a consequence rather than a cause of the pain.

Coping strategies used by chronic pain patients have received considerable study. The best example of this research comes from Keefe and his colleagues (Keefe & Dolan, 1986; Keefe et al., 1989). They have identified a number of coping strategies commonly used by chronic pain patients and have classified these as follows: (1) diverting attention, (2) coping self-statements, (3) praying or hoping, (4) increased behavioral activities, (5) reinterpretation of pain sensation, (6) ignoring pain sensations, (7) catastrophizing. They observed that low back pain patients in particular are prone to try and think of things that might distract them from the pain and to hope and pray that the pain will go away someday. These strategies have also been observed to be generally ineffective as the patients themselves report little improvement following their use. Determining why this is the case remains an important clinical issue. One suggestion is that such cognitive strategies are associated with a high degree of pain behavior overall. Keefe and Dolan proposed that chronic pain patients have difficulty accepting the chronicity of their condition and are prone to cycle through periods of overactivity followed by increased pain and prolonged inactivity. "Catastrophizing" is a cognitive coping strategy defined as "a method of cognitively coping with pain characterized by negative self-statements and overly negative thoughts and ideas about the future." Representative catastrophic cognitions include "It is terrible and I feel it is never going to get better," "I worry all the time about whether it will end," and "I feel like I can't go on." Patients who engage in high levels of catastrophizing have a poor prognosis, unless they learn to identify and change these negative thought patterns.

Both negative and active avoidance cognitive coping strategies do very little, if anything, to direct the patient to subtle sensations associated with muscular hypertension accompanying the pain. Furthermore, if these patients, as some suggest, also possess obsessive-compulsive attributes, then one can understand how pain reduction following an injury might not occur. Directing attention away from the pain is a very common cognitive strategy used by chronic pain patients as they often try to ignore, push on, or otherwise direct their energies and behaviors away from the painful region. One patient remarked, after receiving several sessions of relaxation/ biofeedback training, "What do you want me to do—just tell me what I am supposed to do and I will do it. You mean I don't have to fight the pain, I can lie down when I hurt, I don't have to fight myself!" Avoidant coping styles are largely ineffective and serve only to enhance the anger, frustration, and depression that accompany chronic pain conditions. Previous coping styles associated with struggle and achievement are often effective when the body is sound. With injury, however, such coping styles make recovery very difficult. Unfortunately, they seldom realize that the solution in effect becomes the problem as, the more they try to avoid the problem, the more they brace to the pain and exacerbate the underlying condition:

> An example of this phenomenon comes from a police officer who, prior to a motor vehicle accident resulting in whiplash, was a member of a special tactical forces unit. As a member of this unit, he was trained to ignore personal discomfort, especially as it pertained to bodily pain in the performance of police work. Several months after the accident, he continued to experience severe back pain and associated headaches in the neck and head regions. He eventually returned to work but could no longer engage in active police duty as he had lost most of the mobility in his neck necessary for movement. He remained very apprehensive about having to make sudden movements and further injuring himself. Although a very controlled individual, this injury and his effort to deal with the pain by functioning in spite of it simply worsened the spasms in the neck/shoulder region and made it virtually impossible for him to recover. He became extremely irritable at home, both with wife and children, all of whom could not understand why he would no longer participate in marital and family activities. He repeatedly tried but always had to withdraw because of no longer being able to ignore the pain. On several occasions he admitted having thoughts of using his service revolver to end the pain.

Such cases are very difficult to treat but part of the process requires having the person become aware of sensations of tightness contributing to pain as well as the presence of maladaptive coping styles.

Behavioral approaches to the treatment of low back pain treatment began with Fordyce's (1976, 1988) clinical research. His approach draws on operant learning principles and was developed in response to the lack of efficacy of the traditional medical approaches in treating low back pain. In developing the operant model, Fordyce made important distinctions between pain experience, pain suffering, and pain behavior. Pain is viewed, in accordance with the accepted definition, as an unpleasant sensory and emotional experience. Suffering is defined as an emotional response which can be triggered by nociception as well as by other negative events such as loss of a loved one, fear, and threat. Pain behavior is defined as the things that people do when they are in pain or when they suffer. The distinctions in these three pain attributes are especially vital for understanding patients who fail to recover from acute pain and begin to exhibit a pattern of chronic pain.

The distinction between pain and suffering is quintessential to understanding Fordyce's approach to the chronic back pain patient. He noted that approximately 85% of those who injure their backs return to normal function within a few days or weeks. The problem lies with those who do not follow this course and who have not experienced structural damage to the back. He does not believe that the disease model of pain is very useful for understanding chronic pain conditions. The pain for these individuals needs to be analyzed in terms of pain suffering and pain behavior rather than in terms of pain experience. The question is not so much "Why does this person have pain?" as it is "Why is this person emitting suffering or pain behaviors?" Pain behaviors such as limping, grimacing, bracing, complaining, and inactivity may be initiated by injury but may persist beyond healing because of "powerful consequences in the patient's environment." Pain behaviors may be positively reinforced directly, for example, by attention from a spouse or medical personnel. Pain behaviors may also be maintained by the *escape* from noxious stimulation by the use of drugs or rest, or by the *avoidance* of undesirable activities such as work or unwanted sexual activity. In addition, "well behaviors" (e.g., working) may not be sufficiently reinforcing and the more rewarding pain behaviors may, therefore, be maintained. These many consequences are referred to as 'contingencies' because the occurrence of reinforcers is contingent upon the occurrence of pain behaviors. A pain behavior originally elicited by physical factors may come to occur, totally or in part, in response to reinforcing environmental events.

The goals of an operant treatment approach include: (1) increased activity levels, (2) reduction in pain behaviors, (3) reduction in pain-related medication, (4) restoration or establishment of "well-behaviors," including remediation of social and interpersonal problems; (5) modification of the reinforcing contingencies to pain and well-behaviors in the patient's environment; and (6) reduction in health care utilization related to pain problems. Pain clinics vary considerably in the degree to which they adhere to strictly operant methods in their treatment programs. For example, some programs have patients sign a "contract" in which they agree not to discuss pain during the course of the program. The contract may ask that they learn to "live with the pain" and change those actions, attitudes, and behaviors that are associated with pain. Many individuals find it difficult to accept an approach that does not focus on the pain (Flor, Birbaumer, & Turk, 1990).

The operant approach has been criticized on the grounds that behavioral methods do nothing to alleviate pain and instead only teach patients to be stoical about their pain. Fordyce argued, in defense of the approach, that behavioral techniques do not have as a primary objective the reduction of pain per se. Behavioral treatments are intended to reduce the 'disability' associated with chronic pain problems:

> If a patient is seen only in the light of his or her presumed underlying problem (e.g., hysteria, poor motivation, degenerative disk disease, spinal stenosis, fibromyalgia, pain of unknown origin, etc.), then the patient's potential for

increased functioning may be overlooked or underestimated. In contrast, if the clinician attends to what the patient does or does not do, then it becomes possible to use learning technology to increase, decrease, or maintain selected behaviors to bring about improvements in function. These improvements in function may occur in the absence of changes in the underlying medical or psychological problems. The purpose of behavioral pain management programs is to reduce the excess disability. The fact that some patients increase their function and quality of life without reporting concurrent decreases in pain is not a shortcoming of this treatment approach. For most of these patients there is no alternative. (Fordyce, Roberts, & Sternbach, 1985, p. 121)

Patients in operant programs generally report reductions in pain. It is likely that increases in activity level and reduction in overguarding associated with behavioral techniques are at least partially responsible for the diminished pain. Fordyce's work is especially important for emphasizing that chronic pain is an open system and subject to influence by factors outside the original injury.

Operant programs will often not accept individuals who are engaged in some form of litigation. Pain in the absence of organicity is especially troublesome when litigation is involved. Litigation goes beyond lawsuits and includes compensation and occupational disability (Chapman & Brena, 1989). There is often suspicion from the employer that the patient in question is malingering or has some psychological rather than physical disability which is preventing recovery and return to work. The patients usually resent this interpretation and argue instead that their pain is not being properly diagnosed and treated. Chapman and Brena stated that disability claims for chronic pain have reached "epidemic" levels in the United States and show no sign of decreasing. In operant terms, there are a number of contingencies that lead to disability claims. Following an industrial accident, a worker may be disabled with respect to the original job but able to work at a less demanding task. Unfortunately, the less demanding task is usually associated with a reduction in income. Patients are also afraid of returning to work following long periods of unemployment for a number of reasons, including fear of reinjury, self-doubt, fear of not being able to reinstate the disability. Whether or not a person returns to work may depend as much on social and economic factors as it does on medical factors. In fairness to the injured person, from the moment the injury occurs, the medical system promises that it will be able to "fix" the condition through medication and/or surgery. It is only after all medical efforts fail that the patient is expected to take responsibility for his recovery.

External contingencies are only part of the answer as to why some patients become disabled by back pain in the absence of obvious organicity. Many of these patients seem to consciously or unconsciously resist rehabilitation efforts. Some of this "resistance" undoubtedly has to do with the person's preinjury personality and what the injury means to the person in terms of this personality. Fordyce once remarked that "people hurt a lot less when they have something better to do." Back pain patients resent such statements and are known to starve themselves in the hope of drawing attention to their plight.

Specialized pain clinics go beyond behavioral techniques alone and include a multidisciplinary approach to pain management. Behavior modification, if used at all, is complemented with cognitive behavior therapy, nerve block, TENS, biofeedback, ultrasound, and massage. The consensus is that these programs are effective in increasing nonpain behaviors such as return to work, reduced hospitalization, reduced analgesic use, improved physical capacity, and improved psychological functioning. Positive outcomes are even more impressive when it is recognized that patients attending pain clinics often have "the most recalcitrant problems and are the least likely to benefit from any intervention" (Turk & Rudy, 1990). These patients have generally been treated with all the conventional approaches, including neurological and surgical specialists. There is also evidence that pain clinic patients are more likely, when compared to nonclinic patients, to be experiencing greater intrapersonal and interpersonal difficulties.

In spite of the stated successfulness of pain clinics, there remains concern that claims of success are often exaggerated and dependent on the outcome measures used. Initial successes are also often not maintained. Turk and Rudy (1991) reviewed a number of studies which claimed high success rates initially but which also showed relapse rates of 30% to 70% after a one-year follow-up. Gallon (1989) noted that positive outcomes may be the exception rather than the rule and occur only in very intensive programs. Effective programs, for example, involve full-time patient commitment to program activities and deal with a small number of patients. Programs which are less demanding have produced lower improvement rates and in some instances no differences between treated and nontreated patients. In his study, Gallon assessed, in addition to functional outcome measures, the dimension of subjective pain-related disability. Initially the patients received a community hospital-based outpatient treatment program based on physical therapy, coping with pain skills training, anger management, and biofeedback. Four to six years later, 300 patients were surveyed by telephone to determine their current status. Information was collected regarding current medical status, vocational and compensation status, medication usage, and perception of current pain and disability status as compared to their remembered status at the time of entering the program. Perceived disability status was determined from a scale which assessed amount of pain present, time resting due to pain, amount of disturbed sleep, anxiety/discouragement about pain, amount of activity, etc. The results showed that on objective measures, approximately 50% of the patients were working and 65% were not seeking further medical treatment. The positive outcome of these measures was not matched by positive scores on the perceived disability measure. Only 29% of the subjects rated themselves as much or somewhat improved on this measure. The remainder of the subjects rated themselves as not changed, somewhat worse, or much worse since their pain clinic experience. Patients who failed to improve were still on compensation and many of these reported their condition as "worse." Of patients who had received back surgery since terminating the program, 58% reported themselves as more disabled than they had been at the time of pain program evaluation.

Multidisciplinary approaches to chronic pain management need to strengthen their proficiency at modifying the "internal milieu" maintaining the pain condition, in a fashion similar to the approach proposed for chronic headache conditions. Back pain patients themselves need to recognize their role in modifying the experiential and physiologic aspects of the chronic pain condition and not just nonpain behaviors. Both clinic objectives and patient expectations are often not clear on this issue:

> The vast majority of patients seek [pain clinic] treatment in the hope that their pain will be eliminated. Yet most pain clinics give the explicit message that they will help the patient "learn to live with the pain." This message is incompatible with patients' desires. Although not always as effective as they could be, patients know how to live with pain. . . . They come to a pain clinic because they wish to live *without* pain. Further, many pain clinics emphasize that a central goal of treatment will be elimination of unnecessary analgesic medication. Some patients may be unwilling to consider treatment in such a program for fear of removal of analgesic drugs on which they feel dependent, or fear that without the medication their pain will become intolerable. . . . They may be uncomfortable when terms such as learning, self-regulation, active participation, and personal responsibility are discussed. . . . Perhaps the reasons that patients reject treatment are not poor motivation and secondary gains, . . . but a mismatch between their views of their problem and their treatment goals, which conflict with the rationale offered and the expressed goals of the treatment program. (Turk & Rudy, 1990, pp. 14–16)

The psychobiologic processes which contribute to chronic back pain are rarely appreciated by patients with this condition. Unfortunately, there are no solid physiologic measures or indices of these processes. One hypothesis is that chronic tension in the paraspinal muscles develops as a protective mechanism following injury to the spinal region. It is assumed that increased low back muscle tension leads to a worsening of the pain symptoms. Documenting the presence of such activity with electromyographic (EMG) recordings has not proven to be a simple task. Some investigators have found increased EMG activity from the lumbar region in chronic pain patients as compared to controls, whereas other studies have failed to find patient-control differences. A study of women who experienced severe low back pain during menstruation demonstrated the presence of heightened EMG activity in the low back region which was specific to their descriptions of a personally relevant stressor, that is, they showed greatest increase in spinal EMG activity when describing a personally relevant stressful situation. In the resting condition, their EMGs were no different from normal controls (Dickson-Parnell & Zeichner, 1988). Other researchers have suggested that the problem may be less one of hyperexcitability of muscles and more one of biomechanical limitations. That is, pain patients, following an injury, may engage in a high degree of protective guarding, bracing, and compensatory posturing which limits range of motion and inhibits the appropriate muscle activity that would otherwise provide stability for the lumbar spine (Ahern et al., 1988). The link between heightened EMG and low back pain remains a possibility, and final explanations will likely draw on both models. The future may see an increase in therapeutic effectiveness as pain sufferers become more and more knowledgeable and sophisticated in the use of self-regulation strategies which promote an understanding facilitative of healing and a return to productive life.

CANCER PAIN CONTROL

Cancer pain has special attributes and significance to the patients and their families. Cancer-related pain afflicts millions of people, with surveys suggesting that pain occurs in approximately 40% of patients in all stages of cancer and 66% of patients in advanced cancer. Cancer pain is often poorly managed due to lack of adequate knowledge and fears that the pain is inevitable or that the patient might become addicted to prescribed medications. The three commonest sites of cancer pain are soft tissue, nerve, and bone. Bone is the most frequent site and the origin of the pain is not understood. Inflammation in the region of the cancer is part of the answer as well as pain-producing substances that may be released by the tumor itself.

Untreated cancer pain can force the patient to feel helpless and hopeless, thereby preventing coping with the disease. Liebeskind (1991) suggested that left untreated, pain may directly and/or indirectly through association with stress actually contribute to the spread of cancer. He demonstrated, using an inbred strain of rats with a particular tumor, that the stress of forced swimming decreased NK cell cytotoxicity and increased the number of lung surface metastases. Moreover, animals with cancer exposed to the pain of surgery (laparotomy) also showed increased metastatic growth; whereas animals which received only a surgical anesthetic were unaffected.

The precise stimulus conditions necessary to produce these effects, whether it is the pain itself or the stress reaction caused by it, need still to be determined. What is clear is that pain of sufficient magnitude can, directly or indirectly, suppress immune mechanisms normally serving to defend the body against tumors and thereby cause a marked increase in tumor growth. Melzack has stated it plainly: "Pain . . . can . . . have a major impact on morbidity and mortality . . . it can mean the difference between life and death" . . . (p. 3)

Historically, one of the major difficulties with cancer pain control has been the reluctance to use effective dosages of pain-controlling drugs because of fears of addiction (that is, capable of inducing tolerance and physiological and psychological dependence). According to Melzack (1990), it is rare to see addiction when patients take morphine for cancer pain. Also, patients who use morphine for pain do not develop the rapid physical tolerance to the drug that is often a sign of addiction. Many people who are prone to addiction quickly require markedly escalating doses to achieve a desired change of mood, whereas patients who take the drug to control pain do not need sharply rising doses for relief.

Morphine is the major active ingredient of opium, which has been a medical therapy for longer than 2,000 years. Heroin is a semisynthetic derivative produced by a compound similar in activity to morphine (it takes 3 milligrams of heroin to produce the same analgesic effect of 10 milligrams of morphine). A number of categories of opioid-like receptors are known to exist and narcotic drugs can be classified on the basis of their affinity for a particular receptor category. "Mu" receptors are believed to be involved in blocking mild to moderate pain and are responsive to codeine, oxycodone, and meriperidine (Demerol). Meriperidine is not recommended for chronic pain because prolonged use is associated with the accumulation of the active metabolite normeperidine, which has one-half the analgesic strengh of meperidine and twice the convulsive potential. Morphine would be used for moderate to severe pain and it has high affinity of Mu receptors. Two other categories of receptor which have clinical significance are kappa and sigma. Pentazocaine (Talwin) is the prototypic drug in this receptor category. This drug can produce sedation as well as dysphoria and hallucinations in a small number of patients. Nalbuphine (Nubain) is another example of a kappa-sigma agonist.

There is growing acceptance of the view that the use of narcotics for controlling cancer pain is not necessarily associated with addiction. Indeed, Melzack argued that the use of narcotics for all forms of chronic pain is seldom associated with addictive characteristics. He believes that those individuals who do develop a tolerance and dependence on narcotics most often have a history of psychological disturbance or of drug dependence (the key phrase is "psychological disturbance" as, depending on the definition, it would be possible to cast a very wide or narrow net). Melzack provided an example of a study involving 11,882 patients who were given narcotics to relieve pain stemming from various medical problems; none of the subjects had a history of drug dependence and only four subjects went on to abuse drugs. Tolerance is not only a sign of possible addiction but is also a medical concern in its own right. Side effects of large amounts of morphine include coma and impaired respiration. According to Melzack, little tolerance develops in patients with cancer who take individually adjusted doses of heroin several times a day over long periods. From his own work, he notes that increase in morphine use is usually related to disease progression rather than tolerance.

Another change that has taken place in cancer pain management is the recognition that narcotic drugs for pain relief should be administered on a "round the clock" dosing. Most narcotics have a duration of four to six hours and therefore daily pain control requires four to six doses spaced equally throughout the 24-hour day. As illustrated in Figure 6.7, the standard prescription "PRN" order (pro re nata or "as needed") is not recommended in order to prevent the cyclic recurrence of pain, feelings of despair, and dose escalation. PRN is reserved for episodes of "breakthrough" pain.

> The result of the PRN approach is often a confrontation between the patient and the care giver, who expects morphine analgesia to last for four to six hours. The patient, whose pain has returned earlier than expected, is in agony and pleads to have the next injection. The health-care worker, fearful of causing addiction, refuses to comply. When the pain is finally treated, it may

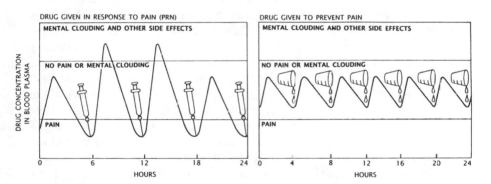

Figure 6.7. Two different approaches to morphine injections for pain control. Left: PRN approach involves giving injections "as needed." Injections are given in response to pain. Right: Morphine is given orally after a specified time interval (e.g., every 4 hours) to prevent pain and to ease the fear of recurring pain. From The Tragedy of Needless Pain, by Ronald Melzack. Copyright © 1990 by Scientific American, Inc. All rights reserved.

be so severe that a large dose has to be given, which increases the likelihood of side effects, such as mental clouding and nausea. Particularly when a patient has a terminal illness, the issue of addiction is meaningless, and delaying relief is cruel. (Melzack, 1990, p. 28)

The more humane way is to give morphine continuously and tailor the amount to each patient. An initial dose of 10 milligrams is given and repeated every four hours. Then over the course of several days or weeks the dose and timing are adjusted until a maintenance regimen is established. For patients having cancer, an approach emphasizing pain prevention is particularly wise. Pain and the fear of pain are perhaps their greatest source of suffering. Bruera and colleagues (Bruera et al., 1989) developed a clinical staging system for cancer pain which takes into account the mechanism of pain (visceral, bone-soft tissue, neuropathic, unknown), pain characteristics, previous narcotic exposure, cognitive function (i.e., memory, space and time orientation), addictive personality, and psychological distress. Patients with good response to narcotic pain management are those with visceral and bone-soft tissue pain, nonincidental pain, normal cognitive function, low psychological distress, low tolerance development, and a negative history for alcoholism or drug addiction.

Methods of continuous drug administration continue to improve. There are now special capsules that release morphine slowly. Also available are special electronically controlled pumps that deliver a steady infusion of medication under the skin. Termed "patient controlled analgesia" (PCA), a timer controls the release of the medication over a period of approximately 10–30 seconds, and then "locks" the patient out until the next timed release. A design objective of the procedure was to eliminate the peaks and troughs of plasma analgesic drug concentrations inherent in parenteral methods. The plasma concentration in which analgesia is experienced is referred to as the "therapeutic window." The window is narrow and is flanked by sedation when plasma levels are too high and pain when plasma levels are too low. PCA is intended to reduce this peak and trough effect by allowing the patient a degree of control in the absence of sedation.

Cancer pain cannot be managed with narcotics alone and needs to be treated in the context of ongoing anticancer treatment, nondrug treatments and psychosocial support. The fostering of empathic and supportive communications is especially important and the use of narcotic medications should always be accompanied by opportunity for ample ventilation of feelings. Fear, anger, depression, and anxiety are major components of the cancer experience. Narcotics, although a powerful treatment aid, should be used with the understanding that the patient's pain needs to be understood and managed within the patient's total ongoing experiences with the disease.

Epilogue
The Challenge

Throughout this book we have explored the interface of thoughts, feelings, bodily sensations, and physiology in an effort to isolate psychobiologic processes which are conducive to health. In topics ranging from somatic awareness, migraine headache, anxiety, depression, pain, psychopharmacology, and cancer the evidence suggests that much can be done to improve health through a better understanding of the individual's psychobiology. With psychophysiologic disorders like headache and chronic pain, as well as mood disorders like anxiety and depression, we possess a good grasp of the psychobiological processes which control these conditions. With cancer, less is known, but the available evidence points to an immunosuppressive coping style which if altered may have both treatment and health promotion potential.

Psychobiologic health represents a progression of efforts to develop models of wellness. In the field of mental health, Cowen (1991) recommended that we move energies and resources from struggling with illness toward building "wellness," i.e., build health rather than fight sickness. He proposed that the pursuit of wellness can best be achieved through the psychological attributes of competence, resilience, and empowerment. Psychological empowerment refers to a sense of control and mastery over the social environment. Providing people with the behavioral and interpersonal skills to achieve greater life satisfaction and gratification would without doubt improve both mental and physical health. If, at the same time, they can learn to develop an experiential awareness of their psychobiology, they are more likely to attain and maintain wellness at all levels.

Our understanding of the nature of psychobiologic processes which contribute to health and illness needs further study. People at any age, from the young to the elderly, can learn to recognize the relationship between their innermost thoughts, feelings, and bodily sensations. At present, this awareness is limited to therapy settings and there is a need for programs which educate the populace at large about the health-enhancing potential of somatic awareness. There is a wisdom of the body which can be utilized to facilitate health and recovery from illness.

Bodily symptoms associated with pain and discomfort can signify both benign and organic conditions. Unfortunately, there is no easy way to know which condition the symptoms reflect. However, there is at times prolonged confusion and doubt when there are, according to the best diagnostic tests available, no signs of organicity. Why then are there symptoms? The elderly in particular are often caught in this dilemma as no one seems to be able to explain their various pains. There is no easy way of assuring individuals of the non-life threatening nature of such symptoms but understanding of the psychobiological possibilities would provide patients and professionals with an alternative.

Psychobiology can be utilized to facilitate "collaborative" relationships between professionals and patients. One of the pleasures of working as a clinical psychologist is the repeated discovery that patients usually understand themselves better than therapists do and it is the two-way exchange of mind-body information inherent to the approach which makes therapy personally rewarding. For patients, it means that their thoughts, feelings, and sensations accompanying the disorder or disease are taken seriously and listened to. Patients are also likely to recognize that they have an active role to play in maintaining their health.

The psychobiology of health, with its emphasis on the individual, will need to be intergrated with the interpersonal aspects of living. Our need for interpersonal relationships has been called the hallmark of the human condition and the adequacy of these relationships has a powerful effect on our psychobiology. In this context, we are reminded of an elderly stroke patient who described each day feeling like the legendary cartoon character with the perpetual black cloud above his head. She described each day praying for death, not because of her stroke-induced physical handicaps but because she now felt that "my husband would be better off if I were dead." We see, from this example, how the presence of a medical condition may extend beyond the disease process and threaten the individual's ability to hold on to cherished interpersonal relationships and the desire to live life itself.

Similarly, personal distress in a family member often equals or exceeds the distress experienced by the patient and makes it very difficult for the ill member to marshal inner resources if he or she must deal with the distress in others. A young woman with cancer, while participating in a study of psychoimmunology, commented that we should be asking psychological questions of her spouse rather than of her. She said that in the two years that she has suffered from cancer no one had ever asked her husband anything regarding his feelings and ability to cope with her disease.

We need to recognize, as professionals and family members, that emotional support, companionship, and sensitive listening constitute powerful psychobiologic therapeutic tools. Nurses are well aware that the momentary holding of a patient's hand, a touch on the shoulder, or a supportive arm can communicate caring and concern. Such forms of touch and communication can lead to a reduction in stress-related symptoms. The psychobiological well-being of professionals and care-givers should not be overlooked as their ability to function at an optimum level requires having the necessary resources to minimize stress within themselves.

Self-help and community groups have unique potential for facilitating shared psychobiologic awareness. Self-help groups involve a "bottom-up" form of participation with heavy reliance placed on the experiential knowledge of the members. An immediate and powerful experience of the new group member is the discovery of and acceptance by others with a similar difficulty. The helper and "helpee" have similar problems and the empathy and "inside understanding" of the problem enable the helper to be particularly effective. Self-help groups are especially powerful for providing members with information about how best to live with a condition. These groups are likely to become more sophisticated in their use of psychobiology in the coming years.

We have entered an era where the recognition of psychobiological factors is becoming as important as physical factors in the determination of health and illness. Society's awareness of the importance of mind-body relationships as "risk" factors in illness will continue to grow. We are witnessing an expansion of the revolution in health promotion to include not only the management of sexual health, substance abuse, and nutrition/weight issues, but also the management of one's psychobiology. How best to achieve this management is a challenge for the future. Ultimately, it may be achieved through a return to more fundamental values, resulting in a greater harmony of our mental, spiritual, and physical selves.

References

Abramson, L. Y., Metalsky, G. I., & Alloy, L. B. (1989). Hopelessness depression: A theory-based subtype of depression. *Psychological Review, 96,* 358–372.

Ader, R., & Cohen, N. (1975). Behaviorally conditioned immunosuppression. *Psychosomatic Medicine, 37,* 333–340.

Ader, R., & Cohen, N. (1982). Behaviorally conditioned immunosuppression and murine systemic lupus erythematosus. *Science, 215,* 1534–1536.

Agras, W. S. (1988). Relaxation training in essential hypertension (pp. 87–110). In R. Ader, H. Weiner, & A. Baum (Eds.), *Experimental foundations of behavioral medicine: Conditioning approaches.* Hillsdale, NJ: Lawrence Erlbaum Associates.

Ahern, D. K., Follick, M. J., Council, J. R., Laser-Wolston, N., & Litchman, H. (1988). Comparison of lumbar paravertebral EMG patterns in chronic low back pain patients and nonpatient controls. *Pain, 34,* 153–160.

Alberts, M. S., Lyons, J. S., Moretti, R. J., & Erickson, J. C. (1989). Psychological interventions in the presurgical period. *International Journal of Psychiatry in Medicine, 19,* 91–106.

Alexander, F. (1950). *Psychosomatic medicine: Its principles and applications.* New York: Norton.

Alloy, L. B., Abramson, L. Y., Metalsky, G. I., & Hartlage, S. (1988). The hopelessness theory of depression: Attributional aspects. *British Journal of Clinical Psychology, 27,* 5–21.

American Psychiatric Association. (1987). *Diagnostic and statistical manual of mental disorders* (3rd ed). Washington, DC: Author.

American Psychological Association. (1990). The Seville statement on violence. *American Psychologist, 45,* 1167–1168.

Amery, W. K., Waelkens, J., & Vandenbergh, V. (1986). Migraine warnings. *Headache, 26,* 60–66.

Andrasik, F., Kabela, E., Quinn, S., Attanasio, V., Blanchard, E. B., & Rosenblum, E. L. (1988). Psychological functioning of children who have recurrent migraine. *Pain, 34,* 43–52.

Angell, M. (1985). Disease as a reflection of the psyche. *New England Journal of Medicine, 312,* 1570–1572.

Angyal, A. (1941). *Foundations for a science of personality.* Cambridge: Harvard University Press.

Antonovsky, A. (1987). *Unraveling the mystery of health: How people manage stress and stay well.* San Francisco: Jossey-Bass.

Ax, A. F. (1953). The physiological differentiation between fear and anger in humans. *Psychosomatic Medicine, 15,* 433–442.

Bakal, D. A., Demjen, S., & Kaganov, J. (1984). The continuous nature of headache susceptibility. *Social Science & Medicine, 19,* 1305–1311.

Barefoot, J. C., Dodge, K. A., Peterson, B. L., Dahlstrom, W. G., & Williams, Jr., R. B. (1989). The Cook-Medley Hostility Scale: Item content and ability to predict survival. *Psychosomatic Medicine, 51,* 46–57.

Barlow, D. H. (1988). *Anxiety and its disorders: The nature and treatment of anxiety and panic.* New York: Guilford Press.

Barsky, A. J. (1988). *Worried sick: Our troubled quest for wellness.* Boston: Little, Brown and Company.

Bartrop, R, W., Luckhurst, E., Lazarus, L., Kiloh, L. G., & Penny, R. (1977). Depressed lymphocyte function after bereavement. *The Lancet, i,* 834–836.

Batson, C. D. (1990). How social an animal?: The human capacity for caring. *American Psychologist, 45,* 336–346.

Beck, A. T. (1967). *Depression: Clinical, experimental, and theoretical aspects.* New York: Harper & Row.

Beck, A. T. (1988). Cognitive approaches to panic disorder: Theory and therapy (pp. 91–109). In S. Rachman & J. D. Maser (Eds.), *Panic: Psychological perspectives.* Hillsdale, NJ: Lawrence Erlbaum Associates.

Beecher, H. K. (1959). *Measurement of subjective responses: Quantitative effects of drugs.* New York: Oxford University Press.

Belsher, G., & Costello, C. G. (1988). Relapse after recovery from unipolar depression: A critical review. *Psychological Bulletin, 104,* 84–96.

Berkman, L. F., & Syme, S. L. (1979). Social networks, host resistance, and mortality: A nine-year follow-up study of Alameda County residents. *American Journal of Epidemiology, 109,* 186–204.

Berkowitz, L. (1990). On the formation and regulation of anger and aggression. *American Psychologist, 45,* 494–503.

Biddle, S. J. H., & Fox, K. R. (1989). *British Journal of Medical Psychology, 62,* 205–216.

Blackburn, I. M., Eunson, K. M., & Bishop, S. (1986). A two-year naturalistic follow-up of depressed patients treated with cognitive therapy, pharmacotherapy, and a combination of both. *Journal of Affective Disorders, 10,* 67–75.

Blix, A. S., Stromme, S. B., & Ursin, H. (1974). Additional heart rate—an indicator of psychological activation. *Aerospace Medicine, 45,* 1219–1222.

Blumer, D., & Heilbronn, M. (1982). Chronic pain as a variant of depressive disease: The pain-prone disorder. *Journal of Nervous and Mental Disease, 170,* 381–406.

Boureau, F., Doubrère, J. F., & Luu, M. (1990). Study of verbal description in neuropathic pain. *Pain, 42,* 145–152.

Brown, G., & Beck, A. T. (1989). The role of imperatives in psychopathology: A reply to Ellis. *Cognitive Therapy and Research, 13,* 315–321.

Brownell, K. D., Marlatt, G. A., Lichtenstein, E., Wilson. G. T. (1986). Understanding and preventing relapse. *American Psychologist, 41,* 765–782.

Bruera, E., MacMillan, K., Hanson, J., & MacDonald, R. N. (1989). The Edmonton staging system for cancer pain: preliminary report. *Pain, 37,* 203–209.

Budzynski, T. H. (1974). *Relaxation training program.* New York: Bio Monitoring Applications.

Burge, S. K. (1988). Posttraumatic stress disorder in victims of rape. *Journal of Traumatic Stress, 1,* 193–210.

Cacioppo, J. T., Andersen, B. L., Turnquist, D. C., & Tassinary, L. G. (1989). *Patient Education and Counseling, 13,* 257–270.

Calabrese, J. R., Kling, M. A., & Gold, P. W. (1987). Alterations in immunocompetence during stress, bereavement, and depression: Focus on neuroendocrine regulation. *The American Journal of Psychiatry, 144,* 1123–1134.

Campbell, J. D. (1978). The child in the sick role: Contributions of age, sex, parental status, and parental values. *Journal of Health and Social Behavior, 19,* 35–51.

Campbell, J. N., Raja, S. N., Cohen, R. H., Manning, D. C., Khan, A. A., & Meyer, R. A. (1989). Peripheral neural mechanisms of nociception (pp. 22–45). In P. D. Wall & R. Melzack (Eds.), *Textbook of pain (2nd ed.).* Edinburgh: Churchill Livingstone.

Cannon, W. B. (1970). *Bodily changes in pain, hunger, fear and rage.* Washington, DC: McGrath. (Original work published 1929)

Carkskadon, M. A., & Dement, W. C. (1989). Normal human sleep: An overview (pp. 3–13). In M. H. Kryger, T. Roth, & W. C. Dement (Eds.), *Principles and practice of sleep medicine.* Philadelphia: W. B. Saunders.

Cassel, E. J. (1982). The nature of suffering and the goals of medicine. *The New England Journal of Medicine, 306,* 639–645.

Cassileth, B. R., Lusk, E. J., Miller, D. S., Brown, L. L., & Miller, C. (1985). *New England Journal of Medicine, 312,* 1551–1555.

Catchlove, R. F. H. (1987). Alexithymia: Socio-cultural implications in patients with chronic pain. *Transcultural Psychiatric Research, 24,* 96–106.

Cella, D. F. (1990). Health promotion in oncology: A cancer wellness doctrine. *Journal of Psychosocial Oncology, 8,* 17–31.

Chapman, S. L., & Brena, S. F. (1989). Pain and litigation (pp. 1032–1041). In P. D. Wall & R. Melzack (Eds.), *Textbook of pain (2nd ed.).* Edinburgh: Churchill Livingstone.

Charlton, B. (1990). A critique of biological psychiatry. *Psychological Medicine, 20,* 3–6.

Chen, A. C. N., Dworkin, S. F., Haug, J., & Gehrig, J. (1989). Topographic brain measures of human pain and pain responsivity. *Pain, 37,* 129–141.

Cioffi, D. (1991). Beyond attentional strategies: A cognitive-perceptual model of somatic interpretation. *Psychological Bulletin, 109,* 25–41.

Cloninger, C. R. (1987). Neurogenetic adaptive mechanisms in alcoholism. *Science, 236,* 410–416.

Cohen, S. & Williamson, G. M. (1991). Stress and infectious disease in humans. *Psychological Bulletin, 109,* 5–24.

Costa, Jr., P. T., & McCrae, R. R. (1987). Neuroticism, somatic complaints, and disease: Is the bark worse than the bite? *Journal of Personality, 55,* 299–316.

Cousins, N. (1989). *Head First.* New York: E.P. Dutton.

Cowen, E. L. (1991). In pursuit of wellness. *American Psychologist, 46,* 404–408.

Craske, M. G., & Barlow, D. H. (1990). Nocturnal panic: Response to hyperventilation and carbon dioxide challenges. *Journal of Abnormal Psychology, 99,* 302–307.

Dana, C. S. (1921). The autonomic seat of the emotions: A discussion of the James-Lange theory. *Archives of Neurological Psychiatry, 6,* 634–639.

Daruna, J. H., & Morgan, J. E. (1990). Psychosocial effects on immune function: Neuroendocrine pathways. *Psychosomatics, 31,* 4–12.

Darwin, C. R. (1965). *The expression of emotions in man and animals.* Chicago: University of Chicago Press. (Original work published 1872)

Davison, G. C. (1966). Anxiety under total curarization: Implications for the role of muscular relaxation in the desensitization of neurotic fears. *Journal of Nervous and Mental Disease, 143,* 443–448.

Demjen, S., Bakal, D. A., & Dunn, B. E. (1990). Cognitive correlates of headache intensity and duration. *Headache, 30,* 423–427.

Dent, J., & Teasdale, J. D. (1988). Negative cognition and persistence of depression. *Journal of Abnormal Psychology, 97,* 29–34.

Depue, R. A., Arbisi, P., Spoont, M. R., Leon, A., & Ainsworth, B. (1989). Dopamine functioning in the behavioral facilitation system and seasonal variation in behavior: Normal population and clinical studies (pp. 230–259). In N. E. Rosenthal & M. C. Blehar (Eds.), *Seasonal affective disorders and psychotherapy.* New York: Guilford Press.

Depue, R. A., & Monroe, S. M. (1986). Conceptualization amd measurement of human disorder in life stress research: The problem of chronic disturbance. *Psychological Bulletin, 99,* 36–51.

Descartes, R. Discourse on Method and Meditations on First Philosophy. (1980). Indianapolis: Hackett Publishing. (Original work published 1637/1641)

Dickson-Parnell, B., & Zeichner, A. (1988). The premenstrual syndrome: psychophysiologic concomitants of perceived stress and low back pain. *Pain, 34,* 161–170.

Di Clemente, R. J., & Temoshok, L. (1985). Psychological adjustments to having cutaneous malignant melanoma as a predictor of follow-up clinical status. *Psychosomatic Medicine, 47,* 81.

Dienstbier, R. A. (1989). Arousal and physiological toughness: Implications for mental and physical health. *Psychological Review, 96,* 84–100.

Donovan, D. M. (1988). Assessment of addictive behaviors: Implications of an emerging biopsychosocial model (pp. 2–48). In D. M. Donovan & G. A. Marlatt (Eds.), *Assessment of Addictive Behaviors,* New York: Guilford Press.

Duckro, P. N. (1990). Biofeedback in the management of headache: Part I. *Headache Quarterly, Current Treatment and research, 1,* 290–298.

Dunkel-Schetter, C. (1984). Social support and cancer: Findings based on patient interviews and their implications. *Journal of Social Issues, 40,* 77–98.

Ekman, P., & Friesen, W. V. (1986). A new pan-cultural facial expression of emotion. *Motivation and Emotion, 10,* 159–168.

Ekman, P., Levenson, R. W., & Friesen, W. V. (1983). Autonomic nervous system activity distinguishes among emotions. *Science, 221,* 1208–1210.

Elkin, I., Shea, T., Watkins, J. T., Imber, S. D., Sotsky, S. M., Collins, J. F., Glass, D. R., Pilkonis, P. A., Leber, W. R., Docherty, J. P., Fiester, S. J., & Parloff, M. B. (1989). National Institute of Mental Health Treatment of Depression Collaborative Research Program. *Archives of General Psychiatry, 46,* 971–982.

Ellis, A. (1987). A sadly neglected cognitive element in depression. *Cognitive Therapy and Research, 11,* 121–146.

Engel, G. L. (1959). "Psychogenic" pain and the pain-prone patient. *American Journal of Medicine, 26,* 899–918.

Engel, G. (1968). A life setting conductive to illness: The giving up-given up complex. *Bulletin of the Menninger Clinic, 32,* 355–365.

Espie, C. A., Brooks, D. N., & Lindsay, W. R. (1989). *Journal of Behaviour Therapy & Experimental Psychiatry, 20,* 143–153.

Esterling, B. A., Antoni, M., Kumar, M., Schneiderman, N. (1990). Emotional repression, stress disclosure responses, and Epstein-Barr viral capsid antigen titres. *Psychosomatic Medicine, 52,* 397–410.

Eysenck, H. J. (1988). Personality, stress, and cancer: Prediction and prophylaxis. *British Journal of Medical Psychology, 61,* 57–75.

Fahrenberg, J. (1986). Psychophysiological individuality: A pattern analytic approach to personality research and psychosomatic medicine. *Advances in Behaviour Research and Therapy, 8,* 43–100.

Fein, G., Van Dyke, C., Davenport, L., Turetsky, B., Brant-Zawadzki, M., Zatz, L., Dillon, W., & Valk, P. (1990). Preservation of normal cognitive functioning in elderly subjects with extensive white-matter lesions of long duration. *Archives of General Psychiatry, 47,* 220–223.

Felton, D. L., & Felton, S. Y. (1988). Sympathetic noradrenergic innervation of immune organs. *Brain, Behavior, and Immunity, 2,* 293–300.

Fields, H. L., & Basbaum, A. I. (1989). Endogenous pain control mechanisms (pp. 206–217). In P. D. Wall & R. Melzack (Eds.), *Textbook of pain (2nd ed.).* Edinburgh: Churchill Livingstone.

Fishbain, D. A., Goldberg, M., Rosomoff, R. S., & Rosomoff, H. L. (1988). Munchausen syndrome presenting with chronic pain: case report. *Pain, 35,* 91–94.

Fisher, S. (1986). *Development and structure of the body image (Vol. 1).* Hillsdale, NJ: Lawrence Erlbaum Associates.

Fisher, S., & Greenberg, R. P. (1989). A second opinion: rethinking the claims of biological psychiatry (pp. 309-336). In S. Fisher & R. P. Greenberg (Eds.), *The limits of biological treatments for psychological distress.* Hillsdale, NJ: Lawrence Erlbaum Associates.

Flament, M. F., Whitaker, A., Rapoport, J. L., Davies, M., Berg, C. Z., Kalikow, K., Sceery, W., & Shaffer, D. (1988). Obsessive compulsive disorder in adolescence: An epidemiological study. *Journal of the American Academy of Child and Adolescent Psychiatry, 42,* 657–666.

Flor, H., Birbaumer, N., & Turk, D. C. (1990). The psychobiology of chronic pain. *Advances in Behaviour Research and Therapy, 12,* 47–84.

Flor, H., & Turk, D. C. (1989). Psychophysiology of chronic pain: Do chronic pain patients exhibit symptom-specific psychophysiological responses? *Psychological Bulletin, 105,* 215–259.

Foa, E. B., & Kozak, M. J. (1986). Emotional processing of fear: Exposure to corrective information. *Psychological Bulletin, 99,* 20–35.

Fordyce, W. E. (1976). *Behavioral methods for chronic pain and illness.* St. Louis, MO: Mosby.

Fordyce, W. E. (1988). Pain and suffering: A reappraisal. *American Psychologist, 43,* 276–283.

Fordyce, W. E., Roberts, A. H., & Sternbach, R. A. (1985). The behavioral management of chronic pain: A response to critics. *Pain, 22,* 113–125.

Frankl, V. E. (1969). Reductionism and nihilism (pp. 396–416). In A. Koestler & J. R. Smythies (Eds.), *Beyond reductionism.* London: Hutchinson.

Friedman, H. S., & Booth-Kewley, S. (1987). The *"Disease-prone personality": A meta-analytic view of the construct. American Psychologist, 42,* 539–555.

Friedman, M., & Rosenman, R. H. (1974). *Type A behavior and your heart.* New York: Alfred A. Knopf.

Funkenstein, D. H. (1955). The physiology of fear and anger. *Scientific American, 192,* 74–80.

Galin, D. (1974). Implications for psychiatry of left and right cerebral specialization. *Archives of General Psychiatry, 31,* 572–583.

Gallon, R. (1989). Perception of disability in chronic back pain patients: a long-term follow-up. *Pain, 37,* 67–75.

Gamsa, A. (1990). Is emotional disturbance a precipitator or a consequence of chronic pain? *Pain, 42,* 183–195.

Gellhorn, E. (1958). The physiological basis of neuromuscular relaxation. *Archives of Internal Medicine, 102,* 392–399.

Gorman, J. M., Liebowitz, M. R., Fyer, A. J., & Stein, J. (1989). A neuroanatomical hypothesis for panic disorder. *American Journal of Psychiatry, 146,* 148–161.

Graham, J. R., & Wolff, H. G. (1938). Mechanisms of migraine headache and action of ergotamine tartrate. *Archives of Neurology and Psychiatry, 39,* 737–763.

Gray, J. A. (1982). *The neuropsychology of anxiety: An enquiry into the functions of the sept-hippocampal system.* New York: Oxford University Press.

Green, J., & Schellenberger, R. (1991). *The dynamics of health and wellness: A biopsychosocial approach.* Fort Worth: Holt, Rinehart and Winston.

Greenberg, D. B. (1990). Neurasthenia in the 1980s: Chronic mononucleosis, chronic fatigue syndrome, and anxiety and depressive disorders. *Psychosomatics, 31,* 129–138.

Greenberg, R. P., & Fisher, S. (1989). Examining antidepressant effectiveness: Findings, ambiguities, and some vexing puzzles (pp. 1–37). In S. Fisher & R. P. Greenberg (Eds.), *The limits of biological treatments for psychological distress.* Hillsdale, NJ: Lawrence Erlbaum Associates.

Greer, S., & Morris, T. (1975). Psychological attributes of women who develop breast cancer: A controlled study. *Journal of Psychosomatic Research, 19,* 147–153.

Greer, S., Morris, T., & Pettingale, K. W. (1979). Psychological response to breast cancer: Effect on outcome. *The Lancet, ii,* 785–787.

Grossarth-Maticek, R., Bastiaans, J., & Kanazir, D. T. (1985). Psychosocial factors as strong predictors of mortality from cancer, ischaemic heart disease and stroke: The Yugoslav prospective study. *Journal of Psychosomatic Research, 29,* 167–176.

Grossarth-Maticek, R., & Eysenck, H. J. (1991a). Creative novation behaviour therapy as a prophylactic treatment for cancer and coronary heart disease: Part I - Description of treatment. *Behaviour Research and Therapy, 29,* 1–16.

Grossarth-Maticek, R., & Eysenck, H. J. (1991b). Creative novation behaviour therapy as a prophylactic treatment for cancer and coronary heart disease: Part II - Effects of treatment. *Behaviour Research and Therapy, 29,* 17–31.

Guidano, V. F., & Liotti, G. (1983). *Cognitive processes and emotional disorders.* New York: Guilford Press.

Halgin, R. P., & Leahy, P. M. (1989). Understanding and treating perfectionistic college students. *Journal of Counseling & Development, 68,* 222–225.

Hanna, T. (1988) *Somatics.* Reading, MA: Addison-Wesley.

Hauri, P. (1989). Primary insomnia (pp. 442–447). In M. H. Kryger, T. Roth, & W. C. Dement (Eds.), *Principles and practice of sleep medicine.* Philadelphia: W. B. Saunders.

Heide, F. J., & Borkovec, T. D. (1984). Relaxation-induced anxiety: Mechanisms and theoretical explanations. *Behaviour Research and Therapy, 22,* pp. 1–12.

Hoffman, R. S. (1988). The psycho-oncologist in a multidisciplinary breast treatment center (pp. 171–193). In C. L. Cooper (Ed.), *Stress and breast cancer.* New York: John Wiley & Sons.

Hollandsworth, J. G. (1986). *Physiology and behavior therapy.* New York: Plenum.

Hollon, S. D., Shelton, R. C., & Loosen, P. T. (1991). Cognitive therapy and pharmacotherapy for depression. *Journal of Consulting and Clinical Psychology, 59,* 88–99.

Holmes, T. H., & Rahe, R. H. (1967). The Social Readjustment Rating Scale. *Journal of Psychosomatic Research, 11,* 213–218.

Horowitz, M. J. (1976). *Stress Response Syndromes.* New York: Aronsen.

Hu, D., & Silberfarb, P. M. (1988). Psychological factors: Do they influence breast cancer? (pp. 27–62). In C. L. Cooper (Ed.), *Stress and breast cancer.* New York: John Wiley & Sons.

Insel, T. R. (1990). Phenomenology of obsessive compulsive disorder. *Journal of Clinical Psychiatry, 51*(Suppl.), 4–8.

Izard, C. E. (1977). *Human emotions.* New York: Plenum.

Izard, C. E. (1990). Facial expressions and the regulation of emotions. *Journal of Personality and Social Psychology, 58,* 487–498.

Jacobson, E. (1938). *Progressive relaxation.* Chicago: University of Chicago Press.

Jaffe, J. H. (1990). Drug addiction and drug abuse (pp. 522–573). In A. G. Gilman, T. W. Rall, A. S. Nies, & P. Taylor (Eds.), *Goodman and Gilman's The pharmacological basis of therapeutics (8th ed.).* New York: Pergamon Press.

James, W. (1890). *The principles of psychology.* New York: Henry Holt.

Janis, I. (1958). *Psychological stress.* New York: Academic Press.

Janis, I. L., & Mann, L. (1977). *Decision making: A psychological analysis of conflict, choice, and commitment.* New York: Free Press.

Jemmott, J. B., III. (1987). Social motives and susceptibility to disease: Stalking individual differences in health risks. *Journal of Personality, 55,* 267–298.

Jensen, T. S., & Rasmussen, P. (1989). Phantom pain and related phenomena after amputation (pp. 508–521). In P. D. Wall & R. Melzack (Eds.), *Textbook of pain (2nd ed.).* Edinburgh: Churchill Livingstone.

Jones, G. E., & Hollandsworth, J. G. (1981). Heart rate discrimination before and after exercise-induced augmented cardiac activity. *Psychophysiology, 18,* 252–257.

Kabat-Zinn, J. (1990). *Full catastrophe living: Using the wisdom of your body and mind to face stress, pain, and illness.* New York: Delacorte Press.

Kannel, W. B. (1987). New perspectives on cardiovascular risk factors. *American Heart Journal, 114,* 1211–1220.

Kaplan, R. M. (1990). Behavior as the central outcome in health care. *American Psychologist, 45,* 1211–1220.

Kaplan, R. M., & Toshima, M. T. (1990). The functional effects of social relationships on chronic illness and disability (pp. 427–453). In B. R. Sarason, I. G. Sarason & G. R. Pierce (Eds.), *Social support: An interactional view.* New York: John Wiley & Sons.

Kasl, S. V., Evans, A. S., & Neiderman, J. C. (1979). Psychosocial risk factors in the development of infectious mononucleosis. *Psychosomatic Medicine, 41,* 445–466.

Katkin, E. S., Blascovich, J., & Koenigsberg, M. R. (1984). Autonomic self-perception and emotion (pp. 117–138). In W. Waid (Ed.), *Sociophysiology.* New York: Springer-Verlag.

Keefe, F. J., Brown, G. K., Wallston, K. A., & Caldwell, D. S. (1989). Coping with rheumatoid arthritis pain: catastrophizing as a maladaptive strategy. *Pain, 37,* 51–56.

Keefe, F. J., & Dolan, E. (1986). Pain behavior and pain coping strategies in low back pain and myofascial pain dysfunction syndrome patients. *Pain, 24,* 49–56.

Kiecolt-Glaser, J., & Glaser, R. (1988). Psychological influences on immunity. *American Psychologist, 43,* 892–898.

Kirmayer, L. J. (1984). Culture, affect, and somatization. Part I. *Transcultural Psychiatric Research Review.* 21: 159–188.

Klopfer, B. (1957). Psychological variables in human cancer. *Journal of Projective Techniques, 31,* 331–340.

Kolb, L. C. (1988). A critical survey of hypotheses regarding posttraumatic stress disorders in light of recent research findings. *Journal of Traumatic Stress, 3,* 291–304.

Korff, J., & Geer, J. H. (1983). The relationship between sexual arousal experience and genital response. *Psychophysiology, 20,* 21–27.

Kripke, D. F., Mullaney, D. J., Savides, T. J., & Gillin, J. C. (1989). Phototherapy for nonseasonal major depressive disorders (342–356). In N. E. Rosenthal & M. C. Blehar (Eds.), *Seasonal affective disorders & phototherapy.* New York: Plenum.

Kroll, J. (1989). Book review: The psychological experience of surgery. *Psychosomatic Medicine, 51,* 463–473.

Krystal, H. (1979). Alexithymia and psychotherapy. *American Journal of Psychotherapy, 33,* 17–31.

Kupfer, D. J., & Frank, E. (1987). Relapse in recurrent unipolar depression. *American Journal of Psychiatry, 115,* 459–464.

Kusnecov, A., King, M. G., & Husband, A. J. (1989). Immunomodulation by behavioural conditioning. *Biological Psychology, 28,* 25–39.

Lacey, J. I. (1959). Psychophysiological approaches to the evaluation of psychotherapeutic process and outcome (pp. 160–208). In E. A. Rubinstein & M. B. Parloff (Eds.), *Research in psychotherapy.* Washington DC: American Psychological Association.

Lachman, S. J. (1972). *Psychosomatic disorders: A behavioristic interpretation.* New York: John Wiley & Sons.

Lader, M., & Tyrer, P. (1975). Vegetative system and emotion (pp. 123–141). In L. Levi (Ed.), *Emotions—Their parameters and measurement.* New York: Raven.

Lang, P. J. (1985). The cognitive psychophysiology of emotion: Fear and anxiety (pp. 131–170). In A. H. Tuma & J. D. Maser (Eds.), *Anxiety and the anxiety disorders.* Hillsdale, NJ: Lawrence Erlbaum Associates.

Lang, P. J. (1988). Fear, anxiety, and panic: Context, cognition, and visceral arousal (pp. 219–236). In S. Rachman & J. D. Maser (Eds.), *Panic: Psychological perspectives.* Hillsdale, NJ: Lawrence Erlbaum Associates.

Lazarus, R. S. (1990). Stress, coping, and illness (pp. 97–120). H. S. Friedman (Ed.), *Personality and disease.* New York: John Wiley & Sons.

Lazarus, R. L., & Folkman, S. (1984). *Stress, appraisal, and coping.* New York: Springer.

LeDoux, J. E. (1987). Emotion (pp. 419–459). In Mountcastle, V. B., Plum, F., & Geiger, S. R. (Eds.), *Handbook of physiology: A critical, comprehensive presentation of physiological knowledge and concepts. Section 1, Vol. V.* Bethesda: American Physiological Society.

Lefkowitz, R. J., Hoffman, B. B., & Taylor, P. (1990). Neurohumoral transmission: The autonomic and somatic motor nervous systems (pp. 84–121). In A. G. Gilman, T. W. Rall, A. S. Nies, & P. Taylor (Eds.), *Goodman and Gilman's The pharmacological basis of therapeutics (8th ed.).* New York: Pergamon Press.

Lehrer, P. M., Woolfolk, R. L., & Goldman, N. (1986). Progressive relaxation then and now: Does change always mean progress? In R. J. Davidson, G. E. Schwartz, & D. Shapiro, (Eds.), *Consciousness and self-regulation: Advances in research and theory, Vol. 4* (pp. 183–216). New York: Plenum.

Levy, S. M., & Wise, B. D. (1988). Psychosocial risk factors and cancer progression (pp. 77–96). In C. L. Cooper (Ed.), *Stress and breast cancer.* New York: John Wiley & Sons.

Lichstein, K. L. (1988). *Clinical relaxation strategies.* New York: John Wiley & Sons.

Liebeskind, J. C., & Paul, L. A. (1977). Psychological and physiological mechanisms of pain. *Annual Review of Psychology, 28,* 41–60.

Liebeskind, J. C. (1991). Pain can kill. *Pain, 44,* 3–4.

Linn, M. W., Linn, B. S., & Harris, R. (1982). Effects of counselling for late stage cancer patients. *Cancer, 49,* 1048-1055.

Lipowski, Z. J. (1986a). Psychosomatic Medicine: Past and present. Part I. Historical background. *Canadian Journal of Psychiatry, 31,* 2–7.

Lipowski, Z. J. (1986b). Psychosomatic Medicine: Past and present. Part II. Current state. *Canadian Journal of Psychiatry, 31,* 8–13.

Lipowski, Z. J. (1988). Somatization: The concept and its clinical application. *American Journal of Psychiatry, 145,* 1358–1368.

Love, A. W., & Peck, C. L. (1987). The MMPI and psychological factors in chronic low back pain: A review. *Pain, 28,* 1–12.

Ludwig, A. M. (1988). *Understanding the alcoholic's mind: The nature of craving and how to control it.* New York: Oxford University Press.

Lynch, J. J., Thomas, S. A., Paskewitz, D. A., Malinow, K. L., & Long, J. M. (1982).

Interpersonal aspects of blood pressure control. *Journal of Nervous and Mental Disease, 170,* 143–153.

Lynch, P. D., Bakal, D. A., Whitelaw, W., & Fung, T. (1991). Chest muscle activity and panic anxiety: A preliminary investigation. *Psychosomatic Medicine, 53,* 80–89.

MacLean, P. D. (1967). The brain in relation to empathy and medical education. *Journal of Nervous and Mental Disease, 144,* 374–382.

Maddi, S. R., Bartone, P. T., & Puccetti, M. C. (1987). Stressful events are indeed a factor in physical illness: Reply to Schroeder and Costa (1984). *Journal of Personality and Social Psychology, 52,* 833–843.

Maier, S. F., & Laudenslager, M. L. (1988). Inescapable shock, shock controllability, and mitogen stimulated lymphocyte proliferation. *Brain, Behavior, and Immunity, 2,* 87–91.

Malliani, A., Pagani, M., & Lombardi, F. (1989). Visceral versus somatic mechanisms (pp. 128–140). In P. D. Wall & R. Melzack (Eds.), *Textbook of pain(2nd ed.).* Edinburgh: Churchill Livingstone.

Malmo, R. B. (1970). Emotions and muscle tension: The story of Anne. *Psychology Today, 3,* 64–67.

Malmo, R. B., & Shagass, C. (1949). Physiologic study of symptom mechanisms in psychiatric patients under stress. *Psychosomatic Medicine, 11,* 25–29.

Marks, I. M., Lelliott, P., Basoglu, M., Noshirvani, H., Monteiro, W., Cohen, D., & Kasvikis, Y. (1988). Clomipramine, self-exposure, and therapist-aided exposure for obsessive-compulsive rituals. *British Journal of Psychiatry, 152,* 522–534.

Marlatt, G. A., & Gordon, J. R. (Eds.). (1985). *Relapse prevention: Maintenance strategies in addictive behavior change.* New York: Guilford Press.

Martin, R. A., & Dobbin, J. P. (1988). Sense of humor, hassles, and immunoglobulin A: Evidence for a stress-moderating effect of humor. *International Journal of Psychiatry in Medicine, 18,* 93–105.

Marty, P., & de M'Uzan, M. (1963). La pensee operatoire. *Review French Psychoanalysis, 27*(Suppl.), 345–356.

Mason, J. W. (1975). A historical view of the stress field. *Journal of Human Stress, 1,* 22–36.

Matthews, K. A. (1988). Coronary heart disease and Type A behaviors: Update on and alternative to the Booth-Kewley & Friedman (1987) quantitative review. *Psychological Bulletin, 104,* 373–380.

McClelland, D. C. (1989). Motivational factors in health and disease. *American Psychologist, 44,* 675–683.

Mechanic, D. (1986). The concept of illness behaviour: culture, situation, and personal predisposition. *Psychological Medicine, 16,* 1–7.

Meichenbaum, D. H., & Deffenbacher, J. L. (1988). Stress Inoculation Training. *The Counselling Psychologist, 16,* 69–90.

Melzack, R. (1973). *The puzzle of pain.* Harmondsworth: Penguin.

Melzack, R. (1987). The short-form McGill Pain Questionnaire. *Pain, 30,* 191–197.

Melzack, R. (1989). Folk medicine and the sensory modulation of pain (pp. 897–905). In P. D. Wall & R. Melzack (Eds.), *Textbook of pain (2nd ed.).* Edinburgh: Churchill Livingstone.

Melzack, R. (1990). The tragedy of needless pain. *Scientific American, 262,* 27–33.

Melzack, R., Taenzer, P., Feldman, P., & Kinch, R. A. (1981). Labour is still painful after prepared childbirth training. *Canadian Medical Association Journal, 125,* 357–363.

Melzack, R., & Wall, P. (1983). *The Challenge of Pain.* New York: Basic Books.

Merskey, H. (1979). Pain terms: A list with definitions and notes on usage. *Pain, 6,* 249–252.

Michelson, L. K., & Marchione, K. (1991). Behavioral, cognitive, and pharmacological treatments of panic disorder with agoraphobia: Critique and synthesis. *Journal of Consulting and Clinical Psychology, 59,* 100–114.

Michultka, D. M., Blanchard, E. B., Appelbaum, K. A., Jaccard, J., & Dentinger, M. P. (1989). The refractory headache patient—II. High medication consumption (analgesic rebound) headache. *Behavior Research and Therapy, 27,* 411–420.

Millan, M. J. (1986). Multiple opioid systems and pain. *Pain, 27,* 303–347.

Moldofsky, H. (1986). Sleep and musculoskeletal pain. *American Journal of Medicine, 81,* (suppl 3A), 85–89.

Monti, P. M., Abrams, R. M., Kadden, R. M., & Cooney, N. L. (1989). *Treating alcohol dependence.* New York: Guilford Press.

Morris, M., Lack, L., & Dawson, D. (1990). Sleep-onset insomniacs have delayed temperature rhythms. *Sleep, 13,* 1–14.

Mukerji, V., Beitman, B. D., Alpert, M. A., Hewett, J. E., & Basha, I. M. (1987). *Journal of Anxiety Disorders, 1,* 41–46.

Nemiah, J. C. (1972). Emotions and physiology: An introduction (pp. 15-29). In Ciba Foundation Symposium 8 (Ed.), *Physiology, emotion, & psychosomatic illness.* Amsterdam: Elsevier.

Ness, T. J., & Gebhart, G. F. (1990). Visceral pain: A review of experimental studies. *Pain, 41,* 167–234.

Nolen-Hoeksema, S. (1987). Sex differences in unipolar depression:Evidence and theory. *Psychological Bulletin, 101,* 259–282.

Ohman, A. (1986). Face the beast and fear the face: Animal and social fears as prototypes for evolutionary analyses of emotion. *Psychophysiology, 23,* 123–145.

Oken, D. (1985). Gastrointestinal disorders (pp. 1121–1132). In H. I. Kaplan & B. J. Sadock (Eds.), *Comprehensive textbook of psychiatry/IV (Vol.2).* Baltimore: Williams & Wilkins.

Ornstein, R., & Sobel, D. (1987). *The healing brain.* New York: Simon and Schuster.

Orth-Gomér, K., & Undén, A. (1990). Type A behavior, social support, and coronary risk: Interaction and significance for mortality in cardiac patients. *Psychosomatic Medicine, 52,* 59–72.

Ost, L., & Sterner, U. (1987). Applied tension: A specific behavioral method for treatment of blood phobia. *Behaviour Research and Therapy, 25,* 25–29.

Pennebaker, J. W. (1988). Confiding traumatic experiences and health (pp. 671-684). In S. Fisher & J. Reason (Eds.), *Handbook of Life Stress, Cognition, and Health.* New York: John Wiley & Sons.

Peroutka, S. (1990). Sumatriptan in acute migraine: Pharmacology and review of world experience. *Headache, 30*(Suppl. 2), 554–560.

Pettingale, K. W., Morris, T., Greer, S., & Haybittle, J. L. (1985). Mental attitudes to cancer: An additional prognostic factor. *The Lancet, i,* 750.

Pilowsky, I. (1990). The concept of abnormal illness behavior. *Psychosomatics, 31,* 207–215.

Pinel, J. P. J. (1990). *Biopsychology.* Boston: Allyn and Bacon.

Pitts, F. N., & McClure, J. N. (1967). Lactate metabolism in anxiety neurosis. *New England Journal of Medicine, 277,* 1329–1336.

Porter, G., & Norris, P. (1985). *Why me?* Walpole, NH: Stillpoint Publishing.

Pribram, K. H. (1976). Self-consciousness and intentionality (pp. 51–100). In G. E. Schwartz & D. Shapiro (Eds.), *Consciousness and self-regulation: Advances in research. Vol. 1.* New York: Plenum.

Rapoport, J. (1989). Serotonergic agents in obsessive-compulsive disorder. *Psychopharmacology Bulletin, 25,* 31–35.

Rasmussen, S. A., & Eisen, J. L. (1990). Epidemiology of obsessive compulsive disorder. *Journal of Clinical Psychiatry, 51*(Suppl.), 10–13.

Richardson, P. H., & Vincent, C. A. (1986). Acupuncture for the treatment of pain: A review of evaluative research. *Pain, 24,* 15–40.

Rickels, K., Case, W. G., Downing, R. W., & Fridman, R. (1986). One-year follow-up of anxious patients treated with diazepam. *Journal of Clinical Psychopharmacology, 6,* 32–36.

Roehrs, T. A., Zorick, F., & Roth, T. (1989). Transient insomnias and insomnias associated with circadian rhythm disorders (pp. 433–441). In M. H. Kryger, T. Roth, & W. C. Dement (Eds.), *Principles and practice of sleep medicine.* Philadelphia: W. B. Saunders.

Rook, K. S. (1984). Promoting social bonding: Strategies for helping the lonely and socially isolated. *American Psychologist, 39,* 1389–1407.

Rosenman, R. H., Brand, R. J., Jenkins, C. D., Friedman, M., Straus, R., & Wurm, M. (1975). Coronary heart disease in the Western Collaborative Group Study: Final follow-up experience of 8 1/2 years. *Journal of the American Medical Association, 233,* 872–877.

Rosenthal, N. E., Sack, D. A., Skwerer, R. G., Jacobsen, F. M., & Wehr, T. A. (1989). Phototherapy for seasonal affective disorder (pp 273–294). In N. E. Rosenthal & M. C. Blehar (Eds.), *Seasonal affective disorders & phototherapy.* New York: Guilford Press.

Rowbotham, M. C., & Fields, H. L. (1989). Post-herpetic neuralgia: the relation of pain complaint, sensory disturbance, and skin temperature. *Pain, 39,* 129–144.

Schachter, S., & Singer, J. E. (1962). Cognitive, social, and physiological determinants of emotional state. *Psychological Review, 69,* 379–399.

Schneiderman, N., Chesney, M. A., & Krantz, D. S. (1989). Biobehavioral aspects of cardiovascular disease: Progress and prospects. *Health Psychology, 8,* 649–676.

Schultz, J. J., & Luthe, W. (1969). Autogenic methods (Vol. 1). In W. Luthe (Ed.), *Autogenic therapy.* New York: Grune & Stratton.

Schwartz, G. E., & Weiss, S. M. (1978). Behavioral medicine revisited: An amended definition. *Journal of Behavioral Medicine, 1,* 249–251.

Searles, J. S. (1988). The role of genetics in the pathogenesis of alcoholism. *Journal of Abnormal Psychology, 97,* 153–167.

Seeman, J. (1989). Toward a positive model of health. *American Psychologist, 44,* 1099–1109.

Selye, H. (1956). *The stress of life.* New York: McGraw-Hill.

Shan, H. (1988). A study of clinical phenomenology of mental disorder caused by qi gong. *Transcultural Psychiatric Research Review, 25,* 299–304.

Shapiro, A. K., & Shapiro, E. (1984). Patient-provider relationships and the placebo effect (pp. 371–383). In J. D. Matarazzo, S. M. Weiss, J. A. Herd, N. E. Miller, & S. M. Weiss (Eds.), *Behavioral health: A handbook of health enhancement and disease prevention.* New York: John Wiley & Sons.

Shapiro, A. P. (1988). Teaching behavioral concepts in cardiovascular disease with remarks on challenges to medical education. In R. Ader, H. Weiner, & A. Baum (Eds.), *Experimental foundations of behavioral medicine: Conditioning approaches* (pp. 195–207). Hillsdale, NJ: Lawrence Erlbaum Associates.

Shapiro, D. (1974). Operant-feedback control of human blood pressure: Some clinical issues. In P. A. Obrist, A. H. Black, J. Brener, & L. V. DiCara (Eds.), *Cardiovascular psychophysiology: Current issues in response mechanisms, biofeedback, and methodology.* Chicago: Aldine.

Shekelle, R. B., Hulley, S. B., Neaton, J. D., Billings, J. H., Borhani, N. O., Gerace, T. A., Jacobs, D. R., Lasser, N. L., Mittlemark, M. B., & Stamler, J. (1985). The MRFIT behavior pattern study: II. Type A behavior and incidence of cororonary heart disease. *American Journal of Epidemiology, 122,* 559–570.

Siegel, S. (1979). The role of conditioning in drug tolerance and addiction. In J. D. Keehn (Ed.), *Psychopathology in animals: Research and clinical implications* (pp. 143–168). New York: Academic Press.

Sifneos, P. E. (1973). The prevalence of 'alexithymic' characteristics in psychosomatic patients. *Psychotherapy and psychosomatics, 22,* 255–262.

Silva, J. M., & Appelbaum, M. I. (1989). Association-dissociation patterns of United States Olympic Marathon Trial Contestants. *Cognitive Therapy and Research, 13,* 185–192.

Simonton, C., Matthews-Simonton, S., & Creighton, J. (1978). *Getting well again.* Los Angeles: J. P. Tarcher.

Sontag, S. (1979). *Illness as metaphor.* New York: Vintage Books.

Sorbi, M., & Tellegen, B. (1988). Stress-coping in migraine. *Social Science and Medicine, 26,* 351–358.

Sperry, R. W. (1987). Structure and significance of the consciousness revolution. *The Journal of Mind and Behavior, 8,* 37–65.

Spiegel, D., Bloom, J. R., Kraemer, H. C., Gottheil, E. Effect of psychosocial treatment on survival of patients with metastatic breast cancer. *The Lancet,* October, 888–891.

Stark, M. J. (1989). A psychoeducational approach to methadone maintenance treatment. *Journal of Substance Abuse Treatment, 6,* 169–181.

Steketee, G., & Foa, E. B. (1985). Obsessive-compulsive disorder (pp. 69-144). In D. H. Barlow (Ed.), *Clinical handbook of psychological disorders.* New York: Guilford Press.

Stolbach, L. L., & Brandt, U. C. (1988). Psychosocial factors in the development and progression of breast cancer. In C. L. Cooper (Ed.), *Stress and breast cancer.* New York: John Wiley & Sons.

Strauss, D. H., Spitzer, R. L., Muskin, P. R. (1990). Maladaptive denial of physical illness: A proposal for DSM-IV. *Americal Journal of Psychiatry, 147,* 1168–1172.

Suarez, E. C., & Williams, R. B. (1989). Situational determinants of cardiovascular and emotional reactivity in high and low hostile men. *Psychosomatic Medicine, 51*, 404–418.

Suinn, R. M. (1990). *Anxiety management training: A behavior therapy.* New York: Plenum.

Talbot, J. D., Marrett, S., Evans, A. C., Meyer, E., Bushnell, M. C., & Duncan, G. H. (1991). Multiple representations of pain in human cerebral cortex. *Science, 251*, 1355–1358.

Tarter, R., & Edwards, K. (1986). Antecedents to alcoholism: Implications for prevention and treatment. *Behavior Therapy, 17*, 346–361.

Temoshok, L. (1990). On attempting to articulate the biopsychosocial model: Psychological-psychophysiological homeostasis. In H. S. Friedman (Ed.), *Personality and disease.* New York: John Wiley & Sons.

Terman, M. (1989). On the question of mechanism in phototherapy for seasonal affective disorder: Considerations of clinical efficacy and epidemiology (pp. 357–376). In N. E. Rosenthal & M. C. Blehar (Eds.), *Seasonal affective disorders & phototherapy.* New York: Guilford Press.

Theorell, T., Orth-Gomer, K., & Eneroth, P. (1990). Slow-reacting immunoglobulin in relation to social support and changes in job strain: A preliminary note. *Psychosomatic Medicine, 52*, 511–516.

Thomson, R. (1982). Side effects and placebo amplification. *British Journal of Psychiatry, 140*, 64–68.

Turk, D. C., & Rudy, T. E. (1990). Neglected factors in chronic pain treatment outcome studies—referral patterns, failure to enter treatment, and attrition. *Pain, 43*, 7–25.

Turk, D. C., & Rudy, T. E. (1991). Neglected topics in the treatment of chronic pain patients—relapse, noncompliance, and adherence enhancement. *Pain, 44*, 5–28.

van den Hout, M. A., van der Molen, G. M., Griez, E., & Lousberg, H. (1987). Specificity of interoceptive fear to panic disorders. *Journal of Psychopathology and Behavioral Assessment, 9*, 99–106.

van der Kolk, B. A. (1988). The trauma spectrum: The interaction of biological and social events in the genesis of the trauma response. *Journal of Traumatic Stress, 3*, 273–290.

van der Ploeg, H. M., Kleijn, W. C., Mook, J., van Donge, M., Pieters, A. M. J., & Leer, J. H. (1989). Rationality and antiemotionality as a risk factor for cancer: Concept differentiation. *Journal of Psychosomatic Research, 33*, 217–225.

van Doornen, L. J. P., & de Geus, E. J. C. (1989). Aerobic fitness and the cardiovascular response to stress. *Psychophysiology, 26*, 17–28.

Van Egeren, L. F., & Sparrow, A. W. (1989). Laboratory stress testing to assess real-life cardiovascular reactivity. *Psychosomatic Medicine, 51*, 1–9.

Van Egeren, L. F., & Sparrow, A. W. (1990). Ambulatory monitoring to assess real-life cardiovascular reactivity in Type A and Type B subjects. *Psychosomatic Medicine, 52*, 297–306.

Vincent, C. A., & Richardson, P. H. (1986). The evaluation of therapeutic acupuncture: Concepts and methods. *Pain, 24*, 1–13.

Vos, H. P. J. (1989). Denial of the inner reality: Observations on drug abuse and addiction based on psychotherapies after treatment in a therapeutic community in the Netherlands. *Journal of Substance Abuse Treatment, 6,* 193–199.

Walker, E. A., Roy-Byrne, P. P., & Katon, W. J. (1990). Irritable bowel syndrome and psychiatric illness. *American Journal of Psychiatry, 147,* 565–572.

Wall, P. D. (1989a). Introduction (pp. 1-18). In P. D. Wall & R. Melzack (Eds.), *Textbook of pain (2nd ed.).* Edinburgh: Churchill Livingstone.

Wall, P. D. (1989b). The dorsal horn (pp. 102–111). In P. D. Wall & R. Melzack (Eds.), *Textbook of pain (2nd ed.).* Edinburgh: Churchill Livingstone.

Walls, E. W., & Philipp, E. E. (1953). *Hilton's rest and pain.* London: G. Bell & Sons. 6th edition. (First published in 1863 by Bell and Daldy, London)

Wapner, S. (1987). A holistic, developmental, systems-oriented environmental psychology: Some beginnings. In D. Stokols & I. Altman (Eds.), *Handbook of environmental psychology* (pp. 1433–1465). New York: Wiley.

Wardle, J. (1990). Behavior therapy and benzodiazepines: Allies or antagonists? *British Journal of Psychiatry, 156,* 163–168.

Wegner, D. M., & Giuliano, T. (1980). Arousal-induced attention to self. *Journal of Personality and Social Psychology, 38,* 719–726.

Welch, K. M. A. (1987). Migraine: A biobehavioral disorder. *Archives of Neurology, 44,* 323–327.

White, G. L., & Mullen, P. E. (1989). *Jealousy: Theory, research, and clinical strategies.* New York: Guilford Press.

Wiener, N. (1954). *The human use of human beings.* New York: Avon.

Wilkinson, M., & Woodrow, J. (1979). Migraine and weather. *Headache, 19,* 375–378.

Williams, J. G. L., Jones, J. R., Workhoven, M. N., & Williams, B. (1975). The psychological control of preoperative anxiety. *Psychophysiology, 12,* 50–54.

Williams, R. J. (1967). *You are extraordinary.* New York: Random House.

Wise, R. (1988). The neurobiology of craving: Implications for the understanding and treatment of addiction. *Journal of Abnormal Psychology, 97,* 118–132.

World Health Organization. (1964). *Basic documents* (15th ed., p. 1). Geneva, Switzerland: Author.

Wuitchik, M., Bakal, D., & Lipshitz, J. (1989). The clinical significance of pain and cognitive activity in latent labor. *Obstetrics and Gynecology, 73,* 35–42.

Yarnitsky, D., Barron, S. A., & Bental, E. (1988). Disappearance of phantom pain after focal brain infarction. *Pain, 32,* 285–287.

Zatzick, D. F., & Dimsdale, J. E. (1990). Cultural variations in response to painful stimuli. *Psychosomatic Medicine, 52,* 544–557.

Index